Ecology without Nature

Ecology without Nature

❧ RETHINKING ENVIRONMENTAL AESTHETICS

TIMOTHY MORTON

HARVARD UNIVERSITY PRESS
Cambridge, Massachusetts, and London, England

First Harvard University Press paperback edition, 2009.

Library of Congress Cataloging-in-Publication Data

Morton, Timothy, 1968–
Ecology without nature : rethinking environmental aesthetics / Timothy Morton.
   p. cm.
  Includes bibliographical references and index.
  ISBN 978-0-674-02434-2 (cloth : alk. paper)
  ISBN 978-0-674-03485-3 (pbk.)
   1. Environmental literature—History and criticism—Theory, etc. 2. English
literature—History and criticism.   3. American literature—History and criticism.
4. Ecology in literature.   5. Environmentalism—Philosophy. 6. Nature in
literature.   7. Philosophy in literature. 8. Romanticism. I. Title.
PR448.E58 M67   2007
820.9'36—dc22   2006051110

Epigraph to Chapter 1, "To the Reader," by Denise Levertov, from
Poems 1960–1967, copyright © 1961 by Denise Levertov. Reprinted by
permission of New Directions Publishing Corp., Pollinger Limited, and the
proprietor.

Pink Floyd, "Grantchester Meadows," *Ummagumma* (EMI, 1969). Words and
Music by Roger Waters. © Copyright 1970 (Renewed) and 1980 Lupus Music
Co. Ltd., London, England. TRO-Hampshire House Publishing Corp., New
York, controls all publication rights for the U.S.A. and Canada. Used by
Permission.

For Kate

Acknowledgments

Writing this book has often called to mind a precarious picture of walking across a minefield with a bouquet of flowers, dressed in the costume of a clown. For those who encouraged me across, I have nothing but thanks: David Clark, Greg Dobbins, Margaret Ferguson, Kate Flint, Denise Gigante, Geoffrey Hartman, Karen Jacobs, Douglas Kahn, Robert Kaufman, Alan Liu, James C. McKusick, David Norbrook, Jeffrey Robinson, Nicholas Roe, David Simpson, Nigel Smith, Jane Stabler, Robert Unger, Karen Weisman, and Michael Ziser. The two anonymous readers appointed by Harvard University Press were extraordinarily encouraging. To David Simpson in particular I owe a debt of gratitude beyond measure, for years of support and friendship. I benefited from a Distinguished Visiting Fellowship at Queen Mary, University of London while copyediting, proofreading, and indexing. Thanks in particular to Richard Schoch and Paul Hamilton. Thanks go to my research assistants, Seth Forrest and Christopher Schaberg, who helped me balance my life, writing, and teaching. I would like to thank all those students, both undergraduates and graduates, who have explored and shared these ideas since 1998, in classes at the University of Colorado and the University of California. In particular, I am grateful to my entire "Ecomimesis" graduate class of Spring 2004, for helping me to work through to the heart and soul of this project: Seth Forrest, Timothy Kreiner, Dalal Mansour, Eric O' Brien, Francisco Reinking, Christopher Schaberg, Daniel Thomas-Glass, Sabrina Tom, Karen Walker, and Clara Van Zanten. And I am equally grateful to my

"Ecology without Nature" class of Spring 2006: Tekla Babyak, Andrew Hageman, Lynn Langemade, Rachel Swinkin, Julie Tran, and Nicholas Valvo. At Harvard University Press, Lindsay Waters has been everything I would wish an editor to be. John Donohue at Westchester Book Services coordinated the copyediting. Last but not least, I don't think the idea of dark ecology would have been possible without a life spent listening to the ethereal splendor of the Cocteau Twins.

I dedicate this book to my love, my wife Kate. She was the first to hear and discuss the ideas set down here. At every moment, she was ready with a comment, a suggestion, a kind word. And she bore our daughter, Claire, the sweetest stranger who ever arrived.

Contents

Ecology without Nature

Toward a Theory of Ecological Criticism

Nobody likes it when you mention the unconscious, and nowadays, hardly anybody likes it when you mention the environment. You risk sounding boring or judgmental or hysterical, or a mixture of all these. But there is a deeper reason. Nobody likes it when you mention the unconscious, not because you are pointing out something obscene that should remain hidden—that is at least partly enjoyable. Nobody likes it because when you mention it, it becomes *conscious*. In the same way, when you mention the environment, you bring it into the foreground. In other words, it stops being the environment. It stops being That Thing Over There that surrounds and sustains us. When you think about where your waste goes, your world starts to shrink. This is the basic message of criticism that speaks up for environmental justice, and it is the basic message of this book.

The main theme of the book is given away in its title. *Ecology without Nature* argues that the very idea of "nature" which so many hold dear will have to wither away in an "ecological" state of human society. Strange as it may sound, the idea of nature is getting in the way of properly ecological forms of culture, philosophy, politics, and art. The book addresses this paradox by considering art above all else, for it is in art that the fantasies we have about nature take shape—and dissolve. In particular, the literature of the Romantic period, commonly seen as crucially about nature, is the target of my investigation, since it still influences the ways in which the ecological imaginary works.

Why Ecology Must Be without Nature

In a study of political theories of nature, John Meyer asserts that ecological writers are preoccupied with the "holy grail" of generating "a new and encompassing worldview."[1] Whatever its content, this view "is regarded as capable of transforming human politics and society."[2] For example, deep ecology asserts that we need to change our view from anthropocentrism to ecocentrism. The idea that a view can change the world is deeply rooted in the Romantic period, as is the notion of worldview itself *(Weltanschauung)*. Coming up with a new worldview means dealing with how humans experience their place in the world. Aesthetics thus performs a crucial role, establishing ways of feeling and perceiving this place. In their collection of narratives on ecological value, Terre Slatterfield and Scott Slovic tell a story about President Clinton's dedication of a wilderness area in Utah: "At the ceremony dedicating the new national monument [Grand Staircacse-Escalante], . . . President [Clinton] held up a copy of [Terry Tempest Williams's] *Testimony* and said, 'This made a difference.' "[3] Slatterfield and Slovic want to demonstrate how narrative is an effective political tool. But their demonstration also turns politics into an aesthetic realm. For Slatterfield and Slovic, narrative is on the side of the affective, and science, which they call a "valuation frame," has blocked or is in "denial" about it.[4] As well as producing arguments, ecological writers fashion compelling *images*—literally, a *view* of the world. These images rely upon a sense of *nature*. But nature keeps giving writers the slip. And in all its confusing, ideological intensity, nature ironically impedes a proper relationship with the earth and its lifeforms, which would, of course, include ethics and science. Nature writing itself has accounted for the way nature gives us the slip. In *Reading the Mountains of Home,* for example, John Elder writes about how the narrative of nature appreciation is complicated by a growing awareness of "historical realities."[5] *Ecology without Nature* systematically attempts to *theorize* this complication.

Conventional ecocriticism is heavily thematic. It discusses ecological writers. It explores elements of ecology, such as animals, plants, or the weather. It investigates varieties of ecological, and ecocritical, language. *Ecology without Nature* does talk about animals, plants, and the weather. It also discusses specific texts and specific writers, composers and artists. It delves into all types of ideas about space and place (global, local, cosmopolitan, regionalist). Such explorations, while valid and important, are not the main point of this book. The goal is to think through an argument about what we mean by the word *environment* itself.

Ecology without Nature develops its argument in three distinct stages: *describing, contextualizing,* and *politicizing.* The first stage is an exploration of environmental art. Along with books such as Angus Fletcher's *A New Theory for American Poetry,* which offers a poetics of environmental form, and Susan Stewart's *Poetry and the Fate of the Senses,* Chapter 1 develops a fresh vocabulary for interpreting environmental art. It moves beyond the simple mention of "environmental" content, and toward the idea of environmental form. Its scope is wide but precise. Without prejudging the results, or focusing on certain favorite themes, how does art convey a sense of space and place? Chapter 1 explores how ultimately, environmental art, whatever its thematic content, is hamstrung by certain formal properties of language. I consider the literary criticism of environmental literature itself to be an example of environmental art.

Chapter 1 lays out a vocabulary for analyzing works in a variety of media. I have taught several classes on kinds of literature that talk about some idea of environment, in which these terms have proved invaluable. But ways of reading the text intrinsically, with an eye to its paradoxes and dilemmas, are always in danger of themselves turning into the special, or utopian, projects they find in the texts they analyze. What I propose instead is that these close reading tools be used to keep one step ahead of the ideological forces that ecological writing generates. I outline a theory of *ambient poetics,* a materialist way of reading texts with a view to how they encode the literal space of their inscription—if there is such a thing—the spaces between the words, the margins of the page, the physical and social environment of the reader. This has a bearing on the poetics of sensibility out of which Romanticism emerged in the late eighteenth century. Environmental aesthetics is frequently, if not always, caught in this form of materialism.

Chapter 2 studies the history and ideology of concepts, beliefs, and practices that make up current obsessions with the environment in all aspects of culture, from wildlife club calendars to experimental noise music. *Ecology without Nature* is one of the few studies that speak about low and high environmental culture in the same breath, treading the path paved by such books as William Cronon's *The Great New Wilderness Debate,* which brought together a variety of thinkers in so-called theory and so-called ecocriticism. How did the current environmentalism arise, and how does it affect our ideas about art and culture? This chapter analyzes the Romantic period as the moment at which the capitalism that now covers the earth began to take effect. Working forward from that moment, the book elaborates ways of understanding the dilemmas and paradoxes facing environmentalisms. In a somewhat more synthetic manner than David Harvey's *Justice, Nature and the Geography of Difference,* Chapter 2 accounts for why post-Romantic writing is obsessed with space and place. It employs my existing research on the history of consumerism, which has established that even forms of rebellion against consumerism, such as environmentalist practices, fall under the consumerist umbrella. Because consumerism is a discourse about identity, the chapter contains detailed readings of passages in environmentalist writing where a narrator, an "I," struggles to situate him- or herself in an environment.

Chapter 3 wonders where we go from here. What kinds of political and social thinking, making, and doing are possible? The book moves from an abstract discussion to a series of attempts to determine precisely what our relationship to environmental art and culture could be, as social, political animals. The chapter explores different ways of taking an artistic stand on environmental issues. It uses as evidence writers such as John Clare and William Blake, who maintained positions outside mainstream Romanticism. Chapter 3 demonstrates that the "Aeolian," ambient poetics outlined in Chapter 1—picking up the vibrations of a material universe and recording them with high fidelity—inevitably ignores the subject, and thus cannot fully come to terms with an ecology that may manifest itself in beings who are also persons—including, perhaps, those other beings we designate as animals.

Chapter 1 offers a theory of environmental art that is both an explication of it and a critical reflection. Chapter 2 offers a theoretical reflection on *this,* the "idea" of environmental art. And Chapter 3 is a further reflection still. This "theory of the theory" is political. Far from achieving greater levels of "theoretical" *abstraction* (abstraction is far from theoretical), the volume "rises" to higher and higher levels of *concreteness. Ecology without Nature* does not float away into the stratosphere. Nor does it quite descend to earth, since the earth starts to look rather different as we proceed.

Ecological writing keeps insisting that we are "embedded" in nature.[6] Nature is a surrounding medium that sustains our being. Due to the properties of the rhetoric that evokes the idea of a surrounding medium, ecological writing can never properly establish that this is nature and thus provide a compelling and consistent aesthetic basis for the new worldview that is meant to change society. It is a small operation, like tipping over a domino. My readings try to be symptomatic rather than comprehensive. I hope that by opening a few well-chosen holes, the entire nasty mess might pour out and dissolve.

Putting something called Nature on a pedestal and admiring it from afar does for the environment what patriarchy does for the figure of Woman. It is a paradoxical act of sadistic admiration. Simone de Beauvoir was one of the first to theorize this transformation of actually existing women into fetish objects.[7] *Ecology without Nature* examines the fine print of how nature has become a transcendental principle. This book sees itself, in the words of its subtitle, as rethinking environmental aesthetics. Environmental art, from low to high, from pastoral kitsch to urban chic, from Thoreau to Sonic Youth, plays with, reinforces, or deconstructs the idea of nature. What emerges from the book is a wider view of the possibilities of environmental art and criticism, the "widescreen" version of ecological culture. This version will be unafraid of difference, of nonidentity, both in textual terms and in terms of race, class, and gender, if indeed textual-critical matters can be separated from race, class, and gender. Ecocriticism has held a special, isolated place in the academy, in part because of the ideological baggage it is lumbered with. My intent is to open it up, to broaden it. Even if a Shakespeare sonnet does not appear explicitly to be "about" gender, nowadays we still want to ask what it might have to do with gender. The time should come when we ask of any text, "What does this say about the environment?" In the current situation we have already decided which texts we will be asking.

Some readers will already have pegged me as a "postmodern theorist" on whom they do not wish to waste their time. I do not believe that there is no such thing as a coral reef. (As it happens, modern industrial processes are ensuring they do not exist, whether I believe in them or not.) I also do not believe that environmental art and ecocriticism are entirely bogus. I do believe that they must be addressed critically, precisely because we care about them and we care about the earth, and, indeed, the future of life-forms on this planet, since humans have developed all the tools necessary for their destruction. As musician David Byrne once wrote, "Nuclear weapons could wipe out life on earth, if used properly."[8] It is vital for us to think and act in more general, wider terms. Particularism can muster a lot of passion, but it can become shortsighted. The reactionary response to wind farms in the United Kingdom, for instance, has tried to bog down environmentalists with the idea that birds will be caught in the blades of the windmills. Yes, we need to cultivate a more comprehensive view of "humanity" and "nature." Before I get accused of being a postmodern nihilist, I thought I would put my heart on the sleeve of this book. It is just that I aim to start with the bad new things, as Brecht once said, rather than try to return to the good old days. I wish to advance ecocritical thinking, not make it impossible. My work is about an "ecology to come," not about no ecology at all. One should view it as a contribution, albeit a long-range one, to the debate opened up by environmental justice ecocriticism.

Actually, postmodernists have a few nasty surprises in store. I do not think there is a "better way" of doing the things I describe in artistic media. Much contemporary artistic practice is predicated on the idea that there *is* a better way of doing things, with an attendant aura of chic that puts down other attempts as less sophisticated. Supposedly, we should all be listening to experimental noise music rather than Beethoven's Pastoral Symphony. We should all be reading Gilles Deleuze and Félix Guattari instead of Aldo Leopold. From the point of view of *Ecology without Nature,* these texts have more similarities than differences.

I do, however, distinguish between postmodernism, as a cultural and ideological form, and *deconstruction. Ecology without Nature* is inspired by the way in which deconstruction searches out, with ruthless and brilliant intensity, points of contradiction and deep hesitation in systems of meaning. If ecological criticism had a more open and honest engagement with deconstruction, it would find a friend rather than an enemy. Ecological criticism is in the habit of attacking, ignoring or vilifying this potential friend. Walter Benn Michaels has tarred both deep ecology and deconstruction with the same brush.[9] Hear, hear. There is indeed a connection between the two, and contra Michaels, I wish heartily to promote it. Just as Derrida explains how *différance* at once underlies and undermines logocentrism, I assert that the rhetorical strategies of nature writing undermine what one could call ecologocentrism.

Ecology without Nature tries not to foster a particular form of aesthetic enjoyment; at least not until the end, when it takes a stab at seeing whether art forms can bear the weight of being critical in the sense that the rest of the book outlines. No one kind of art is exactly "right." I do think that science would benefit from more grounding in philosophy and training in modes of analysis developed in the humanities. But in general the scientisms of current ideology owe less to intrinsically skeptical scientific practice, and more to ideas of *nature,* which set people's hearts beating and stop the thinking process, the one of saying "no" to what you just came up with. Have a look at any recent edition of *Time* or *Newsweek,* which take *Nature,* one of the main science journals, even more seriously than the scientists. In the name of ecology, this book is a searching criticism of a term that holds us back from meaningful engagements with what, in essence, nature is all about: things that are not identical to us or our preformed concepts. For related reasons, I have avoided the habitual discussions of anthropocentrism and anthropomorphism that preoccupy much ecological writing. These terms are not irrelevant. But they beg the question of what precisely counts as *human,* what counts as nature. Instead of pushing around preformed pieces of thought, I have chosen to hesitate at a more basic level, to lodge my criticism in the fissures between such categories.

Throughout this book, I read texts from the Romantic period, not only because they exemplify, but also because they do *not* accord with the various syndromes and symptoms that emerge from this very period. At the precise moment at which the trajectories of modern ecology were appearing, other pathways became possible. I have called on a multitude of art forms that deal with the idea of *environment,* even when this notion does not strictly entail nature in the way of rainforests or human lungs. A book so brief is only able to scratch the surface of the thousands of available examples. I hope that the ones I have chosen are representative, and that they illuminate the theoretical exploration of the idea of the environment. I have chosen to discuss authors of English literature with whom I am familiar: Blake, Coleridge, Levertov, Wordsworth, Mary Shelley, Thoreau, Edward Thomas. Many agree that they are ecological authors, yet their attitudes are not simple and direct, especially in the contexts of the other writers I adduce. I employ a variety of philosophers to help make my case. It is to Marx and Derrida that I owe almost equal debts, for they have enabled me to create the frameworks with which the analysis proceeds. But I am also indebted to Benjamin, Freud, Heidegger, Lacan, Latour, Žižek, and in particular to Hegel, whose idea of the "beautiful soul" has become the single most important notion in the book. I use Theodor Adorno, whose writing has a strong, often explicit ecological flavor. Adorno based much of his work on the idea that modern society engages in a process of domination that establishes and exploits some thing "over there" called nature. His sensitivity to the idea of nuclear annihilation has many parallels with the sensitivity of ecological writing to equally total catastrophes such as global warming. Where the relationships are less clear (for instance, in the case of Descartes, Derrida, or Benjamin), I trust that my text will explain why a certain writer is appearing. And the study introduces some writers as test cases of environmental writing: David Abram, Val Plumwood, Leslie Marmon Silko, and David Toop, among others. Add to these a host of artists and composers: Beethoven, Reich, Cage, Alvin Lucier, Yves Klein, Escher. And along the way we will also be encountering a number of popular products by J. R. R. Tolkien, Pink Floyd, The Orb, and others.

Ecology without Nature covers a lot of ground in a short space. Studies of the idea of nature have appeared before, many times. Diverse accounts of environmentalism and nature writing have emerged. And specifically, scholarship has frequently derived ecology from Romanticism. In a reflexive and systematic way, *Ecology without Nature* accounts for the phenomenon of environmentalism in culture, delving into the details of poetry and prose, and stepping back to see the big picture, while offering a critique of the workings of "Nature" at different levels. It does this by operating principally upon a single pressure point: the idea of "nature writing" or, as this book prefers to call it, *ecomimesis*. The book is thus necessarily one-sided and incomplete, even as it tries to be comprehensive. But I can see no other way of usefully drawing together all the themes I wish to talk about, in a reasonably short volume. I trust that the reader will be able to bring his or her own examples to the discussion, where they are lacking. My own specializations in Romantic studies, food studies, and the study of literature and the environment have necessarily skewed my sense of things.

Environmental Reflections

"A theory of ecological criticism" means at least two things. Clintonian explanations aside, it all depends on what you mean by "of." On the one hand, this book provides a set of theoretical tools for ecological criticism. "A theory of ecological criticism" is an ecocritical theory. On the other hand, the study accounts for the qualities of existing ecocriticism, placing them in context and taking account of their paradoxes, dilemmas, and shortcomings. "A theory of ecological criticism" is a theoretical reflection upon ecocriticism: to criticize the ecocritic.

Ecology without Nature thus hesitates between two places. It wavers both inside and outside ecocriticism. (For reasons given later, I am at pains not to say that the book is in two places at once.) It supports the study of literature and the environment. It is wholeheartedly ecological in its political and philosophical orientation. And yet it does not thump an existing ecocritical tub. It does not mean to undermine ecocriticism entirely. It does not mean to suggest that there is nothing "out there." But *Ecology without Nature* does challenge the assumptions that ground ecocriticism. It does so with the aim not of shutting down ecocriticism, but of opening it up.

Environmentalism is a set of cultural and political responses to a crisis in humans' relationships with their surroundings. Those responses could be scientific, activist, or artistic, or a mixture of all three. Environmentalists try to preserve areas of wilderness or "outstanding natural beauty." They struggle against pollution, including the risks of nuclear technologies and weaponry. They fight for animal rights and vegetarianism in campaigns against hunting and scientific or commercial experimentation on animals. They oppose globalization and the patenting of life-forms.

Environmentalism is broad and inconsistent. You can be a communist environmentalist, or a capitalist one, like the American "wise use" Republicans. You can be a "soft" conservationist, sending money to charities such as Britain's Woodland Trust, or a "hard" one who lives in trees to stop logging and road building. And you could, of course, be both at the same time. You could produce scientific papers on global warming or write "ecocritical" literary essays. You could create poems, or environmental sculpture, or ambient music. You could do environmental philosophy ("ecosophy"), establishing ways of thinking, feeling, and acting based on benign relationships with our environment(s).

Likewise, there are many forms of ecocriticism. Ecofeminist criticism examines the ways in which patriarchy has been responsible for environmental deterioration and destruction, and for sustaining a view of the natural world that oppresses women in the same way as it oppresses animals, life in general, and even matter itself. A form of ecocriticism has emerged from Romantic scholarship, in the work of writers such as Jonathan Bate, Karl Kroeber, and James McKusick.[10] It puts the *critical* back into academic reading in a provocative and accessible way. It is itself an example of a certain aspect of the Romantic literary project to change the world by compelling a strong affective response and a fresh view of things. Then there is environmental justice ecocriticism, which considers how environmental destruction, pollution, and the oppression of specific classes and races go hand in hand.[11]

From an environmentalist point of view, this is not a good time. So why undertake a project that criticizes ecocriticism at all? Why not just let sleeping ecological issues lie? It sounds like a perverse joke. The sky is falling, the globe is warming, the ozone hole persists; people are dying of radiation poisoning and other toxic agents; species are being wiped out, thousands per year; the coral reefs have nearly all gone. Huge globalized corporations are making bids for the necessities of life from water to health care. Environmental legislation is being threatened around the world. What a perfect opportunity to sit back and reflect on ideas of space, subjectivity, environment, and poetics. *Ecology without Nature* claims that there could be no better time.

What is the point of reflecting like this? Some think that ecocriticism needs what it calls "theory" like it needs a hole in the head. Others contend that this aeration is exactly what ecocriticism needs. In the name of ecocriticism itself, scholarship must reflect—theorize, in the broadest sense. Since ecology and ecological politics are beginning to frame other kinds of science, politics, and culture, we must take a step back and examine some of ecology's ideological determinants. This is precisely the opposite of what John Daniel says about the need for a re-enchantment of the world:

> The sky probably is falling. Global warming is happening. But somehow it's not going to work to call people to arms about that and pretend to know what will work. People don't want to feel invalidated in their lives and they don't want to feel that they bear the responsibility of the world on their shoulders. This is why you shouldn't teach kids about the dire straits of the rain forest. You should take kids out to the stream out back and show them water striders.[12]

To speak thus is to use the aesthetic as an anesthetic.

To theorize ecological views is also to bring thinking up to date. Varieties of Romanticism and primitivism have often construed ecological struggle as that of "place" against the encroachments of modern and postmodern "space." In social structure and in thought, goes the argument, place has been ruthlessly corroded by space: all that is solid melts into air. But unless we think about it some more, the cry of "place!" will resound in empty space, to no effect. It is a question of whether you think that the "re-enchantment of the world" will make nice pictures, or whether it is a political practice.

Revolutionary movements such as those in Chiapas, Mexico, have had partial success in reclaiming place from the corrosion of global economics. "Third World" environmentalisms are often passionate defenses of the local against globalization.[13] Simply lauding location in the abstract or in the aesthetic, however—praising a localist poetics, for example, just because it is localist, or proclaiming a "small is beautiful" aestheticized ethics—is in greater measure part of the problem than part of the solution. Our notions of place are retroactive fantasy constructs determined precisely by the corrosive effects of modernity. Place was not lost, though we posit it as something we have lost. Even if place as an actually existing, rich set of relationships between sentient beings does not (yet) exist, place is part of our worldview *right now*—what if it is actually propping up that view? We would be unable to cope with modernity unless we had a few pockets of place in which to store our hope.

Here is the book's *cri de guerre,* but I will be making a lot of small moves before I interrogate such ideas head-on. There are problems in the fine print of how we write about the environment. Underlining some of this fine print will not make the bigger problems go away, but it is a useful start. The initial focus is what marketing and scholarship in the United States calls "nature writing." Under this banner I place most ecocriticism itself, which, if not wholly an instance of nature writing, contains good examples of the genre. This is far from suggesting that nature writing is the only game in town. It is simply that such writing presents significant artistic and philosophical solutions that crystallize all sorts of issues in ecological writing at large. The book goes on to examine much more: philosophy, literature, music, visual art, and multimedia, in an expanding cone of critical analysis.

Ecocritique

In order to have an environment, you have to have a space for it; in order to have an *idea* of an environment, you need ideas of space (and place). If we left our ideas about nature on hold for a moment, instead of introducing them all too soon—they always tend to make us hot under the collar anyway—a clearer picture would emerge of what exactly the idea of "environment" is in the first place. This is not to suggest that if you subtract the rabbits, trees, and skyscrapers, you will be left with something called an environment. That kind of thinking goes too fast for this book. Instead of lumping together a list of things and dubbing it "nature," the aim is to slow down and take the list apart—and to put into question the idea of making a list at all. *Ecology without Nature* takes seriously the idea that truly theoretical reflection is possible only if thinking decelerates. This is not the same thing as becoming numb or stupid. It is finding anomalies, paradoxes, and conundrums in an otherwise smooth-looking stream of ideas.

This slowing-down process has often been aestheticized. When it is called "close reading" it is supposed to convey all sorts of healthy effects on the reader, much like meditation. Like many other forms of criticism, ecocriticism has a canon of works that are better medicine than others. Even though *Ecology without Nature* widens our view of environmental literature to include texts that are not normative in this way, it is possible that it could advocate the medicinal approach in another way. The reading process itself, no matter what its materials, could be thought of as healing balm. But ultimately, theory (and meditation, for that matter) is not supposed to make you a "better person" in any sense. It is supposed to expose hypocrisy, or if you prefer, to examine the ways in which ideological illusions maintain their grip. So *Ecology without Nature* is not an attempt to be slower than thou, in order to outdo the tortoise of close reading, a kind of anti-race toward an aesthetic state of meditative calm that we could then (falsely) associate with some sort of "ecological awareness." This is especially important since ecological ethics can be based on a meditative aesthetic state: for instance, the "appreciative listening" that Michel Serres hopes will replace "mastery and possession."[14] And this ethics of the aesthetic has in general been getting a good run for its money in the recent work of writers such as Elaine Scarry.[15]

The point is not to attain any special state of mind at all. The point is to go against the grain of dominant, normative ideas about nature, but to do so in the name of sentient beings suffering under catastrophic environmental conditions. I say this with all due respect to the deep ecologists who think that humans, being just a viral infection on the planet, will at some point be sneezed away in a wave of extinction, and that, ultimately, we could just sit back and relax in quietude—or hasten our own demise; or act as if we didn't matter at all.

A truly theoretical approach is not allowed to sit smugly outside the area it is examining. It must mix thoroughly with it. Adopting a position that forgoes all others would be all too easy, a naïve negative criticism that is a disguised position all of its own. It is all very well to carp at the desires of others while not owning up to the determinacy of one's own desire. This is a political as well as an intellectual position, one to which ecological thinking is itself prone. After Hegel, I call it *beautiful soul syndrome,* and examine it in Chapter 2. The "beautiful soul" washes his or her hands of the corrupt world, refusing to admit how in this very abstemiousness and distaste he or she participates in the creation of that world. The world-weary soul holds all beliefs and ideas at a distance. The only ethical option is to muck in. Thus, the book does offer its own view of ecology and ecocriticism, not only throughout its sustained critique of other views, but also in its own right.

In places I come close to Hegel's idea that art since Romanticism has been surpassed by philosophy—or even to Oscar Wilde's idea that criticism itself is now the best vehicle for telling us where we are at.[16] But I shy away from being absolute about this, preferring instead to suggest ways of thinking, making, and practicing environmental art, politics, and philosophy. Ecocriticism is too enmeshed in the ideology that churns out stereotypical ideas of nature to be of any use. Indeed, ecocriticism is barely distinguishable from the nature writing that is its object. I want to develop an idea of what "properly critical" might mean.

Timothy Luke employs the term *ecocritique* to describe forms of left ecological criticism.[17] I use the term in a more self-reflexive way than Luke. Ecocritique is critical and self-critical. This is the proper sense of critique, a dialectical form of criticism that bends back upon itself. It was the Frankfurt School that established this notion of *Kritik.* As well as pointing, in a highly politicized way, to society, critique points toward itself. There is always further to go. Ecocritique is permeated with considerations common to other areas in the humanities such as race, class, and gender, which it knows to be deeply intertwined with environmental issues. Ecocritique fearlessly employs the ideas of deconstruction in the service of ecology, rather than, as is all too frequent, flogging the dead horse of "postmodern theory." Ecocritique is similar to queer theory. In the name of all that we value in the idea of "nature," it thoroughly examines how nature is set up as a transcendental, unified, independent category. Ecocritique does not think that it is paradoxical to say, in the name of ecology itself: "down with nature!"

The guiding slogan of ecocritique is: "not afraid of nonidentity." To borrow an argument from Theodor Adorno, a member of the Frankfurt School and one of the guiding lights of this study, the thinking process is in essence the encounter with nonidentity.[18] If not, it is just the manipulation of preformed pieces on a ready-made board. This is also how Hegel distinguished dialectical thinking from sheer logic.[19] There must be a movement at least from A to not-A. At any moment, thought necessarily bumps its head against what it isn't. Thinking must "go somewhere," though whether it goes anywhere particularly solid is up for grabs. This encounter with nonidentity, when considered fully, has profound implications for ecological thinking, ethics, and art. Non-identity has a lineage in nature writing itself, which is why I can write this book at all. Peter Fritzell delineated a difference between naively mimetic and self-reflexive forms of nature writing. In the latter, " 'what nature was really like' is often not what nature was really like (or, for that matter, what it is)."[20]

Natural History Lessons

One of the ideas inhibiting genuinely ecological politics, ethics, philosophy, and art is the idea of nature itself. Nature, a transcendental term in a material mask, stands at the end of a potentially infinite series of other terms that collapse into it, otherwise known as a metonymic list: fish, grass, mountain air, chimpanzees, love, soda water, freedom of choice, heterosexuality, free markets . . . Nature. A metonymic series becomes a metaphor. Writing conjures this notoriously slippery term, useful to ideologies of all kinds in its very slipperiness, in its refusal to maintain any consistency.[21] But consistency is what nature is all about, on another level. Saying that something is unnatural is saying that it does not conform to a norm, so "normal" that it is built into the very fabric of things as they are. So "nature" occupies at least three places in symbolic language. First, it is a mere empty placeholder for a host of other concepts. Second, it has the force of law, a norm against which deviation is measured. Third, "nature" is a Pandora's box, a word that encapsulates a potentially infinite series of disparate fantasy objects. It is this third sense—nature as fantasy—that this book most fully engages. A "discipline" of diving into the Rorschach blobs of others' enjoyment that we commonly call poems seems a highly appropriate way of beginning to engage with how "nature" compels feelings and beliefs.

Nature wavers in between the divine and the material. Far from being something "natural" itself, nature hovers over things like a ghost. It slides over the infinite list of things that evoke it. Nature is thus not unlike "the subject," a being who searches through the entire universe for its reflection, only to find none. If it is just another word for supreme authority, then why not just call it God? But if this God is nothing outside the material world, then why not just call it matter? This was the political dilemma in which Spinoza, and the deists of eighteenth-century Europe, found themselves.[22] Being an "out" atheist was very dangerous in the eighteenth century, as evidenced by the cryptic remarks of Hume and the increasingly cautious approach of Percy Shelley, who had been expelled from Oxford for publishing a pamphlet on atheism. God often appeared on the side of royal authority, and the rising bourgeoisie and associated revolutionary classes wanted another way of being authoritative. "Ecology without nature" means in part that we try to confront some of the intense notions which nature smudges.

Ecological writing is fascinated with the idea of something that exists in between polarized terms such as God and matter, this and that, subject and object. I find John Locke's critique of the idea of ether to be helpful here. Locke's critique appeared toward the beginning of the modern construction of space as an empty set of point coordinates.[23] Numerous holes in materialist, atomist theories were filled by something elemental. Newton's gravity worked because of an ambient *ether* that transmitted the properties of heavy bodies instantaneously, in an analogy for (or as an aspect of) the love of an omnipresent God.[24] If ether is a kind of "ambient fluid" that surrounds all particles, existing "in between" them, then what surrounds the particles of ambient fluid themselves?[25] If nature is sandwiched between terms such as God and matter, what medium keeps the things that are natural sandwiched together? Nature appears to be both lettuce and mayonnaise. Ecological writing shuffles subject and object back and forth so that we may think they have dissolved into each other, though what we usually end up with is a blur this book calls *ambience*.

Later in the modern period, the idea of the nation-state emerged as a way of going beyond the authority of the monarch. The nation all too often depends upon the very same list that evokes the idea of nature. *Nature* and *nation* are very closely intertwined. I show how ecocritique could examine the ways in which nature does not necessarily take us outside society, but actually forms the bedrock of nationalist enjoyment. Nature, practically a synonym for evil in the Middle Ages, was considered the basis of social good by the Romantic period. According to numerous writers such as Rousseau, the framers of the social contract start out in a state of nature. The fact that this state is not much different from the "concrete jungle" of actual historical circumstance has not escaped attention.

In the Enlightenment, nature became a way of establishing racial and sexual identity, and science became the privileged way of demonstrating it. The normal was set up as different from the pathological along the coordinates of the *natural* and the *unnatural*.[26] Nature, by then a scientific term, put a stop to argument or rational inquiry: "Well, it's just in my nature." He is ideological, you are prejudiced, but my ideas are natural. A metaphorical use of Thomas Malthus in the work of Charles Darwin, for example, naturalized, and continues to naturalize, the workings of the "invisible hand" of the free market and the "survival of the fittest"—which is always taken to mean the competitive war of all (owners) against all (workers). Malthus used nature to argue against the continuation of early modern welfare, in a document produced for the government of his age. Sadly, this very thinking is now being used to push down the poor yet further, in the battle of the supposedly ecologically minded against "population growth" (and immigration). Nature, achieved obliquely through turning metonymy into metaphor, becomes an oblique way of talking about politics. What is presented as straightforward, "unmarked," beyond contestation, is warped.

One of the basic problems with nature is that it could be considered either as a *substance*, as a squishy thing in itself, or as *essence*, as an abstract principle that transcends the material realm and even the realm of representation. Edmund Burke considers substance as the stuff of nature in his writing on the sublime.[27] This "substantialism" asserts that there is at least one actually existing thing that embodies a sublime quality (vastness, terror, magnificence). Substantialism tends to promote a monarchist or authoritarian view that there is an external thing to which the subject should bow. Essentialism, on the other hand, has its champion in Immanuel Kant. The sublime thing can never be represented, and indeed, in certain religions, says Kant, there is a prohibition against trying (Judaism, Islam). This essentialism turns out to be politically liberating, on the side of revolutionary republicanism.[28] On the whole, nature writing, and its precursors and family members, mostly in phenomenological and/or Romantic writing, has tended to favor a substantialist view of nature—it is palpable and *there*—despite the explicit politics of the author. Further work in ecocritique should delineate a republican, nonsubstantialist countertradition running through writers such as Milton and Shelley, for whom nature did not stand in for an authority for which you sacrifice your autonomy and reason.

Ecological forms of subjectivity inevitably involve ideas and decisions about *group* identity and behavior. Subjectivity is not simply an individual, and certainly not just an individualist, phenomenon. It is a collective one. Environmental writing is a way of registering the feeling of being surrounded by others, or more abstractly, by an otherness, something that is not the self. Although it may displace the actual social collective and choose to write about surrounding mountains instead, such displacements always say something about the kinds of collective life that ecological writing is envisaging. Fredric Jameson outlines the necessity for criticism to work on ideas of collectivity:

> Anyone who evokes the ultimate value of the community or the collectivity from a left perspective must face three problems: 1) how to distinguish this position radically from communitarianism; 2) how to differentiate the collective project from fascism or nazism; 3) how to relate the social and the economic level—that is, how to use the Marxist analysis of capitalism to demonstrate the unviability of social solutions within that system. As for collective identities, in a historical moment in which individual personal identity has been unmasked as a decentered locus of multiple subject positions, surely it is not too much to ask that something analogous be conceptualized on the collective level.[29]

The idea of the environment is more or less a way of considering groups and collectives—humans surrounded by nature, or in continuity with other beings such as animals and plants. It is about being-with. As Latour has recently pointed out, however, the actual situation is far more drastically collective than that. All kinds of beings, from toxic waste to sea snails, are clamoring for our scientific, political, and artistic attention, and have become part of political life—to the detriment of monolithic conceptions of Nature.[30] To write about ecology is to write about society, and not simply in the weak sense that our ideas of ecology are social constructions. Historical conditions have abolished an extra-social nature to which theories of society can appeal, while at the same time making the beings that fell under this heading impinge ever more urgently upon society.

Different images of the environment suit different kinds of society. Substantialist images of a palpable, distinct "nature" embodied in at least one actually existing phenomenon (a particular species, a particular figure) generate authoritarian forms of collective organization. The deep ecological view of nature as a tangible entity tends this way. Essentialist ideas of a nature that cannot be rendered as an image have supported more egalitarian forms. It would be very helpful if ecocritique simply observed that there were other kinds of models for nature. For instance, the republican (small "r") poetics derived from writers such as Milton and the neglected history of radical environmentalism in the English Revolution convey iconoclastic figures of the environment that transcend discrete forms of representation.[31] Other political forms prohibit graven images of nature. In contrast to the touchy-feely organicism derived from Burkean ideologies of class and tradition, we could think the environment in a more open, rational and differently sensuous manner. The study of iconoclastic representations of space and world recovers fresh ways of thinking and creating. Demonstrating that there are, at least, different sorts of fantasy images of the natural would refresh environmental thinking. But ecocritique does not stop there.

Substance and essence are strangely different from each other. There is no easy way of finding a term that would supersede both at once. If we claim that substance and essence are absolutely different, this is supporting *substantialism*—substance and essence are two entirely different "substances." On this view, essence and substance are like chalk and cheese, apples and oranges. If, on the other hand, we say that essence and substance are different the way black and white, or up and down, are different, then we approach the *essentialist* view—substance and essence are not different all the way down, but are related to one another in opposition. For instance, the substance of things, on this view, is just a variation in their atomic structure, or DNA code. Substance is embodied in at least one thing, but not in others. Essence cannot be embodied. Nature wants to be both substance and essence at the same time. Nature opens up the difference between terms, and erases those very differences, all at once. It is the trees and the wood—and the very *idea* of trees (Greek *hyle*, matter, wood).

The more we study it, the more we see that, beyond the fact that many different people have many different opinions about it, nature in itself flickers between things—it is both/and or neither/nor. This flickering affects how we write about it. Nature is . . . animals, trees, the weather . . . the bioregion, the ecosystem. It is both the set and the contents of the set. It is the world and the entities in that world. It appears like a ghost at the never-arriving end of an infinite series: crabs, waves, lightning, rabbits, silicon . . . Nature. Of all things, nature should be natural. But we cannot point to it. What we usually get is a suggestive effusion on something "Whose dwelling is in the light of setting suns, / In the round ocean, and the living air, / And the blue sky, and in the mind of man," as Wordsworth marvelously put it.[32] Nature becomes supernatural, a process made clear in John Gatta's decisive treatment of the history of Puritan ideas about nature and wilderness (though Gatta sets aside the more radical Puritan possibilities of the Diggers, the mystic Jacob Boehme and the vegetarian Thomas Tryon).[33] Or nature dissolves and we are left with sheer matter, and a sequence of ideas with numerous high points in radical materialist philosophy, such as Spinoza. We want there to be something in between. But would that be natural? Would it not be supernatural? Would that be supernatural like a spirit—more of a refined essence—or a ghost—something more substantial, maybe made of ectoplasm? We could go on splitting hairs infinitely. Our journey to the middle, to the "in between" space, whatever we call it, would go on generating binary pairs, and we would always be coming down on one side or the other, missing the exact center. It does not matter whether this is materialist spirituality, or spiritual materialism. Thinking posits something "over there" that maintains a mysterious allure.

Since the Romantic period, nature has been used to support the capitalist theory of value and to undermine it; to point out what is intrinsically human, and to exclude the human; to inspire kindness and compassion, and to justify competition and cruelty. It is easy to see why M. H. Abrams would have written a book on Romantic poetry called *Natural Supernaturalism*. In short, nature has been on both sides of the equation ever since it was invented. *Ecology without Nature* takes nature out of the equation by exploring the ways in which literary writing tries to conjure it up. We discover how nature always slips out of reach in the very act of grasping it. At the very moment at which writing seems to be dissolving in the face of the compelling reality it is describing, writing overwhelms what it is depicting and makes it impossible to find anything behind its opaque texture. Even as it establishes a middle ground "in between" terms such as subject and object, or inside and outside, nature without fail excludes certain terms, thus reproducing the difference between inside and outside in other ways.[34] Just when it brings us into proximity with the nonhuman "other," nature reestablishes a comfortable distance between "us" and "them." With ecological friends like this, who needs enemies?

Some will accuse me of being a postmodernist, by which they will mean that I believe that the world is made of text, that there is nothing real. Nothing could be further from the truth. The idea of nature is all too real, and it has an all too real effect upon all too real beliefs, practices, and decisions in the all too real world. True, I claim that there is no such "thing" as nature, if by nature we mean some thing that is single, independent, and lasting. But deluded ideas and ideological fixations do exist. "Nature" is a focal point that compels us to assume certain attitudes. Ideology resides in the attitude we assume toward this fascinating object. By dissolving the object, we render the ideological fixation inoperative. At least, that is the plan.

The ecocritical view of "postmodernism," for which "theory" is a shibboleth, has much in common with the English dislike of the French Revolution—indeed, it is in many ways derived from it.[35] "Theory," goes the argument, is cold and abstract, out of touch.[36] It forces organic forms into boxes that cannot do them justice. It is too calculating and rational. "Postmodernism" is just the latest version of this sorry state of affairs. Of course, the English position against the French was its own abstraction, a self-imposed denial of history that had already happened—the beheading of Charles I, for instance.

Academics are never more intellectual than when they are being anti-intellectual. No self-respecting farmer would comport himself or herself quite like Aldo Leopold or Martin Heidegger. What could be more postmodern than a professor reflexively choosing a social and subjective view, such as that of a farmer? What could be more postmodern than ecocriticism, which, far from being naive, consciously blocks its ears to all intellectual developments of the last thirty years, notably (though not necessarily all at once) feminism, anti-racism, anti-homophobia, deconstruction? Just as the Reagan and Bush administrations attempted a re-run of the 1950s, as if the 1960s had never happened, so ecocriticism promises to return to an academy of the past. It is a form of postmodern retro.

If ecocritics dislike what I say, however, so will post-structuralists. Post-structuralism—criticism that acts as if the 1960s *had* occurred—has its own views of nature, though it may not name it so baldly. It is just that these views are supposedly more sophisticated than previous ones. There is still the basic search for something "in between" categories such as subject and object, fact and value. There exists a class divide between the enjoyment-objects of ecocritical-conservative and post-structuralist-radical readers. If ecocritics prefer Aldo Leopold's almanac style, complete with cute illustrations, post-structuralists tend to go for the latest compilation album by an ambient techno DJ. It may not be Beethoven, but it is still polite at a cocktail party or art opening, if not more so. Leopold and The Orb are really two sides of the same coin, according to ecocritique. Whether they are highbrow or middlebrow, installation or pastoral symphony, artworks exhibit what I call *ecomimesis*, a rhetorical form described in detail in Chapter 1, and ex-

plored throughout this book. Thunderbird or Chardonnay, retro or fu-
turistic, it's all the same ecomimesis.

Postmodernism is mired in aestheticism. It freezes irony into an aesthetic pose. When I suggest that we drop the concept of nature, I am
saying that we *really* drop it, rather than try to come up with hastily
conceived, "new and improved" solutions, a new form of advertising
language. This is about what you think "without" means in the title of
this book. Derrida's profound thinking on the "without," the *sans,* in
his writing on negative theology comes to mind. Deconstruction goes
beyond just saying that something exists, even in a "hyperessential"
way beyond being. And it goes beyond saying that things do not exist.[37]
"Ecology without nature" is a relentless questioning of essence, rather
than some special new thing. Sometimes the utopian language of a
writer such as Donna Haraway rushes to jerry-build ideas like "na-
tureculture."[38] These non-natures are still nature, based on hopeful interpretations of emerging ideas across disciplines such as philosophy,
mathematics, and anthropology, ideas that turn out to be highly aesthetic. Chapter 1 focuses on a set of alternatives to traditional ideas of
nature that lie just to the side of it. Assuming that nature itself is too
soft a target these days, I analyze possible ways of thinking the same
idea bigger, wider, or better under the general heading of "ambience."

To get properly beyond postmodernism's pitfalls, genuinely critical
ecocriticism would engage fully with theory. If we consider the nonthe-
ological sense of nature, the term collapses into *impermanence* and *history*—two ways of saying the same thing. Life-forms are constantly
coming and going, mutating and becoming extinct. Biospheres and ecosystems are subject to arising and cessation. Living beings do not form
a solid prehistorical, or nonhistorical ground upon which human history plays. But nature is often wheeled out to adjudicate between what
is fleeting and what is substantial and permanent. Nature smoothes
over uneven history, making its struggles and sufferings illegible. Given
that much ecocriticism and ecological literature is primitivist, it is ironic
that indigenous societies often refer to nature as a shape-shifting trickster rather than as a firm basis. The final word of the history of nature
is that *nature is history*. "Natural beauty, purportedly ahistorical, is at
its core historical."[39]

What Is Nature For?

Ecology without Nature starts as a detailed examination of how art
represents the environment. This helps us to see that "nature" is an ar-

bitrary rhetorical construct, empty of independent, genuine existence behind or beyond the texts we create about it. The rhetoric of nature depends upon something I define as an *ambient poetics,* a way of conjuring up a sense of a surrounding atmosphere or world. My argument follows Angus Fletcher's recent work on an emerging American poetics of the environment.[40] His suggestive idea that the long, sinuous lines in Whitman and his descendants establish ways of reaching out toward and going beyond horizons, and of creating an open-ended idea of nature, is a valuable account of a specific form of poetics. I associate it, as he does, with developments in postmodern and deconstructive thinking. I am, however, less confident than Fletcher of the utopian value of this poetics.

In Chapter 2, we see that this poetics has its own history and that people have invested various ideological meanings in it, over time. When we historicize ambient poetics, we find out that this, too, is devoid of any intrinsic existence or value. Some contemporary artists use ambient poetics to rise above what they see as the kitsch quality of other forms of natural representation. But in so doing, they ignore the ideological qualities of the rhetoric they are using. They risk creating just a "new and improved" version of the kitsch they were trying to escape. The history of ambient poetics depends upon certain forms of identity and subjectivity, which Chapter 2 also discovers to be historical. Chapter 3 goes still further. Rather than resting in historicization, we should begin to politicize environmental art, which means beginning to become less blind to its operations. We ourselves must not venture formulating a "new and improved" version of environmental art. This will involve us in some paradoxes. For example, since there is no escaping kitsch, the only way to "beat" it is to "join" it.

The "thing" we call nature becomes, in the Romantic period and afterward, a way of healing what modern society has damaged.[41] Nature is like that other Romantic-period invention, the aesthetic. The damage done, goes the argument, has sundered subjects from objects, so that human beings are forlornly alienated from their world. Contact with nature, and with the aesthetic, will mend the bridge between subject and object. Romanticism saw the broken bridge as a lamentable fact of philosophical and social life. Post-Kantian philosophy—Schelling and Hegel in Germany, Coleridge in England—often wishes for *reconciliation* of subject and object. If they met under the right circumstances, they would hit it off. Subject and object require a certain environment in which they can join up together. Thus is born the special realms of art and nature, the new secular churches in which subject and object can be remarried.[42]

This all depends upon whether subject and object ever had a relationship in the first place; and indeed, upon whether there *are* such things as subject and object, which leads us to a central knot, the problem posed by some forms of utopian environmental art. If subject and object do not really exist, then why bother trying to reconcile them? Or, if they do exist, why would some fresh amalgamation of the pair be better than what we have now? Would this amalgamation look any different than the subject–object dualism that concerns us? If the solution to subject–object dualism were as easy as changing our minds, then why have countless texts seeking to do exactly that not done so already? If the solution is some sense of an environment, then *what* precisely is it if it is not "around" anything? Will it not tend to collapse either into a subject or an object?

There are at least two ways of looking at these irksome questions. The first examines the idea that we need to "change our minds." Instead of looking for a solution to the subject–object problem, a more paradoxical strategy is in order. It questions what is problematic about the problem itself. If, at bottom, *there is no problem*—if reality is indeed devoid of reified, rigid, or conceptual notions of subject and object, and we coexist in an infinite web of mutual interdependence where there is no boundary or center—why then do we need to make all this ecocritical fuss? Surely therefore, the fuss is like scratching an itch that doesn't exist—thereby bringing it into existence. In which case, one of the targets of genuine critique would be the very (eco)critical languages—the constant elegy for a lost unalienated state, the resort to the aesthetic dimension (experiential/perceptual) rather than ethical-political praxis, the appeal to "solutions," often anti-intellectual, and so on—which sustain the itch, albeit in a subtle way.

The second approach is to wonder whether the problem lies not so much "in our heads" as "out there," in social reality. What if, no matter what we thought about it, certain features of the dreaded dualism were hardwired into our world? Ecocritique, in that case, takes the cry against dualism at least half seriously. It perceives it to be a symptom of a malaise that was not an idea in our heads, but an ideological feature of the way in which the world operates.

Ecocritique is indeed critique; but it is also "eco." My aim is not to poke fun at hopeless attempts to join together what could never be torn asunder, or to supplant ecological thinking with a hipper form of belief, a nihilistic creed that anything goes. The aim is to strengthen environmentalism. Appealing to nature still has a powerful rhetorical effect. In the short term, relatively speaking, nature still has some force. But environmentalism cannot be in the game just for the short term. And that nature remains an effective slogan is a symptom of how far we have *not* come, not of how far we have.

"Ecology without nature" could mean "ecology without a *concept* of the natural." Thinking, when it becomes ideological, tends to fixate on concepts rather than doing what is "natural" to thought, namely, dissolving whatever has taken form. Ecological thinking that was not fixated, that did not stop at a particular concretization of its object, would thus be "without nature." To do ecocritique, we must consider the aesthetic dimension, for the aesthetic has been posited as a nonconceptual realm, a place where our ideas about things drop away. For Adorno, "The iridescence that emanates from artworks, which today taboo all affirmation, is the appearance of the affirmative *ineffabile,* the emergence of the nonexisting as if it did exist."[43] Art gives what is nonconceptual an illusive appearance of form. This is the aim of environmental literature: to encapsulate a utopian image of nature which does not really exist—we have destroyed it; which goes beyond our conceptual grasp. On the other hand, a nonconceptual image can be a compelling focus for an intensely conceptual system—an ideological system. The dense meaninglessness of nature writing can exert a gravitational pull.

The aesthetic is also a product of distance: of human beings from nature, of subjects from objects, of mind from matter. Is it not rather suspiciously anti-ecological? This is a matter for debate in the Frankfurt School. Benjamin's famous description of the aesthetic aura does indeed use an environmental image.[44] Herbert Marcuse claims that "The aesthetic universe is the *Lebenswelt* on which the needs and faculties of freedom depend for their liberation. They cannot develop in an environment shaped by and for aggressive impulses, nor can they be envisaged as the mere effect of a new set of social institutions. They can emerge only in the collective *practice of creating an environment.*"[45] Art could help ecology by modeling an environment based on love (eros) rather than death (thanatos)—as is the current technological-industrial world, according to Marcuse. Marcuse uses *Lebenswelt* (lifeworld), a term developed in phenomenology out of Romanticism's construction of worlds and environments that situate the thinking mind. As we shall see in Chapter 2, this line of enquiry linked together the environment and the aesthetic. No wonder Marcuse thinks of the aesthetic as a "dimension." He writes: "Art breaks open a dimension inaccessible to other experience, a dimension in which human beings, nature, and things no longer stand under the law of the established reality principle."[46] *Dimension,* like the aesthetic itself, sits somewhere between an objective notion (in mathematics, for instance) and a subjective experience. Many of the writers this study encounters treat the aesthetic and nature as if they comprised a single, unified dimension. But even if there were more than one dimension, this would not solve the problems of this intrinsically spatial way of thinking. No matter how many there are, a dimension is something we are *in*—or not—and this assumes a dichotomy between inside and outside, the very thing that has yet to be established.

Adorno is more hesitant than Marcuse. For him, the aesthetic helpfully distances us from something we have a tendency to destroy when we get close to it:

> The distance of the aesthetic realm from that of practical aims appears inner-aesthetically as the distance of aesthetic objects from the observing subject; just as artworks cannot intervene, the subject cannot intervene in them; distance is the primary condition for any closeness to the content of works. This is implicit in Kant's concept of absence of interest, which demands of aesthetic comportment that it not grasp at the object, not devour it.[47]

In this way, the aesthetic promotes nonviolence toward nature. Art is not so much a space of positive qualities (eros), but of negative ones: it stops us from destroying things, if only for a moment. For Benjamin, on the other hand, the aesthetic, in its distancing, alienates us from the world. What we need is some kind of anti-aesthetic strategy. Benjamin finds a model for this in the age of technical reproducibility, where we can download MP3s of Beethoven's Pastoral Symphony, or distribute photocopies of a landscape painting.[48]

It is still uncertain whether the aesthetic is something we should shun, in the name of generating a liberating ecological artistic practice, or whether it is an inevitable fact of life that reappears in ever-subtler guises just as we think we have given it the slip. We could claim that there is a difference between the aesthetic and aestheticization.[49] But this is rather Romantic. It brings to mind the notion of a "good" aesthetic and a "bad" one. The first is good because it resists becoming objectified or turned into a commodity, if only because it ironically internalizes the commodification process. My final chapter (Chapter 3) does not entirely escape this Romantic distinction.

A consideration of the aesthetic is vital, since the aesthetic intertwines with the idea of a surrounding environment or world. The idea of a "good" aesthetic is based on the notion that there is some intrinsic goodness in perception, neither captured nor perverted by the aestheticization process. In some sense this *must* be true! Otherwise it would be well nigh impossible to see the cracks in anyone's aesthetic edifice, no clean eyes with which to see that the emperor has no clothes. Ecocritique is loath to give this clarity a name, for fear that it becomes another blinding art-religion. Despite the appearance of his acid negativity, Adorno is really a Romantic, because he thinks that things could be different, and that art whispers that this is so—even when shouting it has become politically compromised. Benjamin, on the other hand, seems to be ready to see where specific artistic practices might lead us, despite his opposition to the aesthetic aura. So he is another kind of Romantic, an experimental, constructivist sort who sees the aesthetic not as an explicit agenda but as a political "boot-up disk."[50] It appears that even at its metacritical level, this study is caught within the Romanticism it is trying to describe. It remains to be seen whether there are more things in heaven and earth than are dreamed of in Romantic ecology.

You Gotta Get into It if You Wanna Get out of It

Ecological culture is supposed to be soft and organic, old-fashioned and kitschy, while technoculture is hard, cool, and electronic. But there are surprising connections between the imminent ecological catastrophe and the emergence of virtual reality. The connections concern not content but form, and they open up questions of epistemology—how can we know that we know, and how can we verify what we know? Both virtual reality and the ecological panic are about immersive experiences in which our usual reference point, or illusion of one, has been lost. Old ways of thinking, we tell ourselves, are not to be trusted. They helped to get us into this mess in the first place. In virtual reality it becomes impossible to count on an idea of "distance." We feel that we can't achieve a critical purchase, but are instead about to be dissolved into a psychotic aquarium of hallucinatory un-being. Part of the panic is the coming to terms with the idea that "there is no metalanguage"—that there is nowhere outside a signifying system from which to pronounce upon it;

further, that this idea is one of the illusions that the signifying system enables and sustains. Virtual reality and the ecological emergency point out the hard truth that we *never had this position* in the first place. Slavoj Žižek has pointed out the salutary effect that this has, at least when it comes to thinking about virtual reality.[51] We are now compelled to achieve ways of sorting things out without the safety net of distance, ways that are linked to ways of sorting things out ethically and politically.

We are losing touch with a nonexistent measuring stick. One of the symptoms of this is the corrosive effect of thinking about "how far in" to virtual reality or the ecological emergency we have "gone"—is the catastrophe imminent, or are we already "inside" it? The very worry about whether we are inside or outside becomes a symptom of how far *inside* we have gone—the inside/outside distinction has itself begun to be corroded by this way of thinking. Not only that, but the illusory measuring stick, in the shape of modern modes of discovery, technology, and categorization, appears to have been partially responsible for immersing us in toxic panic. Quantum-theory utopianism—Hey look! My mind can influence matter!—is just the upside of an all-too-true embeddedness of dominating mind in dominated world. The idea that we cannot extricate ourselves, far from providing a necessarily blissful narcissistic experience, also induces a terrifying loss of bearings. "Read it in the papers / You hear it in the news / Very few listen / A spew without a view" (Public Image Limited, "Don't Ask Me").[52]

The idea of drowning in an epistemological sea, as toxic as the mercury-filled physical one, is more than unpleasant. Are we thus condemned to insanity? Romantic art, with its engagement with immersion *and* the strange thing called nature, can give us some clues. The function of *Romantic irony* is to show how far the narrator, who is thought to sit sideways to his or her narrative, is actually dissolved in it, part of it, indistinguishable from it. Since we are still within the Romantic period in a number of very significant ways, as this book demonstrates, it is highly appropriate that we consider how Romantic poetics tackled ideas of immersion.

The so-called ecological crisis, which is also a crisis of reason, has the urgency of being about our physical survival. If it were just a matter of virtual reality, we could imagine that at least we would remain alive, psychotic but alive, in the worst case scenario. When the immersive world is also toxic—when it is not actually just a matter of phenomena appearing on a screen, but of chemicals penetrating our cells—the stakes get higher. None of this is remotely funny, or just an intellectual exercise. The disorientation of virtual reality—wondering how far immersed we have become in a world with no metalanguage—is as nothing compared with the disorientation of global warming—exactly the same wondering, with extra added death and destruction. The already existing ecological emergency resembles the anxiety about virtual reality—that we will be drowned in a psychotic soup where we won't be able to tell one thing from another—only it also involves the possibility of our own death. It is very hard to get used to the idea that the catastrophe, far from being imminent, *has already taken place.*

More haste, less speed. This is the ideal moment for us to slow down as Derrida encouraged us to do, and *not* act (out), but instead to read the linkage between an apparently technocultural-aesthetic issue and an apparently wet and organic one. This book will take the injunction to hurry up and do nothing seriously. Exploring the aesthetics of this frightening and seductive immersion will be how it works its way out of the maze. Instead of talking about content—software and wetware—I explore the realm of *form.* This is not by any means because I think that there are, or ever were, purely aesthetic solutions to our social and political problems. It is more that the very act of scrutinizing the aesthetics of the issue at hand encourages the beginnings of a critical view. This is an argument about close reading, which has always tried to be both up close, and distant, at the same time. At a subtle level, it may be impossible to forget the aesthetic dimension altogether, and in that sense, my approach *is* a kind of aesthetic solution!

Teasing out just how paradoxical this is will become one of the book's testing problems as it tries to maintain the appropriate degree of slow reading. Distance and proximity are aestheticized terms. They imply a perceiving subject and a perceived object. They are part of Immanuel Kant's language of aesthetics—in order to have aesthetic appreciation, you have to have an appropriate distance toward the aesthetic "thing."[53] We keep hearing that we can no longer just sit back and be spectators when it comes to the environmental events around us. The original advertising of virtual reality was an incitement to get into it and dissolve our boundaries. I am banking on the idea that shedding some critical light on ideas of distance and proximity will be of help. So let us begin by examining some artistic forms that play with these terms, whether they are explicitly "environmental" or not.

CHAPTER ONE

The Art of Environmental Language

"I Can't Believe It Isn't Nature!"

As you read, a white bear leisurely
pees, dyeing the snow
saffron,

and as you read, many gods
lie among lianas: eyes of obsidian
are watching the generations of leaves,

and as you read
the sea is turning its dark pages,
turning
its dark pages.

— DENISE LEVERTOV, "TO THE READER"

As I write this, I am sitting on the seashore. The gentle sound of waves lapping against my deck chair coincides with the sound of my fingers typing away at the laptop. Overhead the cry of a gull pierces the twilit sky, conjuring up a sensation of distance. The smoke trail of an ocean liner disappears over the far horizon. The surrounding air is moist and smells of seaweed. The crackle of pebbles on the shore as the waves roll in reminds me of England, summer holidays on stony beaches.

No—that was pure fiction; just a tease. As I write this, a western scrub jay is chattering outside my window, harmonizing with the quiet scratch of my pen on this piece of paper. The sound of Debussy's *Trio for Flute, Viola, and Harp* falls gently around me from the speakers in the living room. The coolness of the air conditioning suggests the blazing heat of the Californian afternoon. A crop-spraying plane buzzes low overhead.

That was also just fiction. What's really happening as I write this: a digital camera is resting silently on a copy of an anthology of Romantic poetry. The sound of Ligeti fills the headphones, chiming with a signal from the dishwashing machine. The smell of sweet pea–scented bubble bath seems artificial in comparison to the aroma of freshly mowed grass outside the window. An ant crawls down my computer screen.

The more I try to evoke where I am—the "I" who is writing this text—the more phrases and figures of speech I must employ. I must get involved in a process of writing, the very writing that I am *not* describing when I evoke the environment in which writing is taking place. The more convincingly I render my surroundings, the more figurative language I end up with. The more I try to show you what lies beyond this page, the more of a page I have. And the more of a fictional "I" I have—splitting "me" into the one who is writing and the one who is being written about—the less convincing I sound.

My attempt to break the spell of language results in a further involvement in that very spell. Perhaps this environmental language offers a digression from the main point. Or perhaps it is a compelling illustration, or an indication of my sincerity. The writing breaks out of philosophical or literary fictional or poetic modes into a journal style, something with a date or a time marker, something with a signature—and thus falls back into the writing it was trying to escape.[1] Many different types of literature try it. Consider the beginning of Charles Dickens's *Bleak House* with its journal-style evocation of Michaelmas term and its all-pervasive London fog.[2]

The "as I write" tag is optional, being nearly always implicit in the narrative mode of this rhetoric, which has a decidedly ecological usage.[3] But in attempting to exit the generic horizon that contains it, or any suggestion of rhetorical strategy altogether ("This isn't writing, it's the real thing!"), the "as I write" gesture enters an ineluctable gravitational field. It cannot achieve escape velocity from writing itself. The more the narrator evokes a surrounding world, the more the reader consumes a potentially interminable stream of opaque scribbles, figures, and tropes. It is like the house in Lewis Carroll's *Alice Through the Looking-Glass.* Try as she might to leave the front garden, Alice finds herself back at the front door. Denise Levertov's poem "To the Reader" inverts "as I write" into "as you read." But the effect is the same, or even stronger, for, as in advertising language, "you" becomes a niche in the text, specifically designed for the actual reader.[4]

This rhetorical strategy appears with astounding frequency in a variety of ecological texts. In trying to evoke a sense of the reality of nature, many texts suggest, often explicitly, that (1) this reality is solid, veridical, and independent (notably of the writing process itself) and that (2) it would be better for the reader to experience it directly rather than just read about it. But in making their case these texts are pulled into the orbit of writing, with its slippery, tricksterish qualities of never quite meaning what it says or saying what it means—"turning / its dark pages." Never mind that for many cultures nature is a trickster, and literary illusion would aptly summon its ever-changing, elusive "essence." The rhetorical device usually serves the purpose of coming clean about something "really" occurring, definitively "outside" the text, both authentic and authenticating.

Ecomimesis: Nature Writing and the Nature of Writing

The device—I call it *ecomimesis*—wants to go beyond the aesthetic dimension altogether. It wants to break out of the normative aesthetic frame, go beyond art. Introducing *Walden,* Thoreau writes: "When I wrote the following pages . . . I lived alone, in the woods, a mile from any neighbor, in a house which I had built myself, on the shore of Walden Pond, in Concord, Massachusetts, and earned my living by the labor of my hands only."[5] There is nothing more "literary" than this activity of acknowledging, in the negative, the suction of fictional writing.[6] And it is not a matter of being more, or less, sophisticated than others. The kitsch of an Aldo Leopold, writing a journal (an "almanac") to convey nature in a suitable (non)aesthetic form, meets the avant-garde strategy of a minimalist painter who puts an empty frame in an art gallery, or a pile of "stuff" without a surrounding frame; or a John Cage, making music out of silence or out of ambient noise.[7] Leopold's *A Sand County Almanac* tries to escape the pull of the literary, in much the same way as avant-garde art tries to escape the conventional aesthetic. Levertov's "To the Reader" *is* highly literary, going so far as to compare the rolling waves with the turning of a text's pages. There is no guilt about writing here. Levertov does point beyond the specific event of the words on the page, the voice intoning the words. But somehow "To the Reader" achieves a sense of the surrounding environment, not by being less artful, but by being more so. This conscious, reflexive, postmodern version is all the *more* ecomimetic for that.

Contemporary art evokes what is often excluded in our view of the picture: its surrounding frame, the space of the gallery itself, the institution of art altogether. In a very significant way, these experiments are *environmental.* Only the taste and habits of the academy have prevented us from seeing the connection between this supposedly "sophisticated" art and the kitsch we know as "nature writing." Roland Barthes writes, in a passage of avant-garde ecomimesis, about the experience of walking through a dry riverbed. The experience, he writes, is analogous to that of what he calls *text*—an infinite play of interweaving signs:

> The reader of the Text may be compared to someone at a loose end . . . this passably empty subject strolls—it is what happened to the author of these lines, then it was that he had a vivid idea of the Text—on the side of a valley, a *oued* [Arabic: a streambed that is usually dry except during the rainy season] flowing down below (*oued* is there to bear witness to a certain feeling of unfamiliarity); what he perceives is multiple, irreducible, coming from a disconnected, heterogeneous variety of substances and perspectives: lights, colours, vegetation, heat, air, slender explosions of noises, scant cries of birds, children's voices from over on the other side, passages, gestures, clothes of inhabitants near or far away.[8]

We normally think of nature writing as having a certain kind of content—say the Lake District. But here we have the orientalist desert. This is orientalist ecomimesis, in contrast to the familiar Eurocentric or American variety. It succinctly demonstrates how avant-garde ecomimesis is cut from the same cloth as the kitsch variety, despite apparent differences (the one organicist, the other artificial, the one about being "home," the other about being "away," and so on). *Oued* conjures up an opaque, exotic land teeming with what Barthes calls "half-identifiable" significance.[9] Barthes opens up this vision with a string of words that confirm the supposed mysteriousness of the Arabic word rather than explaining it. The word itself is treated as foreign, and so is the climate and environment that it signifies: a wet season and a dry season, a river where people walk, evoking the medieval *monde renversé* or world turned upside down. This is not a world you could live in, but a world you could visit, as a tourist. All the traits of ecomimesis are there: the authenticating "it is what happened to the author of these lines," bringing us into a shared, virtual present time of reading and narrating; the paratactic list; the imagery of disjointed phenomena surrounding the narrator; the quietness (not silence, not full sound) of the "slender explosions" and "scant cries" that evoke the distance between the hearer and the sound source. Here in the very gospel of poststructuralism, of the supposedly antinatural bliss of sheer textuality, we find ecomimesis. Barthes offers us a vivid evocation of atmosphere.

An Ambient Poetics

Strong ecomimesis purports to evoke the here and now of writing. It is an inside-out form of "situatedness" rhetoric. Rather than describe "where I am coming from" ("as a blue-blooded young Portuguese hot dog salesman"), I invoke "where I am" ("as I write this, the smell of hot dogs wafts through the Lisbon night air"). The reader glimpses the environment rather than the person. But the effect is much the same. Ecomimesis is an authenticating device. *Weak* ecomimesis operates whenever writing evokes an environment. Rhetoric used to have a whole panoply of terms for this weak form of ecomimesis: *geographia* (the description of earth or land), *topographia* (place), *chorographia* (nation), *chronographia* (time), *hydrographia* (water), *anemographia* (wind), *dendrographia* (trees).[10] (Angus Fletcher has resuscitated *chorographia* to describe exactly what I am after in this chapter, the "environment-poem.")[11] But the emphasis on situatedness is distinct and modern. Situatedness is a rhetoric that David Simpson has linked to the urgency of impending and "threateningly nondiscriminatory" ecological peril. Situatedness is pervasive, he argues, because "no one now thinks himself immune from radical threat."[12] The particular raises its lone voice in the jaws of general doom.

Ecomimesis is a pressure point, crystallizing a vast and complex ideological network of beliefs, practices, and processes in and around the idea of the natural world. It is extraordinarily common, both in nature writing and in ecological criticism. Consider Lawrence Buell's *The Environmental Imagination:* "The grove of second-growth pine trees that sway at this moment of writing, with their blue-yellow-green five-needle clusters above spiky circles of atrophied lower limbs."[13] Or James McKusick: "As I write these words, I peer out of the window of my study across open fields and gnarled trees crusted with ice. Beyond those trees I see cars and trucks dashing along a busy interstate highway past dirty piles of melting snow that still remain from last week's snowstorm. This is the city of Baltimore, where I live."[14] For ecological criticism to be properly critical, it must get a purchase on ecomimesis. Ecomimesis is a mixture of *excursus* and *exemplum.* *Excursus* is a "tale, or interpolated anecdote, which follows the exposition and illustrates or amplifies some point in it." *Exemplum,* also known as *paradigma,* or *paradiegesis,* is "an example cited, either true or feigned; [an] illustrative story."[15] What then, of the specific features of ecomimesis? *Paradiegesis* specifically implies narrative. But first some remarks about the descriptive properties of ecomimesis are in order.

Ecomimesis involves a poetics of *ambience.* Ambience denotes a sense of a circumambient, or surrounding, *world.* It suggests something material and physical, though somewhat intangible, as if space itself had a material aspect—an idea that should not, after Einstein, appear strange. Ambience derives from the Latin *ambo,* "on both sides." Ambient poetics could apply as easily to music, sculpture, or performance art as it could to writing. Ambience, that which surrounds on both sides, can refer to the margins of a page, the silence before and after music, the frame and walls around a picture, the decorative spaces of a building *(parergon),* including *niches* for sculpture—a word that was later taken up in ecological language.[16] Ambience gives rise to a highly specific version: the *nature* rendered by ecomimesis. In the realm of music, Beethoven's Pastoral Symphony is ambient, as is Vaughan Williams's Fifth Symphony; but so are the works of Brian Eno (and explicitly so). Eno's own case for ambience employs ideas that are commonly associated with artifice rather than with nature, such as the notion that music could be like perfume or a "tint."[17] But as we have seen, ecomimesis is not necessarily on the side of nature.

I choose the word *ambience* in part to make strange the idea of environment, which is all too often associated with a particular view of nature. Ambience has a very long history in Western philosophy and literature. Leo Spitzer has traced the jagged evolution of the senses of "ambience" from the time of the pre-Socratic philosophers to Heidegger and beyond.[18] Throughout this history the environment has been associated with a surrounding atmosphere, more or less palpable, yet ethereal and subtle. It is the job of ecomimesis to convey this sense of atmosphere. Let us examine thoroughly the most salient features of this ambient poetics.

There are six main elements: *rendering,* the *medial,* the *timbral,* the *Aeolian, tone,* and, most fundamentally, the *re-mark.* These terms overlap, and are somewhat arbitrary and vague. Rendering refers to the result of ambient poetics, its telos. Tone describes the material makeup. Medial, Aeolian, and timbral refer to technical or "efficient" processes—effects. I have borrowed these terms from many types of media: film (rendering), music (the Aeolian, the timbral, tone), poetry (the Aeolian), painting (re-mark), and writing (tone). The fact that the terminology derives from diverse forms reflects the significance of multimedia in general, and synesthesia in particular, in inspiring the notion of an ambient poetics. New kinds of art and aesthetics have provoked literary criticism, art history, and musicology to acknowledge the role of the environmental.[19]

The different elements of ambient poetics are all present to some degree in ecomimesis. More formally experimental ecomimesis, such as sound art, uses these elements to affect layers of significance other than just imagery: rhythm, lineation, and typography, for instance. Less experimental ecomimesis restricts itself to imagery alone. A realist novel or a philosophical essay that contained ecomimesis might not suddenly break out into Mallarméan experiments with crossed-out words—or, if it were an essay by Jacques Derrida, it might.

Rendering

First and foremost, ambient poetics is a *rendering*. I mean this in the sense developed by the concrete music composer and cinema theorist Michel Chion.[20] Rendering is technically what visual- and sonic-effects artists do to a film to generate a more or less consistent sense of atmosphere or world. After the action has been shot and the computer and other effects pasted into the film, the entire shot is "rendered," so that all the filmic elements will simulate, say, a sunny day in the Alps, rather than a wet night in the tropics. This rendering, like Jean Baudrillard's idea of the simulacrum, pertains to a copy without an original.[21] There was no "real" sunny day. Rendering nevertheless bathes all the filmic elements in the atmosphere of the sunny day.

Is rendering a significant aesthetic phenomenon, or a non-aesthetic or anti-aesthetic one? Rendering attempts to simulate reality itself: to tear to pieces the aesthetic screen that separates the perceiving subject from the object. The idea is that we obtain an *immediate* world, a directly perceived reality beyond our understanding. When ecomimesis renders an environment, it is implicitly saying: "This environment is real; do not think that there is an aesthetic framework here." All signals that we are in a constructed realm have been minimized. Alternatively, even when the perceiver proceeds by "cynical reason," we know very well that we are being deceived, but our disbelief is willingly suspended. Or we choose to enjoy the rendering as if it were not artificial. Rendering encourages us to switch off our aesthetic vigilance. But even if we know very well that it is a special effect, we enjoy the deception. Despite inevitable failure, how well the narrator imparts a sense of immediacy! As Slatterfield and Slovic say about their collection of ecological narratives, it calls on "the use of a living, breathing narrator (a kind of affective presence) to enhance a story's capacity to include the reader in the told experience."[22] Francis Ponge's view of *adéquation* (an idea that we will see is important for Heidegger) is similar. Buell has used this notion to suggest that no matter how stylized it is, language can render real things, that is, ecological ones.[23]

Art since the age of sensibility has sought this immediacy. If only the poet could do a rubbing of his or her brain, and transmit the feelings to us directly. This is the logic of a certain type of Romanticism, and doubtless of realism, naturalism, and impressionism (and expressionism, and so forth). We have only to think of surrealism and automatic writing, a "direct" rendering of unconscious processes; of abstract expressionism with its monumental canvases; of concrete music's sampling and splicing of environmental sound (by Luc Ferrari, for instance); or of environmental art that creates a "space" we must inhabit, if only for a while. Nam June Paik's *TV Garden* (1982).[24] turns televisions broadcasting images of leaping dancers into budding flowers. It is immersive yet humorous and ironical in a way that is, in Schiller's language, sentimental rather than naive.

Rendering practices risk forgetting the other side of Romanticism, the value of hesitation and irony. They overlook why Wordsworth insisted that poetry not only is "the spontaneous overflow of powerful feelings," but also is "recollected in tranquility." Although reflection then dissolves this tranquility until "an emotion, similar to that which was before the subject of contemplation, is gradually produced, and does itself actually exist in the mind," the process thus becomes delayed and mediated.[25] Already we can see cracks in the ecomimetic illusion of immediacy.

The Medial: Contact as Content

The *medial* derives from the argument in Roman Jakobson's "Closing Statement," with its analyses of phatic statements.[26] Jakobson explores six aspects of communication and their attendant literary effects. These effects are achieved by foregrounding one of the parts of communication. The six parts are addresser, addressee, message, code, contact, and context. Emphasizing the addresser gives us a "conative" statement that directly focuses on the intentions of the receiver of the message: "You must feel that Jakbson's model is valid." Stressing the addresser results in an "emotive" statement: "Let me tell you how I feel about Jakobson." Foregrounding the message itself results in a poetic statement, since Jakobson, a structuralist, thinks that poetic language is peculiarly self-referential. If the code is foregrounded, we obtain a "metalinguistic" statement: "You can't say that! It isn't allowed in structuralist theories of language." If we focus on the context, we get a "referential" statement: "This is a message about Jakobson's six-part model of communication."

If we foreground the *contact*, we obtain a phatic statement (Greek *phasis*, speech). "Can you read this awfully small typeface?" "This telephone line is very crackly. Call me back in five minutes—I can't hear you." "Check, check, check one, microphone check." "Testing, testing." "You're on the air." The contact is the dimension—as literally as you would like to understand that word—in which communication takes place. Phatic statements make us aware of the actual air between us, or the electromagnetic field that makes it possible to listen to recorded music, or see a movie. They point out the atmosphere in which the message is transmitted. Jakobson claimed that talking birds share this function alone, of all the different types of communication.[27] Future ecocriticism must take the phatic dimension of language into account. When exploring the radically new environment of the moon, the first words between the American astronauts and Houston were phatic: "You can go ahead with the TV now, we're standing by." The environmental aspect of phatic communication explains the popularity in contemporary ambient electronic music of samples from radio talk shows ("Hello, you're on the air"), scanned telephone conversations and other phatic phenomena.[28]

I prefer the term *medial* rather than *phatic,* because I see no reason that a statement that foregrounds the medium should necessarily have to do with *speech* per se. *Medial* writing, for instance, highlights the page on which the words were written, or the graphics out of which they were composed. Medial statements pertain to perception. Usually we spend our lives ignoring the contact. When the medium of communication becomes impeded or thickened, we become aware of it, just as snow makes us painfully aware of walking. The Russian Formalists, the precursors of the structuralists, described literariness as an impeding of the normative processes of language. Viktor Shklovsky declared, "The technique of art is to make objects 'unfamiliar' . . . to increase the difficulty and length of perception because the process of perception is an aesthetic end in itself and must be prolonged."[29] When the phone is not working properly, we notice it as a medium of transmission. The converse is also true: to point out the medium in which communication is taking place is to interrupt that communication. Notice how the black marks on this page are separated from the edge by an empty margin of blank paper?

When ecomimesis points out the environment, it performs a medial function, either at the level of content or at the level of form. *Contact* becomes *content.* Ecomimesis interrupts the flow of an argument or a sequence of narrative events, thus making us aware of the atmosphere "around" the action or the environment in which or about which the philosopher is writing. Avant-garde and experimental artworks that are not directly ecological in content are environmental in form, since they contain medial elements. Keith Rowe, guitarist in the improvisational music group AMM, talks of the inclusion of "un-intention" (his technical term for silence) in the paintings of Mark Rothko. Un-intention generates a certain atmosphere surrounding Rothko's giant squares of vibrating color.[30] Maurice Blanchot traced the earliest moment of this feature of art to what he calls the *désœuvrement* ("unworking") in Romantic poetry.[31] This unworking accounts for the automated feel of ambient poetics, the "found" quality, the sense that it is working "all by itself" or "coming from nowhere" (see the subsection after next).

"As I write" (birds are singing, the grass is growing) is a medial statement. Literally, and the medial is always literal to some extent, the dimension is the page we are reading. The idea is to reinforce the illusion that the dimension of reading is the same as inscription: that reader and writer inhabit the same dimension, the same *place*. Our awareness of this dimension is available precisely because its transparency has been impeded by the addition of the exuberant, exorbitant ecomimesis to the argument. The "as," poised between "since" and "when," between a temporal marker and an indicator of logical analogy, seduces us from one level of rhetoric to the next. We enter the warm bath of ambient ecomimesis.

Here comes the twist. One of the media that medial statements can point out is the very medium of the voice or of writing itself. Since the sound of music is available via the medium of, say, a violin, then a medial musical passage would make us aware of the "violin-ness" of the sound—its timbre. The timbre is the quality with which the sound-emitting matter is vibrating. So one of the contents of a medial message could be the medium in *this* sense. This undermines the normal distinction we make between medium as atmosphere or environment—as a background or "field"—and medium as material thing—something in the foreground. In general, ambient poetics seeks to undermine the normal distinction between background and foreground.

Medial statements can include media in the sense of timbre. Surely this is why much experimental "noise" music—which seeks precisely to undo the boundary between what we consider noise and what we consider sound—is interested in timbre. Cage's prepared piano makes us aware of the materiality of the piano, the fact that it is made of taut vibrating strings inside a hard wooden box. The sustain pedal, invented in the Romantic period as an addition to the pianoforte, performs this function itself. Conversely, the sustained vibration of a note or drone makes us aware of the space in which the vibration is occurring. Ambient music can render a picture of an environment using sound effects (birdsong, waves) or make us aware of the space in which we are sitting through drones, reverberation, and feedback. The object, the material, of concrete music is timbre. Linguistic art can do the same. At the end of Levertov's "To the Reader," we don't know what is written on the "dark pages"—they are obscure as well as visually dark. We become aware of the text as material, as paper and pages, and the physical rhythm of turning. The turn (Italian: *volta*) is a moment in a sonnet at which the thought processes in the sonnet begin to shift. It is also a trope, a rhetorical turning. And it is the *clinamen* of Lucretius, the turn or swerve of particles that brings about the generation of worlds. Levertov's "turning" is a trope that physicalizes the notion of troping or of *volta*, of switching from one idea to another, of negation.

In Thoreau's *Walden* the distant sound of bells brings to mind the atmosphere in which they resonate:

> All sound heard at the greatest possible distance produces one and the same effect, a vibration of the universal lyre, just as the intervening atmosphere makes a distant ridge of earth interesting to our eyes by the azure tint it imparts to it. There came to me in this case a melody which the air had strained, and which had conversed with every leaf and needle of the wood, that portion of sound which the elements had taken up and modulated and echoed from vale to vale. The echo is, to some extent, an original sound, and therein is the magic and charm of it. It is not merely a repetition of what was worth repeating in the bell, but partly the voice of the wood; the same trivial words and notes sung by a wood-nymph.[32]

In this remarkable passage, Thoreau theorizes the medial quality of ambient poetics. Notice how "strained," "air," and "melody" are all synonyms for music. Thoreau is describing how sound is "filtered"—a common idea since the advent of the synthesizer, which electronically filters sound waves. An echo is evidence of a medium of the air that intervenes between things like a bell and the human ear, but also of wood that vibrates. We shall see, however, that we cannot be as confident as Thoreau about the "original" quality of echoed sound. The echo undermines notions of originality and presence.

The Timbral

The *timbral* is about sound in its physicality, rather than about its symbolic meaning ("timbral" comes from *timbre*, "The character or quality of a musical or vocal sound (distinct from its pitch and intensity) depending upon the particular voice or instrument producing it").[33] Timbre, which initially meant a particular percussion instrument, either a drum or a bell without a clapper ("tambourine" is a related word), came to describe the way sound strikes or stamps (French *timbrer*) our ears, sometime around the late Romantic and Victorian periods. Timbre derives from the Greek *tympanon*. The taut skin of the drum, even of the eardrum, separates the inside from the outside like a margin, and gives rise to resonant sound when struck. The *tympan* in a printing press makes sure the paper is flat enough to register the type correctly. Is this drum, this margin, part of the inside or the outside? Derrida has shown how this suggestive term evokes the difficulty of distinguishing properly between inside and outside.[34]

The timbral voice is vivid with the resonance of the lungs, throat, saliva, teeth, and skull: the grain of the voice, as Barthes called it.[35] Far from the transcendental "Voice" of Derridean theory, this voice does not edit out its material embodiment. Lacan's "llanguage," "lalangue," is the meaningless fluctuation of tongue-enjoyment.[36] This meaningless fluctuation makes us think about a space (the mouth) that is thoroughly material.[37] Nursery rhymes enable the baby to hear the sound of the parent's voice, rather than any specific words. One of the strongest ambient effects is the rendering of this timbral voice. Our own body is one of the uncanniest phenomena we could ever encounter. What is closest to home is also the strangest—the look and sound of our own throat. Thus, timbral statements can be strongly medial, evoking the medium that utters them. And medial statements can be timbral, pointing out the physicality and materiality of the language. This is strongly environmental. A guitar note brings to mind the wood out of which it is made. The timbral and the medial are two ways of describing the same thing. This axiom asserts that at bottom, foreground and background are more than intertwined.

Martin Heidegger affirms that we never hear sound in the abstract. Instead, we hear the way *things* (a very rich word for Heidegger) *sound*, in an almost active sense of the verb. We hear "the storm whistling in the chimney," the sound of the wind *in* the door, the wail of the hound *across* the moor.[38] For Heidegger there is no such thing as a "pure" tone all by itself. Here is a paradox. The perceptual phenomena we have been exploring possess material thingliness. They are inseparable from matter, including fields of force. Even a supposedly "pure" tone such as a sine wave still emerges from material (say, an electrical circuit), and is amplified and transmitted by various materials and energy fields. For Heidegger, the idea of "pure" sound derives from a notion of the thing as a sensory manifold (a mixture of how things feel, touch, taste, and so on): "the *aistheton,* that which is perceptible by sensations."[39] But such ideas risk suggesting that there is nothing other than subjective experience. Modern art and theory, however, experiment with pure tone. We could point to the use of sheer sound or color in art—Yves Klein's and Derek Jarman's use of blue are extreme examples. Klein's pure blue canvases hang in numerous galleries. He wrote of International Klein Blue, a special suspension of ultramarine (crystals of ground lapis lazuli) in a clear commercial binder, Rhodopas: "IKB / spirit in matter."[40] We could also invoke the interpretation of sheer sound or color in psychoanalytic and literary theory.[41]

Whether we think of nature as an environment, or as other beings (animals, plants, and so on), it keeps collapsing either into subjectivity or into objectivity. It is very hard, perhaps impossible, to keep nature just where it appears—somewhere in between. The difficulty used to be resolved by ideas such as that of the elements. Before they became specific atoms in the periodic table, the elements were manifolds of what we conventionally separate as "subjectivity" and "objectivity." The philosophy of elements bears strong resemblances to phenomenology. We still describe verse as liquid, rhetoric as fiery or earthy. Thinking in elemental terms is thinking that matter has certain intrinsic qualities— *wateriness* is not just "painted on" to the surface of the thing called water; water is watery through and through. These terms have gradually come to have a purely subjective sense (this room *feels* dry; I am *hot tempered*). Like timbre and tone (see the later subsection), the elemental is a way of describing a "thing" that is also an "environment." It is substantial, yet surrounding. The Classical elements (fire, water, earth, air) were about the body as much as they were about the atmosphere.

The Aeolian

The *Aeolian* ensures that ambient poetics establishes a sense of processes continuing without a subject or an author. The Aeolian has no obvious source. "Acousmatic" sound, for instance, is disembodied sound emanating from an unseen source. It comes "from nowhere," or it is inextricably bound up with the space in which it is heard. Consider the voice-over in a movie. It does not originate anywhere in the picture on the screen. Cinematic "rendering" employs acousmatic sound to fill the auditorium (surround sound). The specific sound form of a particular place is reproduced, rather than sheer silence. Jet planes unseen on the film's surface appear to fly overhead. The surrounding quiet of a desert of shifting sands is heard as we watch the protagonist recalling his or her experiences there. Experimental music contains examples of acousmatic sound, emerging from loudspeakers. So does the everyday technology of listening to recorded sound: "The true threat of phonography came not from its ability to displace a voice but its ability to displace a person's *own* voice."[42]

In poetry, images can appear to arise without or despite the narrator's control. A poem called "A Geology," in *Cascadia*, Brenda Hillman's experiment with L=A=N=G=U=A=G=E poetry, is both a montage of descriptions of California through geologic time and an account of getting over an addiction. It is impossible to determine which layer has priority. Each layer minimizes the input of a conscious subject: by comparison with geology, addiction and withdrawal are intensely physical processes that must be endured. The form of the poem heightens the physicality by playing with typographical arrangement. There is often something going on in the margin, out of reach of our reading gaze. One metaphor blends into another in a disturbing, punning way that makes it impossible to decide which level of reality is, to use a geological figure, the bedrock.

A certain degree of audiovisual hallucination happens when we read poetry, as Celeste Langan has demonstrated concerning Walter Scott's long narrative poem *The Lay of the Last Minstrel*.[43] Aeolian phenomena are necessarily synesthetic, and synesthesia may not give rise to a holistic pattern. Because we cannot directly perceive the source, those organs of our perception *not* engaged by the disembodied event become occupied with different phenomena. This is the import of contemporary sound art, comprising productions that are supposed to be different from conventional music. Sound art is sometimes exhibited in places traditionally reserved for visual art. In these environments, there is less focus on the musicians (if any) and the music (if any). Acousmatic sound can compel us to a state of distraction rather than aesthetic absorption. This is not inevitable: synaesthesia could give rise to an even more compelling form of *Gesamtkunstwerk* than immersive Wagnerian forms.

The idea of sounds without a source has come under attack from proponents of acoustic ecology. R. Murray Schafer, who coined the term *soundscape* in 1967, labeled it schizophonia. Acoustic ecology criticizes disembodiment as a feature of modern alienation. Like other forms of Romanticism, acoustic ecology yearns for an organic world of face-to-face contact in which the sound of things corresponds to the way they appear to the senses and to a certain concept of the natural. The Aeolian provokes anxiety, because built into it is a hesitation between an *obscure* source and *no* source at all. If the source is obscure, the phenomenon dwells in our world. We need to expand our perception to take stock of it. It is like what Tzvetan Todorov calls the supernatural uncanny: an unusual occurrence that is ultimately explicable.[44] If, however, there is no source at all, the phenomenon does not reside in our world. It radically bisects it. This is akin to Todorov's supernatural marvelous: an event that must be believed on its own terms. We thus face a choice between a transcendental experience and a psychotic one. Most ecomimesis wants to reassure us that the source is merely obscure—we should just open our ears and eyes *more*. But this obscurity is always underwritten by a more threatening void, since this very void is what gives ecomimesis its divine intensity, its admonishing tone of "Shh! Listen!" Even at the very depth of the illusion of rendering, there is a blankness that is structural to our acceptance of the illusion itself.

Tone: Intensity, Stasis, Suspension

Ambience is an expansion of the space-time continuum in an artwork, to the point at which time comes to a standstill. To investigate this, let us rescue the idea of *tone* from its awful fate in American high schools. Tone is a notoriously casual term. It has something kitsch about it: it is too emotional, too physical. When we consider it closely, tone has a more precise significance. It refers to the quality of vibration. Tone can denote the tension in a string or muscle (muscle tone), or a certain pitch: the way in which matter is vibrating. It also, significantly, refers to a notion of place; hence "ecotone," a zone of ecological transition. A rough aesthetic equivalent is the German *Stimmung* ("mood," "attunement"), used by Alexander von Humboldt in his description of how different art emerges from different climates, and Immanuel Kant in his analysis of the sublime.[45] Tone accounts materially for that slippery word *atmosphere*. Multimedia, music, and visual art play with atmosphere as instrument and as raw material. There is a literary analogy in environmental writing and forms of poetics going back to the culture of sensibility in the eighteenth century.[46]

Tone is useful because it ambiguously refers both to the body and to the environment. For "the body" (as it is so often called in contemporary art and theory) *is* the environment, in the conventional, vulgar

Cartesian sense. "We inhabit the body" like a person living in a house. Environmental art makes us aware of our ears, just as much as it makes us aware of the atmosphere. But in so doing, it nudges us out of the vulgar Cartesianism, like phenomenological philosophy. The linkage of perceiver and perceived is a predominant theme in Maurice Merleau-Ponty's phenomenology.[47] There also exists a British lineage. Lockean empiricism asserts that reality will be different for different perceivers.[48] Later in the eighteenth century, the discourse of sentimentality, which registered truth on the body, was developed into an ethics in Adam Smith's *Theory of Moral Sentiments,* with implications for the evolution of the novel.[49] Synesthetic works of art try to disrupt our sense of being centered, located in a specific place, inhabiting "the body" from a central point. Our senses are disoriented; we notice that our gaze is "over there," our hearing is "outside" the room we are sitting in.

Bodily processes are cyclic. Plateaus of tension and relaxation take place over time. The narrative aspect of ecomimesis generates tone. Specifically, this is a strong form of ekphrasis (*descriptio,* vivid description). Ekphrasis exists when a narrator says "picture this." It often takes a visual form, but traditionally ekphrasis can embody any sensory input, and thus it is appropriate to our multimedia age.[50] Vivid description slows down or suspends narrative time. Let us distinguish between *plot*—the events of a narrative in chronological sequence—and *story*—the events in the order in which the narrator tells them. Suppose that in the plot, event B follows event A after an interval of five seconds, but that in the story an intervening ekphrasis is inserted that takes several pages for the reader to get through, such as Homer's description of Achilles' shield during the intense description of battle at the end of the *Iliad.* The effect on the reader is that the time of narration is held in stasis. In narrative, suspension occurs when the time of the plot (the events as they would have occurred in "real time") diverges widely from the time of the story (the events as they are narrated).

In the second decade of the nineteenth century, Sir Thomas Raffles enjoyed the repetitive music of the Indonesian gamelan, and Leonhard Huizinga later declared, "It is a 'state,' such as moonlight poured over the fields."[51] Static sound became a basis of contemporary music, as composers such as Claude Debussy incorporated into their compositions what they had learned from the gamelan since its appearance at the *Exposition Universelle* in Paris (1889). Stasis becomes audible in musical *suspension,* where one layer of sound changes more slowly than another layer. Disco music compels dancers to stay on the dance floor not only because it involves repetitive beats, but also because it sustains suspended chords that do not progress from A to B, but remain "in between" without resolution. This can only be a matter of semblance, even in visual art. Since repetition is itself a function of difference, funk, then disco, then hip-hop, then house, were progressively able to mine ever more deeply the basic blues structure for a sweet spot, a suspended chord pulsating in rhythmic space. Tone is another word for this sweet spot, somewhere within the third part of a four-part blues, always near the resolution but never quite making it.

This is how ambience enters the time dimension. Tone is a matter of quantity, whether of rhythm or imagery: strictly speaking, the amplitude of vibrations. An AA rhyme scheme increases the energy level of a poem, as would a preponderance of repeated beats. A more complex rhyme scheme, a less repetitive rhythmic structure, renders the text "cooler." Texts also exploit negative rhythm to generate tone. The absence of sound or graphic marks can be as potent as their presence. Gaps between stanzas, and other kinds of broken lineation, create tone out of sheer blankness. In terms of imagery, tone is also quantitative. It is not necessarily a matter of *what sort* of imagery, just *how much*. Just as words come in phrases, imagery comes in clusters. Metonymic listing can generate an overwhelming tone. As with rhythm, there is such a thing as negative imagery, or *apophasis*—saying something in the negative. Negative theology asserts that God is not big, small, white, black, here, there . . . Extreme negativity consists in ellipsis (. . .) or silence. Even more extreme is placing a word under erasure, as Mallarmé does (or consider Heidegger's word ~~Being~~). How do you pronounce a crossed-out word? The erasure compels us to pay attention to the word as graphic mark, and to the paper on which it is written (and the silence of the unspoken). Think of the use of shadow in drawing, or silence in music. Cage scored optional quantities of silence of exactly the same length as positive musical phrases, for the performer to substitute spontaneously.

A text can describe something by delineating it negatively. *Occupatio* gives apophasis a self-reflexive twist, consisting in complaining about how words fail our ability to describe something. This negative delineation is especially important in ambient poetics. Since ambience tries to evoke the background *as* background—to drag it into the foreground would dissolve it—it must resort to oblique rhetorical strategies. There is a school of thought that negative ecology, like negative theology, is a more apt description of nature. I remain convinced by

Derrida's remarks that negative theology is still plagued by the meta-physical.[52] It is probable that a negative poetics of the environment also suffers from these symptoms.[53]

Kant's view of the sublime provides a limit case for this section of the argument, much more so than that of Burke, who evokes the sublime in actually existing things rather than in mental experience. If Kant himself, transcendental idealist that he is, provides tools for reading ambient poetics, how much more would someone inclined toward materialism or empiricism do the same? The sheer quantity of nature writing is a cause of its power. And what could be more evocative of this than a swathe of blankness, language that evokes an endless murmuring or scribbling, or glittering color, or the diffusion of a huge cloud of scent? This language establishes a plateau on which all signals are equal in intensity—which might as well be silence. A negative quantity, the absence of something "there," evokes a sense of sheer space. In Kant's terms, our mind recognizes its power to imagine what is not there: *"Sublime is what even to be able to think proves that the mind has a power surpassing any standard of sense."*[54] Kant demonstrates this by taking us on a journey of quantity, from the size of a tree, through that of a mountain, to the magnitude of the earth, and finally to "the immense multitude of such Milky Way systems."[55] The sublime transports the mind from the external world to the internal one.

Negative quantity has become a powerful tool of modern art, but also of modern ideology. For example, consider the use of silence in nationalist rituals. This surely explains the cenotaph, the empty tomb of the unknown soldier. Before Cage, the two minutes' silence on Armistice Day was intended from its inception as a radio broadcast that would make Britons aware of their country's dead. The composer Jonty Semper recently combined every available BBC recording of the two minutes' silence, complete with newsreel hiss, birds calling, cannons firing, and rain.[56] The design that won the commission for Ground Zero in New York City is entitled "Reflections of Absence."

Negative quantity, signified through ellipsis, or some other effect, is a suggestive transportation point in the text, which allows subjectivity to beam down into it. The Romantic bohemian consumerist, Thomas De Quincey, experimented with his own kinds of psychic and physical intensity in taking opium. De Quincey theorizes how, from the reader's (or listener's, or dancer's) point of view, tone gives us pause. This pausing is not a mere hiatus or stopping. It is rather a staying-in-place endowed with its own intensity. There is "not much going on," which is not the same as no information at all. We are thrown back on the here-and-now of bodily sensation. In the anechoic chamber at Harvard, Cage heard the sound of his own body as if it were amplified.[57] This heightening of awareness takes place in what De Quincey calls *parenthesis* or *syncope*.[58] Syncope commonly refers to abbreviation, and, more rarely, to a loss of consciousness, but De Quincey makes the term experiential.[59] Parenthesis usually places a phrase or sentence inside another one, but De Quincey extends the term toward the notion of tone, a plateau or suspension, what Wordsworth called a "spot of time."

Re-Mark: "I Can't Believe It Isn't Art"
We generally take one kind of medium to be the *background:* the ambient air or electromagnetic field, the paper on which text appears. The other kind of medium, the one we explored as the timbral, appears as *foreground.* A disembodied Aeolian sound emanates "from the background" but appears "in the foreground." With Aeolian events, we have a paradoxical situation in which background and foreground have collapsed in one sense, but persist in another sense.

We are approaching the fundamental properties of ambient poetics, the basis of ecomimesis. Background and foreground rely upon distinguishing between here and there, this and that. We talk about "background noise," while music appears as in the foreground, terms indicating distinct political and historical bearings.[60] Background music, Muzak, or specifically ambient music, attempt to undo the normal difference between foreground and background. The Aeolian attempts to undo the difference between a perceptual event upon which we can focus, and one that appears to surround us and which cannot be directly brought "in front of" the sense organs without losing its environing properties. Current neurophysiology has suggested that a receptor in the hypothalamus, Alpha-7, enables the distinction between foreground and background sound. A breakdown in the neurotransmission across this receptor may in part be responsible for schizophrenic symptoms such as hearing voices (foreground phenomena) emanating from sonic sources (radiators, air vents) that are normally considered as lying in the background.[61]

Alvin Lucier's *I Am Sitting in a Room* (1970) is a powerful demonstration of the shifting and intertwined qualities of foreground and background.[62] A voice speaking in a room is recorded over and over again, such that each previous recording becomes what is then re-recorded in the same room. The text that Lucier reads is about this pro-

cess. It is medial. After a short while, the recording picks up the resonance of the room and feeds it back, amplifying and articulating it
through the sound of the speaking voice. (Likewise, amplifier feedback
in general lets us hear the sound of the technical medium of transmission.) We lose the words and gain the sound of the room "itself." I put
"itself" in quotation marks because what we come to realize is that the
voice and the room are mutually determining. One does not precede the
other. The work is situated on a wavering margin between words and
music, and between music and sheer sound, and ultimately between
sound (foreground) and noise (background). Retroactively, we realize
that the room was present in the voice at the very beginning of the process. The voice was always already in its environment. "I am sitting in a
room" sits in a room. There was never a point of "hand-over" at which
the sound of the voice "in itself" modulated into the sound of the room
"in itself." Voice is to room, not even as sound source to medium, but
as tongue to bell. They were always implicated in each other. This art is
as environmental as writing about birds and trees, if not more so, because it tries directly to *render* the actual (sensation of) environment altogether. We could easily think of visual equivalents, such as environmental sculpture. Andy Goldsworthy's work gradually dissolves into its
site.[63]

Aesthetic, and furthermore, metaphysical distinctions, involve dis-
criminations between inside and outside.[64] We can be sure that this discrimination is metaphysical, since really what we are dealing with is the
idea of *medium,* split into two aspects (foreground and background).
We must be careful not to assert that a medium exists "before" the split
occurs, since the notion of medium depends upon this very split (between "here" and "there"). There is a Buddhist saying that reality is
"not one, and not two." Dualistic interpretations are highly dubious.
But so are monist ones—there is no (single, independent, lasting)
"thing" underneath the dualist concept. Otherwise Alvin Lucier would
not have been able to generate *I Am Sitting in a Room.*

How does the split that separates background and foreground occur?
There is a device that produces it in art. Jacques Derrida has brilliantly
analyzed it in such works as *Dissemination* and *The Truth in Painting.*
He calls it the *re-mark.*[65] The re-mark is the fundamental property of
ambience, its basic gesture. The re-mark is a kind of echo. It is a special
mark (or a series of them) that makes us aware that we are in the presence of (significant) marks. How do you discriminate between the letters on this page and random patches of dirt, or patches of paint and

"extraneous" matter on the canvas? Or between *noise* and *sound* (how about *harmony* and *dissonance*)? Or between *graphics* and *letters?* Or a nonspecific *smell* and a specific or significant *scent?* Or, even more subtly, between a ringing bell and a sounding tongue?[66] Between a substance and its attributes? A re-mark differentiates between *space* and *place*. In modern life this distinction is between *objective* (space) and *subjective* (place) phenomena.[67] Every time I teach a class on ecological language, at least one student asserts that "place" is what a person makes of "space," without reference to an outside. Even when it is external, place has become something that people *do,* or construct; a space that, as it were, *happens to* someone. Despite the rigidity of the student response, I am suggesting here that subjectivity and objectivity are just a hair's breadth (if that) away from each other. The illusive play of the re-mark establishes their difference out of an undifferentiated ground.

In T. S. Eliot's poetry, how do we recognize that some image of an external thing is actually an "objective correlative" for a subjective state? Some very small flicker occurs. A re-mark flips an "objective" image into a "subjective" one. The re-mark is minimalistic. It doesn't take much for ecomimesis to suggest a quality of place. The subjective value that shines out of places such as Thoreau's Walden Pond emanates from minute, as well as from larger, signals in the text. To identify the re-mark is to answer the question: how little does the text need to differentiate between foreground and background, or between space and place?

It is a truism that contemporary art tries to challenge such distinctions. But the re-mark occurs more widely. The re-mark is behind the humor of the Charlie Brown cartoons. When the bird Woodstock speaks, we don't know what he is saying, but we know *that he is speaking,* because the little squiggles above his head are placed in a speech bubble, which performs the action of the re-mark and makes us pay attention to *these* squiggles as meaningful in some unspecified way. (Woodstock himself, who appeared after the Woodstock festival, is close to the subject of this book, insofar as he embodies the natural world "beyond" Snoopy's garden lawn.)

Gestalt psychology establishes a rigid distinction between figure and ground such that figure and ground entail each other (the faces and candlestick illusion is the classic example), while it remains strictly impossible to see both as figure, or both as ground, at the same time. The re-mark is a quantal event. What happens at the level of the re-mark resembles what happens in quantum physics, at the level of the very small. This sounds abstruse, even mystical, but really I mean it in a very straightforward sense. The occurrence of the re-mark is always a "one-shot deal." In quantum mechanics, a *choice* presents itself between waves and particles. We could measure things one way or another; never as an amalgam of the two simultaneously.[68] Until the measurement takes place, both possibilities are superposed, one on the other. Reality, at that "moment" (though that word only makes sense after the quantum wave reduction), is only a series of probabilities.

We cannot claim that there is a special entity that exists as a combination of both wave and particle. There is *nothing underneath* the wave/particle distinction. The same is true of the re-mark. Either the inside/outside distinction is constituted, or not—in which case the distinction will appear at another date, in another place. The level of the re-mark is a fundamentally indeterminate one, at which a squiggle could be either just a squiggle or a letter. However close we get to the (admittedly artificial) boundary between inside and outside (sound/noise, smell/scent, squiggle/letter), we won't find anything in between. This is related to a mathematical paradox. It is impossible to establish in advance (using an algorithm) whether a point will lie on the boundary of a set, even a very simple one: "Imagine two algorithms generating the digits 0.99999 . . . and 1.0000 . . . respectively, but we might never know if the 9s, or the 0s, are going to continue indefinitely, so that the two numbers are equal, or whether some other digit will eventually appear, and the numbers are unequal."[69]

The brilliance of ambient rhetoric is to make it appear as if, for a fleeting second, there *is* something in between. Calling William Wordsworth a minimalist, Geoffrey Hartman praises the idea of Wordsworthian nature as a contemplative space in his book on culture: "The spacious ambience of nature when treated with respect, allows physical and emotional freedom; it is an outdoor room essential to thought and untraumatic (that is, relatively unforced) development."[70] This "outdoor room" is the result of ambient rhetoric (and a certain attachment to an idea of a temperate climate; untraumatic development would be less possible if one were freezing to death). This is not to say that ambience is not incarnated in physical things. Ambient rhetoric is present, for instance, in the common suburban lawn, which acts as an extension of the inside of the house and is referred to as a carpet.[71] Actually existing spaces can have ambient qualities; otherwise, certain forms of contemporary architecture would not be possible.

Margin (French *marge*) denotes a border or an edge, hence "seashore." Indeed, if current industrial policies remain unchecked, these very spaces, such as coral reefs, and liminal species (Latin, *limen,* boundary) such as amphibians, will be increasingly at risk of being wiped out. But because of the logic of the re-mark, such spaces, whether they are outside or inside our heads, embody what is, at bottom, illusory. I mean here to support these margins. As a matter of urgency, we just *cannot* go on thinking of them as "in between." We must choose to include them on this side of human social practices, to factor them in to our political and ethical decisions. As Bruno Latour states, "Political philosophy . . . finds itself confronted with the obligation to *internalize* the environment that it had viewed up to now as another world."[72]

Since it appears to lie in between oppositional entities, the effect of ambience is always *anamorphic*—it can only be glimpsed as a fleeting, dissolving presence that flickers across our perception and cannot be brought front and center. Georges Bataille was substantializing it too much when he labeled what he called the *informe* "unassimilable waste," but it is a suggestive image for the ecological critic, preoccupied with waste products that will not be flushed away.[73] Minimalist experiments with empty frames and also with frameless and formless "found objects" or installations make this apparent.[74] In these works, art tries to sneak a glimpse of itself from the side, or from ground level, like an animal.[75] We have returned to the idea of *rendering,* but with greater understanding. Rendering appears to dissolve the aesthetic dimension because it depends upon a certain necessarily finite play with the *re-mark.* The more extreme the play, the more art collapses into non-art. Hence the infamous stories of janitors clearing away installations, thinking they were just random piles of paintbrushes and pots of paint. There is a politics to this aesthetics. It says that if we point out where the waste goes, we won't be able to keep ourselves from taking greater care of our world. In the rhetoric of juxtaposing contents and frame, product and waste, the anti-aesthetics of the high avant-garde meets more common varieties of ecological language.

A question to which we shall return: does not this collapse of art into non-art actually paradoxically serve to *hold open* the space of the aesthetic "until something better comes along" in an age where all art has been commercialized?[76] And therefore is not the collapse a strongly Romantic gesture of defying the commodity world? I reiterate that this is not to say that there do not exist actual anamorphic life-forms. These very life-forms (coral, sea slugs, invertebrates) are vital for sustaining life on earth. Because they have no distinct shape, it is very hard to make them cute, to turn them into objects of consumerist environmental sympathy. A doe-eyed coral reef is more likely to elicit a gasp of horror than a coo of identification.

Although it tries with all its might to give the illusion of doing so, ambient poetics will *never* actually dissolve the difference between inside and outside. The re-mark either undoes the distinction altogether, in which case there is nothing to perceive, or it establishes it in the first place, in which case there is something to perceive, with a boundary. On this point, there is an absolute difference between my argument and that of Jean-François Lyotard. Lyotard claims that there is such a thing as *nuance,* some quality of color or sound that exists "in between" inside and outside.[77] I am claiming that you will never be able to find some "thing" in between, however close to the boundary line you get. It is like those tests at the optometrist's, when slightly different lenses are presented: "Do you prefer number one, or number two?" However similar the lenses, there is never a way of seeing "in between" the first and second lens. The choice is always starkly and straightforwardly between "one" and "two." Lyotard is one of those post-structuralist thinkers who, however nihilistic he appears, actually believes in something—a "better" something than what is available through normal aesthetics, to be sure, but something nevertheless. I, on the other hand, do not think that ambience will save us from anything.

If "new and improved" versions of continuity between inside and outside, such as *nuance,* are suspect in their attempt to smooth over the quantum difference that the re-mark establishes, then magical forms of differentiation—for example, ones that are miraculously "nonhierarchical" or "nonlinear"—are out of bounds too. These forms, such as Gilles Deleuze and Félix Guattari's idea of the "rhizome," are also post-structuralist fantasies that seek to do away with the strange, bumpy divisions between things. "Rhizomes," so the story goes, are better than hierarchical "trees" of information, because they do not discriminate between different levels of importance.[78] A rhizome is a sprout of a plant such as a potato, which grows, when compared with plants that must deal with gravity, in a seemingly indiscriminate manner, sometimes putting out a new fruit, sometimes carrying on growing.

This image has become very popular in fashionable sound art circles, in part because of the popularization of Deleuze and Guattari in techno music by DJ Spooky (the author of a "rhizomic" study, *Rhythm Science*), and others such as David Toop, an ambient composer and writer of books on ambient music and sound art.[79] The compositional technique of bricolage or pastiche, a collage of snatches and samples of music, lends itself to the idea that this music does not depend upon normative hierarchies such as beginning/end, background/foreground, high/low, and so forth. The *nouveau roman* of the 1960s (Robbe-Grillet) took this principle down to the very level of the syntax of the individual sentence, whose subject would change alarmingly somewhere in the middle. The snobbery of contemporary music criticism and fashion readily corrects the idea that a real disruption of norms has taken place. Some rhizomes are more rhizomic than others.

If the function of rhizome is to join and therefore to differentiate, then how can it do it in a "better way" than a binary play of difference, without collapsing difference into identity? If sound *b* grows "rhizomically" out of sound *a*, then is it the same sound, or a different sound? If I am retrofitting my car, tacking on found pieces here and there and ignoring the factory specifications, does it stop being the same car at some point? If it is now a "different" car, then in what consists the rhizomic thread connecting the "two" cars? If it is the "same" car, then surely there is no point in talking about a connection, rhizomic or not, between two things, since only one thing exists. If I have somehow produced a "quasi-car" that exists "between" the original car and an entirely different one, then this car will suffer from the same problems—is it different or the same?

If we try to avoid the idea of hierarchy (between inside and outside, say), with the language of rhizome, we will be left with the same conundrum, dressed up in chic language, as the one we confronted earlier. Moreover, there is an aesthetic politics of the rhizome, which promotes rhizome for rhizome's sake.[80] Thinking that you are doing something new by mixing different sounds together from different sources, or inventing new ways of mimicking real or imaginary sounds, is the very form of modern music production, and has been so at least since the emergence of capitalist demands for fresh product. Rhizomic writing, visual art, architecture, and multimedia all suffer the same ironic fate.

Scholarship in auditory cultural studies, which studies the history of sonic environments, has tended to see sound along a continuum, even as a circle (or "O factor") that traces a smooth transition from "primal cries" through speech to music, then to ambient sound and back again to cries.[81] But the quantum character of the re-mark assures that there is no genuine continuum and that the transition from one sound to the next will be very bumpy. The bumps themselves are formed by all kinds of ideological and philosophical processes.

None of this is to claim that inside and outside "really" exist. In fact, understanding the re-mark means radically questioning the genuine existence of these categories, far more than clinging to an aesthetic amalgam of the two, especially a "new and improved" version, such as ambience. Ambience suggests that there is a special kind of noise-sound, or sound-noise; a noise that is also a sound, a sound that is also a noise. Somehow, however, we can still tell the difference between the two. Somewhere that is *both* inside *and* outside suffers from this wish to have it both ways. Somewhere that is *neither* inside *nor* outside is strictly inconceivable. Believing that such a place exists is sheer nihilism.

Ecorhapsody and Ecodidacticism: Turn On, Tune In, Get Out

"Ecomimesis" is a rough Greek translation for "nature writing." It is the mimesis of the *oikos* (Greek "home"). I have been arguing that there is an intense and specific form of ecomimesis. Let us consider more carefully what *mimesis* signifies. We have seen how ecomimesis is a rendering. Rather than a weak representation, or imitation, this is a strong, magical form, a compelling illusion rather than a simple copy. Plato's idea of mimesis is more appropriate here than Aristotle's. Aristotle considers mimesis to be simple imitation, as when an actor acts a role.[82] For Plato mimesis is a divinely inspired form of madness. This is not simply a matter of copying forms, but of being plugged in to a source of inspiration, "mainlining" reality.

The poet is a *rhapsode,* and mimesis is a form of *rhapsody.* A rhapsode is *"one who stitches or strings songs together: one who recited Epic poems, a rhapsodist;* sometimes . . . *the bard who recited his own poem,* but mostly . . . *a class of persons who got their living by reciting the poems of Homer:* hence the poems of Homer came to be divided into certain lengths called *rhapsodies,* i.e. *lays* or *cantos,* which were recited at one time."[83] Even in the case of "the bard who recited his own poem," not to mention the idea of a class of readers, rhapsody embodies a notion of reading rather than writing, of recording or transmitting rather than spontaneous production. During the later eighteenth century, "rhapsody" and "rhapsode" became associated with irrational, nonfactual language, and with the notion of "miscellany," a popular literary term at the time, indicating an almost random "threading" of topics.[84] The earlier sense of rhapsody as a threading of memorized verses extends to suggest juxtaposed poems. The expanded definition of rhapsody still gestures toward reading. Ecological rhapsody is a reading of the book of nature.

In Plato's *Ion*, Socrates does not exactly condemn poetry, as one might expect; rather, he places poetry outside the sphere of rational thinking. Such thinking involves a self-possessed subject, or "mastery."[85] Poetry, however, is the invasion of divine madness. Socrates addresses the rhapsode Ion:

> It's a divine power that moves you, as a "Magnetic" stone moves iron rings . . . This stone not only pulls those rings, if they're iron, it also puts power *in* the rings, so that they in turn can do just what the stone does . . . so that there's sometimes a very long chain of iron pieces and rings hanging from one another . . . In the same way, the Muse makes some people inspired herself, and then through those who are inspired a chain of other enthusiasts is suspended.[86]

The magnet is a suggestive image of ambient poetics. The "divine power" exerts a force we now call a magnetic field, in which things become charged with energy. Poetic power emanates from beyond the subject. Inspiration derives from the environment. Plato depicts inspiration as a transmogrification of human into beast: "Poets tell us that they gather songs at honey-flowing springs, from glades and gardens of the Muses, and that they bear songs to us as bees carry honey, flying like bees. And what they say is true. For a poet is an airy thing . . . and he is not able to make poetry until he becomes inspired and goes out of his mind and his intellect is no longer in him."[87] The poet literally "goes out of his mind," like a bee leaving the hive to gather honey from a flower. The poet is an *enthusiast*: literally, he or she buzzes within (Greek, *enthuein*).[88] The environment ("glades and gardens of the Muses") is "out of our mind." Poetry *is* a medium, the contact. The poet becomes the servant of the medium, its gardener.[89] Ion becomes the puppet of fiction: "when *I* tell a sad story, my eyes are full of tears; and when I tell a story that's frightening or awful, my hair stands on end with fear and my heart jumps."[90] The mind lets go while the body takes over.

Whether or not it is written for recitation, ecomimesis embodies this automatic quality in its form. It is as if the narrator turns on a spigot, out of which flows a potentially endless stream of metonymic associations: "Dionysiac parousia [presence] is confirmed by the common mark of the sudden and spontaneous, the *automaton*, another technical term for Dionysian epiphany."[91] Surrealist "automatic writing" develops this desire to render—not just to copy, however perfectly, but actually to *transmit*—something that circumvents the conscious will.[92] André Breton describes how the automatic writer becomes a recording device: "The expression 'all is written,' it seems to me, must be literally held to. All is written on the blank page, and writers make far too much ado about something that is like a revelation or a *photographic* development."[93] Some Romantic poems try to look like psychological curiosities, such as Coleridge's "Kubla Khan." Wordsworth placed lines of poetry on or in the earth, trying to turn them into found objects.[94] Just as individualism and private space were opening up, so collectivity and nonpersonal, or transpersonal, environmental space became artistically exciting.

Ecorhapsody is a mode of ecomimesis. The environment in general manifests in some specific element, as if it were magnetically charged. (I often wonder whether ecological writing is at bottom nothing other than the poetics of these fields altogether. If it were not for the gravitational field, the earth would have no atmosphere at all.) The general enters the realm of the particular. An abstraction passes into an empirical domain. "Oh there is blessing in this gentle breeze."[95] Wordsworth's apostrophe to the ambient air is a fitting way to begin a poem about the formation of a poet's mind in dialectical relation with the world that surrounds him. The image suggests that significance and inspiration come from "elsewhere," even if that elsewhere is really an analogue for somewhere "in" the poet's mind. This elsewhere is beyond concept, but palpable, like the air. It exists in between somewhere so different that it is utterly unknown, and "here," the place of the subject.

Schopenhauer, Nietzsche, and Heidegger based theories of poetics on notions of attunement to and immersion in an environment, which bring to mind the idea of rhapsody. Schopenhauer's view of lyric is that "the subjective disposition . . . imparts its own hue to the perceived surrounding, and conversely, the surroundings communicate the reflex of their color to the will."[96] For Nietzsche, the Dionysian aspect of art, embodied in the Greek chorus, is an immersion in phenomena, a blissful, intoxicated collapse of the Schopenhauerian *principium individuationis* (principle of individuation).[97] For Heidegger, poetics in general is a right reading of the environment—a monitoring, though he would not approve of the technological metaphor. In Heidegger's description of a van Gogh painting, the environment resonates in a pair of peasant shoes. Beyond its particular shape and texture, this environment is an inkling of Being itself, which Heidegger calls *Dasein*—"being there":

> As long as we only imagine a pair of shoes in general, or simply look at the empty, unused shoes as they merely stand there in the picture, we shall never discover what the equipmental being of the equipment truly is. From Van Gogh's painting we cannot even tell where these shoes stand. There is nothing surrounding this pair of peasant shoes in or to which

they might belong—only an undefined space. There are not even clods of soil from the field or the field-path sticking to them, which would at least hint at their use. A pair of peasant shoes and nothing more. And yet—

From the dark opening of the worn insides of the shoes the toilsome tread of the worker stares forth. In the stiffly rugged heaviness of the shoes there is the accumulated tenacity of her slow trudge through the far-spreading and ever-uniform furrows of the field swept by a raw wind. On the leather lie the dampness and richness of the soil. Under the soles slides the loneliness of the field-path as evening falls. In the shoes vibrates the silent call of the earth, its quiet gift of the ripening grain and its unexplained self-refusal in the fallow desolation of the wintry field. This equipment is pervaded by uncomplaining anxiety as to the certainty of bread, the wordless joy of having once more withstood want, the trembling before the impending childbed and shivering at the surrounding menace of death. This equipment belongs to the *earth,* and it is protected in the *world* of the peasant woman. From out of this protected belonging equipment itself rises to its resting-within-itself.[98]

"In the shoes vibrates the silent call of the earth": the language wants us to hear this non-sound, almost a subsonic (empirical but inaudible) sound. Beyond a certain feeling, rhapsody is most properly the *tone* of the environment, registered in discrete things that, simply because they are discrete, are no longer just in the background, but have been pulled into the foreground. Rhapsody is the resonance of the background in the foreground: "In the vicinity of the work [of art] we were suddenly somewhere else than we usually tend to be."[99] The very space inside the shoes, "the dark opening of the worn insides," speaks of the outside. It all depends on what "in" means—inside? In the shoes' material? In our idea of the shoes?

Heidegger's locative vagueness has a precise function. As he develops his view of art as a "happening of truth" in the revealing of the "thingly" character of the thing, it becomes clear that this view is deeply rhapsodic. Rather than trying to be adequate to a real pair of shoes—Heidegger criticizes the idea that art is, in the medieval terminology, a kind of *adaequatio*—the artwork embodies the historical-cultural "world" in which it was made, and the "earth" out of which it emerges and which, in Heidegger's words, "shelters" it, "makes space for that spaciousness." In a Greek temple in a "rock-cleft valley," we glimpse the way Greek culture organized "birth and death, disaster and blessing, victory and disgrace, endurance and decline"; and "The luster and gleam of the stone, though itself apparently glowing only by the grace of the sun, yet first brings to light the light of the day, the breadth of the sky, the darkness of the night."[100] Unlike the transcendental,

Neoplatonic realm, to which representation can only be adequate, Heidegger posits a beyond that is also right here. No wonder ecopoetics, which wants to convey both *here* and a sense of *beyond*, often looks to Heidegger. But as we saw in the analysis of the Aeolian, what is obscure (beyond) opens up the possibility of a threatening void, an inert or dark spot that fascinates ecopoetics and which ecopoetics wants to paint over.

Ecorhapsody mobilizes class, as we shall see when we examine ambience as a function of automation in the following chapter. For Heidegger "man is the shepherd of Being"—he might as well have said that man is the rhapsode of being, a romanticized worker whose job is to hold it in mind.[101] Aristotle's pragmatic definition of mimesis links humans to animals: man is the "most imitative of creatures."[102] Ecorhapsody can also mobilize species. Despite his comparison of poets to bees, Plato's view of rhapsody removes humans from the animal realm. Likewise, Heidegger said explicitly that animals lacked precisely a sense of their environment as a surrounding "world."[103] More recently, David Abram has tried to link environmental poetics to an attunement to the animal aspects of human being.[104] There is a zero-sum game going on here, however one thinks of animals. Either one is more conscious and less attuned to the world, or more sensitive to the world and less conscious.

What would a rhapsodic tuning-in look like? The environment produces a certain tone inside a railway carriage in Edward Thomas's "Adlestrop":

> Yes. I remember Adlestrop—
> The name, because one afternoon
> Of heat the express-train drew up there
> Unwontedly. It was late June.
>
> The steam hissed. Someone cleared his throat.
> No one left and no one came
> On the bare platform. What I saw
> Was Adlestrop—only the name
>
> And willows, and willow-herb, and grass,
> And meadowsweet, and haycocks dry,
> No whit less still and lonely fair
> Than the high cloudlets in the sky.
>
> And for that minute a blackbird sang
> Close by, and round him, mistier,

Farther and farther, all the birds
Of Oxfordshire and Gloucestershire.[105]

The sheer name of a train station gives rise to a whole sequence of surrounding impressions. The first seem insignificant. The hissing steam and the clearing throat are timbral. They are functions of the physicality of the train and its passengers. Before we get a positive description of the surrounding world, there is an uncanny sense of something lurking just beyond our ken. It is a present absence made vivid by the "don't think of a pink elephant" quality of "No one left and no one came / On the bare platform" (6–7), a good example of the "negative quantity" described earlier as a feature of ambient tone.

We look back at the beginning of the poem—one of the features of silent reading is that we can scan backward—and find it changed. The poem was already an answer to a question hanging in the air: "Yes. I remember Adlestrop" (1). Whether or not the narrator posed the question, the "Yes" medially acknowledges the communication dimension. Moreover, before the paratactic rhapsody beginning with "And" (9) there is a blank space, unmarked with words. It serves as the re-mark that opens the inside of the carriage to the outside world. It distinguishes the inside from the outside and their attendant associations (industry/nature, stillness/movement, intimate/panoramic). A linking and a de-linking, a spacing, opens up before we know it. We can only know it after the fact. "Adlestrop" always already existed within a larger textual field. The poem itself has an "elsewhere" whence it arises, in the definite yet nonconceptual sense outlined earlier. In the same way, the station name, "Adlestrop," always existed within a wider environment. Ian Hamilton Finlay's sculpture *Starlit Waters* (1967) consists of the carved wooden phrase "Starlit Waters" enveloped by a fishing net, as if the title were the name of a boat; a name that also refers to the environment around it. So while the poem, moving forward, widens out to include this environment, if we look backward, we see that there already was one. This sensation creeps up on us uncannily. It is as if we had never left. The medium that contains the poem, for which Oxfordshire and Gloucestershire are in some ways just analogues, tugs at us.

That "and" in the third verse amplifies the reader's awareness out of the carriage to include a widening circle of things, "farther and farther." "It was late June" (4): the innocent-seeming "It was" contains its own haunting rhapsodic tone. Emmanuel Levinas has examined the effect of the "there is" (French *il y a*; German *Es gibt*). What is the "it" when we say "it is raining"? The "it" is Being for Heidegger, "a presence of absence," since it cannot exist on its own.[106] For Levinas the *it* is the horrifying—that is, literally flesh-creeping—quality of sheer existence. This is the horror of what Levinas characterizes as experience in a Cartesian world, despite himself, if we are to believe his citation of Pascal, who wrote of Cartesian space that its silence filled him with dread.[107]

There is "transcends inwardness as well as exteriority," subject and object. Levinas writes:

> When the forms of things are dissolved in the night, the darkness of the night, which is neither an object nor the quality of an object, invades like a presence. In the night, where we are riven to it, we are not dealing with anything. But this nothing is not that of pure nothingness. There is no longer *this* or *that;* there is not "something." But this universal absence is in its turn a presence, an absolutely unavoidable presence. It is not the dialectical counterpart of absence, and we do not grasp it through a thought. It is immediately there. There is no discourse. Nothing responds to us, but this silence; the voice of this silence is understood and frightens like the silence of those infinite spaces Pascal speaks of. *There is,* in general, without it mattering what there is, without our being able to fix a substantive to this term. *There is* is an impersonal form, like in it rains, or it is warm. Its anonymity is essential. The mind does not find itself faced with an apprehended exterior. The exterior—if one insists on this term—remains uncorrelated with an interior. It is no longer given. It is no longer a world. What we call the I is itself submerged by the night, invaded, depersonalized, stifled by it. The disappearance of all things and of the I leaves what cannot disappear, the sheer fact of being in which *one* participates, whether one wants to or not, without having taken the initiative, anonymously. Being remains, like a field of forces, like a heavy atmosphere belonging to no one, universal, returning in the midst of the negation which put it aside, and in all the powers to which that negation may be multiplied.

It is or *there is* makes us aware of *tone,* both inside and outside our bodies. There is more or less tension in the environment: "The rustling of the *there is* . . . is horror."[108] Levinas's onomatopoeia is disembodied. The *there is* is an automated process.

The environment just happens around us, without our intention. Or it is the objectified, perhaps unintended consequence of an intention—intention's echo. Levertov figures nature as a series of reading-writing processes continuing in some other key, around and beyond the act of reading the written text. The earth (in Heidegger's sense) continues behind our backs, "over there." Levertov makes a poem about *that,* turning inside out the normative subject of lyric which, as writers from

Schopenhauer to Allen Grossman have observed, is the ego (Grossman's suggestive phrase is "the genre of the other mind"[109] Instead of getting to know the narrator's sense of self, of "I," the narrator forces us to attune to *it*. Instead of *here is,* the poem says *there is.*

Ecorhapsody operates through parataxis and metonymy. The general shines in the particular after a lot of rubbing, each phrase trying to coax a new sparkle. Lists have a tempo or *phase.* They can also have varied moments of intensity or tone. Shifts in phase and tone evoke a force from "elsewhere" within the text itself. Levertov's poem has intense tone. Three stanzas of similar length accumulate three strong images. The final image has a slower phase than the others, since it is repeated: "the sea is turning its dark pages, / turning / its dark pages" (8–10). Our eyes must "turn" from one line to the next to follow the syntax, producing a rhythmical slowing-down that echoes the way the image coagulates and hangs at the bottom of the poem.

Ecorhapsodic lists are suffused with enjoyment, never directly available, off to the side, just around the corner, in the next item on the list. In ecorhapsodic mimesis, we can always admire but never touch. One way to radicalize ecorhapsody is to shatter the aesthetic distance that enables the sliding of desire. Coleridge opts radically for "hot" rather than "cool" (aesthetic) contemplation in *The Ancient Mariner.* When the Mariner "loses himself" rhapsodically in the water snakes (4.272–287), the proximity of the disgusting object punctures the normative aesthetic distance associated with "good taste," the product of eighteenth-century aesthetic development.[110] Likewise, the drinking and eating of Orphic substances in "Kubla Khan" turns the poet into the target of a ritualized disgust ("Weave a circle round him thrice, / And close your eyes with holy dread," (51–52)).[111] Like Keats, Coleridge approaches hyperbolic enjoyment, undermining the distance and mastery of the anthropocentric human subject. There are poetic traditions within Romanticism that run counter to the expectations of ecomimesis.

Ecodidacticism is an often deliberately oblique quality by which ecomimesis makes us exclaim, "Oh! Nature!" There are two levels of didacticism. Ecomimesis points us in the direction of nature, which is meant to teach us something. In "Adlestrop," the expansion of awareness outside the railway carriage eventually makes us aware of the counties of Oxfordshire and Gloucestershire. No longer are we in a purely abstract space of hissing and throat clearing, but we are in a highly significant place charged with national identity. There may be explicit instructions about how to look for natural things. For instance, we could be advised on how to set up our equipment—a tent, some binoculars—so as to see birds or flowers more vividly. But ecomimesis may contain another command, one that does not involve instruments but evokes nature as noninstrumental or anti-technological. This is the order to *stop reading* and "go out into" nature. The injunction is to "Look up!" from one's book, as Wordsworth's "The Tables Turned" puts it. To read an injunction to stop reading is paradoxical. A 1970s children's television program in the United Kingdom was called *Why Don't You Just Turn off Your Television Set and Go and Do Something More Interesting Instead?* Of course, it was always more interesting to watch other people doing it on the TV (see "Reality Writing" in Chapter 2). And there is always *some* instrumentality—this noninstrumental nature is *for* something, if only, in a circular fashion, to teach us the value of the noninstrumental. Ecodidacticism thus participates in the Kantian aesthetic of purposiveness without a purpose.

There is a very intense moment of ecodidacticism in Thoreau's *The Maine Woods*. The high ecomimetic tone, a veritable forest of phrases that stretches over the best part of the first hundred pages in the Penguin edition, finally gives way to Thoreau's realization, as he narrates the descent of Mount Katahdin, that this is "primeval, untamed, and forever untamable *Nature*."[112] Thoreau mythologizes the mountain as a powerfully nonhuman realm:

> It is difficult to conceive of a region uninhabited by man. We habitually presume his presence and influence everywhere. And yet we have not seen pure Nature, unless we have seen her thus vast and drear and inhuman, though in the midst of cities. Nature was here something savage and awful, though beautiful. I looked with awe at the ground I trod on, to see what the Powers had made there, the form and fashion and material of their work. This was that earth of which we have heard, made out of Chaos and Old Night. Here was no man's garden, but the unhandseled globe. It was not lawn, nor pasture, nor mead, nor woodland, nor lea, or arable, nor waste land. It was the fresh and natural surface of the planet Earth, as it was made forever and ever,—to be the dwelling of man, we say,—so Nature made it, and man may use it if he can. Man was not to be associated with it. It was Matter, vast, terrific,—not his Mother Earth that we have heard of, not for him to tread on, or be buried in,—no, it were being too familiar even to let his bones lie there,—the home, this, of Necessity and Fate.[113]

The Greek Titans (Chaos, Night) bestow upon this wilderness a sense of something primitive, something that many previous societies superseded. "Unhandseled" is the key word. It is derived from an Old English noun for money or a gift, as an offering that inaugurates something (earnest money); a luckpenny, or token of good luck; a first installment; or an offering inaugurating the new year.[114] Thoreau describes the wilderness as never having entered into any economic transaction. Even a precapitalist term from old-fashioned rituals is inappropriate. The more modern (Enlightenment) gods of "Nature ... Matter ... Necessity and Fate" lose something in this linguistic transaction. They lose all trace of rationality.

Didacticism blends with rhapsody, as Thoreau's rhetoric injects the feel of nonhuman nature into our very minds:

> What is it to be admitted to a museum, to see a myriad of particular things, compared with being shown some star's surface, some hard matter in its home! I stand in awe of my body, this matter to which I am bound has become so strange to me. I fear not spirits, ghosts, of which I am one,—*that* my body might,—but I fear bodies, I tremble to meet them. What is this titan that has possession of me? Talk of mysteries! Think of our life in nature,—daily to be shown matter, to come into contact with it,—rocks, trees, wind on our cheeks! the *solid* earth! the *actual* world! the *common sense! Contact! Contact! Who* are we? *Where* are we?[115]

The italics at the end perform the role of the *re-mark*. They announce a heightened tone, inviting the reader to imagine his or her vocal muscles tightening. They put our body into the text, which had been gliding along of its own accord for almost a hundred pages. This far into *The Maine Woods,* we are embedded in the "contact" of a text, and here we are made to wonder at how far in we have gone. Textual pressure renders an environmental one. Despite the wealth of texts on the Maine Woods, the rhetoric evokes an utterly pristine zone.[116] Even when the narrator is apparently screaming in our face *("Contact! Contact!"),* the message hovers off to one side. It appears to inhabit an entirely different dimension, like the skull in Hans Holbein's painting *The Ambassadors.* Nature loses its nature when we look at it head on. We can only glimpse it anamorphically—as a distortion, as a shapeless thing, or as the way in which other things lose their shape. This "shapeless thing" is the very *form* of ecological writing.

Ecomimesis as Fantasy: Are You Experienced?

Why is ambient rhetoric, with its basic feature of the re-mark, vital to ecomimesis? Ecological writing wants to undo habitual distinctions between nature and ourselves. It is supposed not just to describe, but also to provide a working model for a dissolving of the difference between subject and object, a dualism seen as the fundamental philosophical reason for human beings' destruction of the environment. If we could not merely figure out but actually *experience* the fact that we were embedded in our world, then we would be less likely to destroy it. The subject–object dualism depends upon a distinction between inside and outside. The subject is "this," "over here," inside; the object is "that," "over there," outside. Various metaphysical systems support this distinction, and not just in the West. The Hindu idea of *tat tvam asi* for instance ("thou art that"), is posited as the pinnacle of self-realization. Indeed, it has been a function of the orientalism of ecological criticism that it has usually considered the West to be hopelessly mired in Cartesian dualism, while other, more exotic or primitive cultures benefit from a more embedded view.[117] Since our thinking appears compromised beyond repair, the new ecological view derives from an aesthetic *experience* of the natural world.[118]

Val Plumwood's *Environmental Culture,* a philosophical text, contains ecomimesis. None is more sustained than a passage from the chapter "Towards a Materialist Spirituality of Place." The chapter concludes Plumwood's investigation of how notions of reason should be refashioned to suit a moment of ecological crisis. Plumwood tries to find an "alternative paradigm" to Lockean theories of land ownership in a sense of communication: "making ownership out in the essentially narrative terms of naming and interpreting in the land, in telling its story in ways that show a deep and loving acquaintance with it and a history of dialogical interaction."[119] The effect of the passage is cumulative:

A world perceived in communicative and narrative terms is certainly far richer and more exciting than the self-enclosed world of meaningless and silent objects exclusionary, monological and commodity thinking creates, reflecting back to us only the echo of our own desires. The communicativity and intentionality of more-than-human others is often the key to the power of place. As dusk gathers beyond my desk and the light glows green, the forest around me comes alive with a sublime and delicate sound like the chiming of countless little silver bells. The sound is almost the only sign to human senses of the innumerable tiny rainforest tree crickets who rub their wings and legs together to make it. It evokes the enchantment of late summer in the cool, misty mountain forest of my Australian home more richly and sensually than any human description, any photograph, map or calendar. As the year turns, this dusk song gives way to others, in regular succession, for the twilight is a sensory and communicative space of much significance for forest dwellers. The erotic tinkling of the crickets holds the space until the first cool weather. That is the time for the squeals of the Little Red Flying Foxes feeding on nectar-filled white Pinkwood flowers. Then, in the chilly violet twilights of late autumn, the silence may be broke by a Lyrebird calling late from nest or perch. Or, if you are lucky, you may hear a distant Powerful Owl hoot and cry for love. In the frosty stillness of moon-silver nights in May or June, you should listen for the Sooty Owl's shuddering, ghostly, scream, and for the questing bass of a mal Barking Owl from June to August, while the courting Mountain Thrushes still play their early evening flutes. August brings forth the first Boobrook Owl duets—his baritone to her soprano—that signal spring, foreshadowing their cheerful but impassioned mating operettas of September and October. November to January is the best time for the great frog choruses, although these in turn have their negotiated spaces and species successions throughout the year. But from midsummer onwards the lusty tree frogs retire and dewfall brings out the whole droning orchestras of mole crickets, each drone, it seems, equipped with an ear-splitting vibrator designed to guide in a flying evening mate. When they too begin to retire in February, the cycle starts once more as the gentle love-songs of the dew-crickets fill the twilight autumn air again until the first cold spell.[120]

The idea of dialogue, taken from Mikhail Bakhtin and Jürgen Habermas in equal measure, is important to Plumwood. But the form this particular passage takes, even as it demonstrates a dialogue with other sentient beings, is not itself a dialogue. This is not to argue against Plumwood's thesis, or to catch it in the act of betraying itself; for example, by finding that this is actually an example of individualist monologue. This passage is not a monologue. It is more like a jungle of writing, twisting, and writhing to such an extent that it almost appears autonomous from the text that surrounds it. It requires more and more of itself to justify itself. There is no logical conclusion. There are notes of instrumental didacticism: "you should listen . . . November to January is the best time for. . . ." But there is an overwhelming, seductively noninstrumental quality to the whole thing. What is it doing almost at the end of Plumwood's book? It is providing a *fantasy,* an aesthetic playground in which the ideas in the book appear incarnated, a literary gravitational field generated by the sheer quantity of vivid description (ekphrasis). Plumwood's ecomimesis is ambient in relation to the main argument. It hovers to one side of it, not directly supporting it but making it aesthetically appealing.

We might think that Plumwood's rhetoric is just a special feature of a religious form of ecological discourse. We might think that it need not concern us very much, if we are ready to take it with a pinch of salt. But this language demands a genuine response. Moreover, it is strikingly the same when writing tries to invoke a sheer sense of environment as if for its own sake. Experimental art likewise models utopian spaces, rather than simply describing something. Take a look at the sophisticated evocation of ambient sound, at the very beginning of David Toop's *Ocean of Sound*:

> Sitting quietly in never-never land, I am listening to summer fleas jump off my small female cat on to the polished wood floor. Outside, starlings are squabbling in the fig tree and from behind me I can hear swifts wheeling over rooftops. An ambulance siren, full panic mode, passes from behind the left centre of my head to starboard front. Next door, the neighbours are screaming—". . . fuck you . . . I didn't . . . get out that door . . ."—but I tune that out. The ambient hum of night air and low frequency motor vehicle drone merges with insect hum called back from the 1970s, a country garden somewhere, high summer in the afternoon. The snow has settled. I can smell woodsmoke. Looking for fires I open the front door, peer into the shining dark and hear stillness. Not country stillness but urban shutdown. So tranquil.
>
> Truthfully, I am lying in intensive care. Wired, plugged and electronically connected, I have glided from coma into a sonic simulation of past, and passed, life. As befits an altered state, the memories have been superimposed, stripped of context, conflated from seasons, times, eras, moments, even fictions, into a concentrated essence of my existence in the sound-world.
>
> These sounds reconnect me to a world from which I had disengaged. Sound places us in the real universe. Looking ahead, I can see a plane enlivened by visually represented objects. I can touch within a limited radius. I can smell a body, a glass of beer, burning dust. But sound comes from everywhere, unbidden. My brain seeks it out, sorts it, makes me feel the immensity of the universe even when I have no wish to look or absorb.[121]

The passage continues for another page. Toop does not argue, but renders, like Plumwood. He is both rhapsodic and didactic—"Sound places us in the real universe." The imagery is more self-reflexive than Plumwood's. The sounds are juxtaposed memories rather than an actually existing "soundscape." This is a construct, says the passage. The narrator wants us to know that this is a simulation. But despite this, perhaps even because of it, the passage is compelling. It strives to authenticate the "I" by situating it: "Sitting quietly . . . I am listening," albeit in "never-never land." Whether the space being evoked is supposed to be real or taken as unreal, the same rhetorical strategies apply: authentication, rendering, the Aeolian, and other ambient effects such as suspension and stasis.

If, as demonstrated, the dissolution of inside and outside is strictly impossible—though ecomimesis puts a lot of effort into simulating it—then ecomimesis is a form of ideological fantasy. When ambient rhetoric tries to blur inside and outside, or abolish them, or superimpose them, it generates an inconsistent "thing." Lyotard's "nuance" exists somewhere "in between" the normative colors, or in between the normative notes of a musical scale. This "in between" is better described as ambience, with "nuance" as an aspect of tone. Students of literature should be beginning to recognize what is going on here. It is commonly called *the aesthetic*. But Lyotard asserts that nuance is beyond normal aesthetic categories and hence, he hopes, the problems associated with the aesthetic: notably, that it does not really collapse the subject–object dualism, either by reconciling subject to object, or by undoing the distinction altogether. Ambience, or nuance, are "new and improved" versions of the aesthetic. In bursting the bubble of the aesthetic, we find ourselves in a new, potentially even more compelling, bubble.

Nevertheless, the fantastic inconsistency of ambience makes it possible to do critique. Ambience is what Jacques Lacan would have called a *sinthome*. The sinthome is the materially embodied, meaningless, and inconsistent kernel of "idiotic enjoyment" that sustains an otherwise discursive ideological field.[122] The sinthome of homophobia, for instance, might be an image of the "queer," or certain kinds of sex act. Ideology resides in the distance we assume toward this fantasy object. By collapsing the distance we undermine the potency of the ideological field. Within every field is a symptom, and every symptom can be made to vomit forth a sinthome. By assuming with pride the word *queer*, the gay movement disabled the ideological field that sustains homophobia. This paradoxical act of identification with the fantasy object of ideology could be mirrored in critical analysis, by the relentless close reading of texts, not in order to achieve some tasteful distance toward them, but precisely in order to "mess around" with them, or as my students sometimes say in horror, "dissect."

A word about "objects." I have modified the term *sinthome*. What Lacan applies to an objectal substance could apply to surrounding space. This involves an inversion. Imagine the sinthome not as figure but as ground: a potent, non-neutral ground, a giant stain. This would square well with the vaginal connotations of the sinthome, in patriarchy a *wound* that is also a *space*.[123] When I refer to ambience as a fantasy thing, the terminology is not quite exact—fantasy space is more like it.

If it is to have teeth, ecocritique must be self-critical. Ecocritique is a twofold process, consisting both in exuberant friendliness and disarming skepticism. The approach is not to be confused with nihilism. We are treading a path between saying that something called nature exists, and saying that nothing exists at all. We are not claiming that some entity lies between these views. We are dealing with the raw materials of ideology, the stuff that generates seductive images of "nature." That is why it is important to go as "far in" to the notion of nature in ecomimesis as possible. In the name of ecology itself, we should pull out all the plugs. This is radically different from a "new historicist" approach, in which our own analysis, rightly wary of the aesthetic dimension, ironically recreates the very aesthetic distance it is criticizing, by holding the artwork at a disdainful distance. At its best, historicism claims that there is no single solid subject of history. But it also risks casting a negative aura around the aesthetic object, one of phobic distance. It re-creates history in the image of a self-contained, richly ambivalent poem as read by one of the New Critics like Cleanth Brooks.

Do we find any inconsistencies in nature writing? There is a profound inconsistency between ambience, the way ecomimesis operates, and ecomimesis itself. The poetics of the echo, for example, interferes with the fantasy that ecomimesis is immediate. This immediacy must be an illusion that the narrator manages to pull off, with varying degrees of success. And even if successful, the illusion is not an accurate rendering of the environment. We can only perceive things *after* they have arisen, never before and never at exactly the same time. In this sense, all experience is only passing memory. Ambient poetics, amplifying this quality, is imbued with the uncanny, but there is a disjunction with ecomimesis at this point. Ecomimesis resists the uncanny, in its effort to present an original, pristine nature not "infected" with the consciousness, the mentality, or the desire of the perceiver, unless it is deemed to be "natural." Ecomimesis wants to deliver nature in the raw, but it always arrives with a slight smell of burning.

Echoes are inescapable features of ambience. Some nature writers think that they are receiving a direct transmission from nature, when in fact they are watching a mirror of the mind. There is a choice between honesty and hypocrisy. We can admit that all we can sense of nature is an echo of our "sounding out" of it. We posit nature retroactively. Narcissus is only aware of his beloved Echo through the repetition of his words. This was formalized in Renaissance verse when "Echo" repeats the last syllables of a verse. This is a basic mimetic function of some animals: the echolocation of bats "sounds out" the dimensions of a place, a phenomenon exploited by Alvin Lucier in *Vespers,* in which musicians use electronic devices that emit pulses of sound for the same purpose. For Narcissus to love Echo properly, he must love her as the trace of his voice reflected in the sheer extension of matter: the vibrational qualities of air, the reflective properties of water. To remain true to Echo he must remain "faithful" to the fact that she only exists as a "faithful" reproduction of his voice. Narcissism appears on both sides of the equation.[124] Narcissism is on the side of self-absorption disguised as immersion in, or contact with, another being (called Nature). And narcissism is on the side of the subject who cynically knows "very well" that he or she is in an echo chamber.

The exuberant immediacy of ecorhapsody contradicts the melancholic delay of the ambient effects out of which it is made. Ecorhapsody suggests that we can have the real deal, nature as it is, even while it consists of a list of elements, which only gestures toward the real. Ecodidacticism infers that nature and self are connected, and in so doing short-circuits the paradoxes of ambient rhetoric. Consider the trope of chiasmus: I am you and what I see is me; I am he as you are he as you are me and we are all together.[125] Merleau-Ponty describes experience as a "chiasm," an intertwining of what is sensed with the one who is sensing.[126] Such ideas are very suggestive for ecological poetics, since they provide a way of determining that the self and its world are intertwined. Chiasmus does not solve anything, because in order to work, both terms must be *preserved* even as they are cancelled at another level. Think of an optical illusion that confuses background and foreground, such as the faces/candlestick, or a work by M. C. Escher, playing with simplistic cubes without proper foreshortening, such that the front and back faces have the same size.[127] It becomes impossible to say which face is at the front. The trick operates on two levels. On the first level, we perceive a breakdown of our normal distinction between background and foreground, but on the second, this distinction is preserved. In order for the first level to be effective, the second level must also be effective. What is given with one gesture is paradoxically taken away with another. Term x dissolves into term y, but retains the form of term x. Otherwise we would not be able to recognize that it had dissolved! All we would be left with would be term y. So when nature writing collapses self and nature, it prizes them apart on another level.

What if, however, the chiasmus did not want us to solve it, to hold both its terms properly together in our mind? What if the philosophical musing that chiasmus lets loose concealed a meaningless, "sprouting" enjoyment? This is where the sinthome, the kernel of idiotic enjoyment, operates. One would expect a poetics of rendering to be interested in employing the sinthome. A simple way of recognizing the sinthome is to wonder what all this nature writing is *for*. There is just so much of it; a potentially infinite supply. Nature writing tries to evoke this sense of sheer stuff. The form of Chinese painting called "mountains and rivers without end" was borrowed for Gary Snyder's huge poem sequence of the same name.[128] At most points in the giant scroll on which the mountains and rivers are painted, except at the beginning and at the end, there is the sense that the scroll could go on forever. There is just a vast proliferation of brushstrokes. In the same way, nature writing in general is sinthomic, a sprawl of sheer *text*. By analogy, "nature" is a gigantic swathe of sheer *life,* or *stuff*. This stuff is always eluding conceptuality, not because it transcends the material realm, but because it is relentlessly material. Our conceptual mind keeps slipping off its surface. Snyder's poem tries to capture, to render, this quality as an experience of Buddhist *shunyata* or emptiness, though the term evokes the idea of *nothingness* rather than the "something-ness" I am aiming at here.

Western explorations of Buddhism aside, we are not far from the notion of a life-substance that emerged in *Lebensphilosophie* in Schelling and others, from which existential and psychoanalytic ideas, not to mention literary ones, of *life* are derived. Nature, after all, according to modern (post-Romantic) thinking, is what sprouts; it is the state of stimulation, of metabolism between the inside and the outside. It is the state of swelling and opening to the outside—or orgasm, as Lamarck put it.[129] Paul Ricoeur's idea of metaphor also leaps to mind. Ricoeur states, "*Lively* expression is that which expresses existence as *alive.*"[130] Nature writing embodies this orgasmic view of life (French, *jouissance*) in the aesthetic form of endless textuality. Thoreau's *The Maine Woods* does not even try to tell us something, but appears merely to be a journal, something artless that falls out of normal conventions of literary narrative. Didacticism becomes an orgasmic peak rather than a sober reflection. But nature writing involves us in a basic paradox. The more nature we have, and therefore the more "lively expression," the more writing we have. The paradox is present in the very phrase "nature writing." Is nature to be thought of as writing? Or is writing a natural process, in the sense that Byron meant when he referred to the "lava" of imagination?[131] Nature writing is a dense chiasmus.

For Ricoeur, "All *mimesis,* even creative—nay, *especially* creative—*mimesis,* takes place within the horizons of a being-in-the-world which it makes present."[132] This sounds like a positive theory of ecomimesis, which wants to fit nature like skin fits a hand—it *is* the hand. Adorno's remarks on the way some art "steps out" into nature, collapsing the barrier between art and non-art, are appropriate here:

> Authentic artworks, which hold fast to the idea of reconciliation with nature by making themselves completely a second nature, have consistently felt the urge, as if in need of a breath of fresh air, to step outside of themselves. Since identity is not to be their last word, they have sought consolation in first nature . . . The extent to which this taking a breath depends on what is mediated, on the world of conventions, is unmistakable. Over long periods the feeling of natural beauty intensified with the suffering of the subject thrown back on himself in a mangled and administered world; the experience bears the mark of Weltschmerz. Even Kant had misgivings about the art made by human beings and conventionally opposed to nature . . . The gesture of stepping out into the open is shared . . . with the artworks of their time. Kant lodged the sublime—and probably along with it all beauty that rises above the mere play of form—in nature.[133]

Adorno asserts that sometimes art needs to "take a breath," to renounce the hard work of dominating nature in the name of art. Instead of shaping natural materials into sculpture, perhaps sculpture should dissolve back into nature, as in the work of Andy Goldsworthy. Nature writing is another way of saying artless art. The sinthome is necessarily inconsistent. There is no genuine material embodiment of an ideological system. The presence of chiasmus should alert to an intense, sinthomic level, which does not make sense but just *is*, beyond the pleasant mirror effect of chiasmus itself.

Presence and absence are intertwined in difference. Ecomimetic tone—the bodily sensation of thereness—is compromised by the inescapable dimension of time. Ecological writing may want to drag us into the here and now, in a mystical or primitivist or exoticist gesture that seeks to sweep away bad Western cunning. The past is just an illusion. The future is yet to come. Dig the present! But when we get there, we discover that the here and now does not exist either. The here and now has come to be associated with a certain meditative calm and quiet. Yet quiet—even more so silence—is always elsewhere. It is someone else's, somewhere else (Cage: "all of the sound we don't intend").[134] Quietness is a common effect of ambient music, which strives to be below the threshold of regular listening. Quietness strives toward the pregnant pause: syncope. Syncope is thus always the effect of tone—there is always some information (in the cybernetic sense), and in order to differentiate it there must be some roughness, some *noise*. Quiet is the idea of tone we almost can't perceive, tone that is constantly vanishing. It is not necessarily relaxed or peaceful. The syncope

De Quincey analyzes—the silence in *Macbeth* after the murder of King Duncan—is unbearably tense. The narrative cliché "It's quiet—too quiet" speaks the truth that as soon as we perceive it, quiet becomes saturated with tone and therefore intense. Quiet itself is stimulating.

Like death, quiescence is always further to the side of the margin of the paper than where we rest our reading gaze. But we can still glimpse it out of the corners of our eyes. Freud tries to give an ambience to death, an experiential quality, as if we could experience it on *this* side. Life yearns toward, in James Strachey's poetic translation, "the quiescence of the inorganic world."[135] This haunting phrase is more than what Freud might be suggesting, however. "Quiescence" implies something still living, where "inertia" would have brought it to a dead stop. We want to experience ourselves as objects. In other words, consciousness tries to feel what it is like to be a purely extended thing (*res extensa,* in Cartesian terms).

Nirvana has a utopian edge and is relevant in this life, as Adorno recognized. One can imagine it as an experience rather than as the dissolution of experience:

> A mankind which no longer knows want will begin to have an inkling of the delusory, futile nature of all the arrangements hitherto made in order to escape want, which used wealth to reproduce want on a larger scale. Enjoyment itself would be affected, just as its present framework is inseparable from operating, planning, having one's way, subjugating. *Rien faire comme une bête,* lying on water and looking peacefully at the sky, "being, nothing else, without any further definition and fulfilment," might take the place of process, act, satisfaction, and so truly keep the promise of dialectical logic that it would culminate in its origin. None of the abstract concepts comes closer to fulfilled utopia than that of eternal peace.[136]

Blankness and silence thus convey, in extremis, either a state in which nothing *must* be done, or one in which nothing *needs* to be done. Ecomimesis strains to see outside itself, in a dialectic of life and death: a rhythm that alternates between incorporating the environment and becoming tenser, versus relaxing into an inorganic state (becoming the environment). Peeping round the corner at a state where there are no humans, no readers—trying to see our own death—is a common ecological fantasy, as Mary Shelley demonstrated very early in her science-fiction work, *The Last Man,* in which the reader gets to contemplate a world without humans.[137] When we try to see our own death, the "we" who are seeing remain alive.

Wordsworth is the Romantic master of tone, and the ironic ways in which consciousness floats around it, recalls it, alters it. Through simple repetition, he suggests the tension of a sigh or a sob, a physical tightening or relaxing, within the act of reading the poem. Tone appears to float above or behind the sheer linguistic surface.[138] The notion of repetition brings up another feature of ambient poetics. *Retroactivity* compels us to look back, or listen back, through time to posit something new, to reframe or to alter what we have been perceiving. We can't be sure that we have been in a suspension until we have left it; retroactively, we know that the narrative has been circling around on itself. Likewise, the environment becomes audible as an echo, as after-image.[139]

Even though Hegel attributes pure repetition to cultures existing outside his concept of history (such as Africa), repetition persists within the very teleological structures of high Romanticism. Here I concur with James Snead, who identified countercurrents of European philosophy and culture that celebrated the idea of repetition.[140] Repetition is the subject of Wordsworth's "There was a Boy," a "lyrical ballad" about a boy who hoots to owls, repeating their sounds across a lake.

> There was a Boy, ye knew him well, ye Cliffs
> And Islands of Winander! many a time,
> At evening, when the stars had just begun
> To move along the edges of the hills,
> Rising or setting, would he stand alone,
> Beneath the trees, or by the glimmering lake,
> And there, with fingers interwoven, both hands
> Press'd closely palm to palm and to his mouth
> Uplifted, he, as through an instrument,
> Blew mimic hootings to the silent owls
> That they might answer him. And they would shout
> Across the wat'ry vale and shout again
> Responsive to his call, with quivering peals,
> And long halloos, and screams, and echoes loud
> Redoubled and redoubled, a wild scene
> Of mirth and jocund din. And, when it chanced
> That pauses of deep silence mock'd his skill,
> Then, sometimes, in that silence, while he hung
> Listening, a gentle shock of mild surprize
> Has carried far into his heart the voice
> Of mountain torrents, or the visible scene
> Would enter unawares into his mind
> With all its solemn imagery, its rocks,

Its woods, and that uncertain heaven, receiv'd
Into the bosom of the steady lake.

　Fair are the woods, and beauteous is the spot,
The vale where he was born: the Church-yard hangs
Upon a slope above the village school,
And there along that bank when I have pass'd
At evening, I believe, that near his grave
A full half-hour together I have stood,
Mute—for he died when he was ten years old.[141]

De Quincey was immensely fond of the suspension or parenthesis in the middle, when we read that the owls sometimes do not respond to the boy's "mimic hootings" (10), and that in the silence he becomes aware of his environment. Out for a walk one evening with William Wordsworth, De Quincey's mind is opened to an awareness of ambience: "No sound came up through the winding valleys that stretched to the north, and the few cottage lights, gleaming at wide distances from recesses amidst the rocky hills, had long been extinct."[142] The apophasis of "no sound" makes us *hear* the *absence* of sound—ambient poetics resounds with this logic, the same as that which applies in "don't think of a pink elephant!"

De Quincey continues: "Once, when he was slowly rising from his effort, his eye caught a bright star that was glittering between the brow of Seat Sandal and of the mighty Helvellyn." Wordsworth declares " 'if, under any circumstances, the attention is energetically braced up to an act of steady observation, or of steady expectation, then, if this intense condition of vigilance should suddenly relax, at that moment any beautiful, any impressive visual object, or collection of objects, falling upon the eye, is carried to the heart with a power not known under other circumstances.' " This unexpected consequence of a meditative state should be familiar to anyone who has practiced meditation. Wordsworth explains:

Just now, my ear was placed upon the stretch, in order to catch any sound of wheels that might come down upon the lake of Wythburn from the Keswick road; at the very instant when I raised my head from the ground, in final abandonment of hope for this night, at the very instant when the organs of attention were all at once relaxing from their tension, the bright star hanging in the air above those outlines of massy blackness fell suddenly upon my eye, and penetrated my capacity of apprehension with a pathos and a sense of the infinite, that would not have arrested me under other circumstances.[143]

Wordsworth outlines a minimalist sensory attunement, like meditation, one of surprising surprise, we might say—of a surprise that remains surprise because it does not participate in what Wordsworth
himself called the "gross and violent stimulants" of the poetics of sensibility.[144]

We find out that we have been standing beside the boy's grave all the
time we were reading of the boy's exploits in the woods, returning the
echoes of the owls. Looking back from the end of the poem we posit the
boy's death and our identification with him, in a tranquil, sweet quietness. The whole poem becomes an "echo" of the boy. We can only become aware that we were in a space of identification after the fact. This
awareness is always uncanny—familiar yet strange, and even more so,
familiarly strange, based on minimal clues such as the repetition of
"hung" (18) and "hangs" (27), the position of both of which at the
ends of lines makes us hang suspended in mid-page. The ultimate uncanny experience is recognizing the strange as a familiar feature of the
familiar. Freud explained that the uncanny was associated with the
compulsion to repeat. In ambient poetics, the uncanny works such that
the space-time of the text turns out to have changed, almost impercep-
tibly. We become attuned to this quality *before* the text is read, before
it begins. So the sense is that the change *will have occurred*. This quality
of future anteriority is built into the work—an uncannily proleptic
backward glance. We get the uncanny sense that at some time in the un-
folding of the text, we will look back and all will have changed. Like a
loud sound heard from far away, the retroactivity effect in "There was
a Boy" makes sure that the poem is not just a plateau of tone.

The actual "moment," if there is one at all, since it only *becomes* actual retroactively, is a blankness. This is rendered in Wordsworth's
poem by the subtle use of blank space and lineation. "But" would have
differentiated things more than "And"—which is why Wordsworth
does not use it (16). Ambient poetics has a mournful quality even when
its explicit topic is not mourning (in fact, "There was a Boy" *is* a work
of mourning). I am saying "mournful" here, but I am not distinguishing, as Freud did, between mourning and melancholia, which
boils down to a distinction between proper and improper digestion. In
some sense, "proper" mourning would always be too late. Having fully
digested the lost object, we could never taste it again. As a section in
Chapter 3 will suggest, melancholy is more apt, even more ethically appropriate, to an ecological situation in which the worst has already
happened, and in which we find ourselves, like Wordsworth's narrator,

or a character in *noir* fiction, already fully implicated. In Galenic medicine, melancholy was the humor that was closest to the earth.

The moment of contact is always in the past. In this sense we never actually have it or inhabit it. We posit it afterward. An echo can only reach our ears after the sound has caused the medium to vibrate. According to the theory of relativity, all perceptual phenomena exist in the past, reaching our senses at a later date—even light, even gravity, which Newton thought was instantaneous. So the uncanny, future-anterior, retroactive—and, moreover, melancholic—qualities of ambient poetics are, ironically, accurate. They track the inevitable too-lateness of the way in which things arise. This point becomes very important when we assess why environmental writing is at such pains to convey a sense of immediacy. The immediacy is what "Romantic ecology" wants to hear in the echoes of the owls across the lake. In an astonishing bait and switch, Wordsworth withdraws this immediacy even as he appears to offer it.

The sublimity of sheer tone turns out to be dangerous for ecomimesis. Kant explicitly forbids the sublime to refer to anything "teleological." Thus a text cannot celebrate the environmental capacity of the environment and remain sublime, no matter how much the author piles phrase on phrase. Kant puts it this way:

> When we judge the sight of the ocean we must not do so on the basis of how we *think* it, enriched with all sorts of knowledge which we possess (but which is not contained in the direct intuition), e.g., as a vast realm of aquatic creatures, or as the great reservoir supplying the water for the vapors that impregnate the air with clouds for the benefit of the land, or again as an element that, while separating continents from one another, yet makes possible the greatest communication among them; for all such judgments will be teleological. Instead we must be able to view the ocean as poets do, merely in terms of what manifests itself to the eye—e.g., if we observe it while it is calm, as a clear mirror of water bounded only by the sky; or, if it turbulent, as being like an abyss threatening to engulf everything—and yet find it sublime.[145]

This goes for any environment, real or imagined: "when we call the sight of the starry sky *sublime,* we must not base our judgment upon any concepts of worlds that are inhabited by rational beings." Tone comes into the orbit of the sublime, but ecomimesis deflects it, if it remains at all representational. The content of ecomimesis is thus at war with its form. Tone also threatens to collapse into sheer stimulation, what Kant calls "mere sensations of an object (gratification or pain)."[146]

Tone is either too abstract, or not abstract enough, for ecomimesis. Ambient poetics complicates and even disables the aims of ecomimesis, which tries to get around these complications by viewing the environment "as poets do"—that is, as an aesthetic object, or even as an analogue for the aesthetic altogether. That way the ambience of the textual environment can have just the right amount of abstraction—too little and it becomes sheer sensation; too much and it turns into something teleological. But maintaining the appropriate distance is tricky.

Ecomimesis is a specific rhetoric that generates a fantasy of nature as a surrounding atmosphere, palpable but shapeless. The ambient poetics that establishes this experience interferes with attempts to set up a unified, transcendent nature that could become a symptomatic fantasy thing. Critical close reading elicits the inconsistent properties of this ambient poetics. Ambience compromises ecomimesis because the very processes that try to convey the illusion of immediacy and naturalness keep dispelling it from within. In the language of Julia Kristeva, ambience is the *genotext* to the *phenotext* of ecomimesis. Kristeva defines the genotext: "[Genotext] will include semiotic processes but also the advent of the symbolic. The former includes drives, their disposition and their division of the body, plus the ecological and social system surrounding the body, such as objects and pre-Oedipal relations with parents. The latter encompasses the emergence of object and subject, and the constitution of nuclei of meaning involving categories: semantic and categorical fields."[147] The genotext generates the phenotext, "language that serves to communicate." Surging, pulsing "quanta" (Kristeva's word) are the "underlying foundation" of language.[148] Ironically, the genotext *is* the environment, the matrix in which the subject is born and grows ("the ecological and social system surrounding the body" is part of it). It is this very environment that inhibits ecomimesis from firmly establishing an essential or substantial environmental nature of any kind. And, even more ironically, especially for Kristeva herself, who believed that the genotext had a revolutionary potential, one of the ways in which this happens is that the Cartesian self that floats above phenomena keeps rearing its ugly head, ironically in those very texts that try to flatten the distinction between subjectivity an objectivity.

In sum, one of the principal complaints against establishing a vivid, solidly real nature "out there" or "over there" is that it just fails to be convincing. This lack of believability penetrates to the very core of ecomimesis, the most potent rhetorical device for establishing a sense of nature. The inherent instability of language, and of the human and nonhuman worlds, ensure that ecomimesis fails to deliver.

Let me say right here that the attempt to forge art and concepts that lie "in between" traditional ideas of inside and outside is noble, exciting, and the only reason why I can write this book at all. The problem comes when we start to think that there is something behind or beyond or above (in other words, outside!) the inside–outside distinction. *Not* that the distinction is real; it is entirely spurious. Thus, it is wrong to claim that there is something more real beyond inside and outside, whether that thing is a world of (sacred) nature (traditional ecological language) or machines (Deleuze and Guattari world). Yet it is equally wrong to say that there is nothing, to "believe in nothing," as it were, and to say that he or she who has the best argument is the right one—pure nihilism. There is *not even nothing* beyond inside and outside. Getting used to that could take a lifetime, or more.

Romanticism and the Environmental Subject

Even the elementary concepts of time and space have
begun to vacillate. Space is killed by the railways. I feel
as if the mountains and forests of all countries were ad-
vancing on Paris. Even now, I can smell the German
linden trees; the North Sea's breakers are rolling
against my door.

—HEINRICH HEINE

We now begin to contextualize ambience, the texture of ecomimesis.
Contextualization is necessarily incomplete: there is always more where
that came from. And almost any text contains weak ecomimesis. We
can safely conclude that ecomimesis exists in various cultures. Consider
Basho: "The frog jumps into the old pond / The sound of the water."[1]
The final line of the haiku mimics-evokes the plop of the frog, the trace
of the sound, the presence of an ear and a mind that hears, all contained
in a "world." Our sense of the broad scope of ambience is right and
proper. Any formalist definition of literary effects can be broadly applied. And if ambience were not a feature of rhetorical and artistic production in general, this study would have no basis.

Since all texts coordinate relationships between inside and outside,
ambience, and in particular the function of the re-mark, its fundamental component, is an aspect of every text. The associated distinctions (background/foreground, sound/noise, graphics/sign, smell/scent),
fall into place "after" the text has established this basic relationship.
We can expect to find ambient qualities in any artwork whatsoever. We
need not restrict ourselves to works that are specifically ambient, and
especially not that subset of works that contain ecomimesis. In a world
properly attuned to the environment, we would read poems with an eye
to ecology, no matter what their content.

The universality of ambient poetics is also a condition of the very
long history of ideas such as *milieu* and *ambience,* as Leo Spitzer
demonstrated. Spitzer painstakingly charts a long reduction of ambi-

ence from a spiritual term to a scientific and sociological notion (the Enlightenment idea of *milieu*), and finally, one that suggests the form of the commodity. Restaurants have ambience. Spitzer begins with the intuition that ambience tries to name "an anti-Cartesian desire to penetrate 'les sombres tunnels de l' inexprimable.'" The Greek *periechon* (surrounding "air" or atmosphere) had a spiritual quality. Plato and Sextus Empiricus considered it to be an active force. The more pragmatic Aristotle still used *periechon* to suggest that all things had their place, their specific surroundings. The replacement of this notion with one of abstract space has developed in natural philosophy since the Renaissance. But the idea of a specific surrounding medium was even present in Descartes (the *matière subtile* adopted in Newton's idea of ether). This is rather curious, if we accept the common idea expressed by Spitzer himself at the start of the essay, that ambience fills a need for something discarded in post-Cartesian thinking. It sounds a note we will hear again: we cannot ignore Descartes.[2]

Spitzer argues that the very thinkers whose ideas undermine these usages introduce them, to protect us against what they have clearly discovered—vast empty space.[3] This vastness subverts the significant, particular, local embeddedness that ecological writing tries to bring back. Once we accept that there is an "impossible point of view" of space itself, from which all other points of view are equally (in)significant, imagining that there are (however many) unique viewpoints from within a horizon which are unequal but significant, begins to become increasingly fraught with difficulty. The global starts to pervade the local, not just socially but also philosophically.[4] Even postmodern ideas of numerous, possibly infinite, viewpoints that are incommensurable and discrete appear against this general background. The very idea that "there is no metalanguage" is posed from this "point of view." The gradual divestment of the aura of ambience is precisely why it is a good term to use in searching out the inconsistencies of ecomimesis.

None of this gets rid of the need to trace precise historical determinations and emphases, genealogies, and lineages. Ideological determination depends not just upon the *content* and *form* of an artwork or rhetorical device, but also upon the *subject position* that it establishes. The artwork hails us, establishing a certain range of attitudes. When we consider the relationships of subjectivity to ambient poetics, we will discover consistent veins of historical and ideological patterning. Ironically, the thought of something "in between" beings becomes hard to think, at exactly the moment at which "the environment" rears its ugly, irradiated, toxic head. I am thus not confident that we can invent a "new and improved" way of talking about the local, or embeddedness, even if we resort to flashy new words like "network" or "web." Rather than nature, it is the *subject* with which this chapter concludes.

This chapter contains three different kinds of historical account, which in turn read the form, content, and subject positions of contemporary society. Marx delineates the social and economic form. Next comes a history of ideas, in which I explore the terms *world, state, system, field,* and *body.* I then investigate the idea of a certain *subject,* emerging in the Romantic period: the beautiful soul. A historical perspective can induce a certain feeling of distance, even smugness. That is why this book has a third chapter, which explores future possibilities. Chapter 2 does not just provide a historical background for the speculations of the following one. It delves further into what nature might be. We will revisit the "encounter with nonidentity" spoken of previously. *Ecology without Nature* gradually amplifies this encounter. It appeared in Chapter 1 as the way in which environmental writing establishes corners and edges that make it hard to maintain a solid center. Ambience is what environmental writing is after, and ambience is its ultimate nemesis. These distortions reappear here in more conscious form, as "strangers"—human others, animals, and other beings who wander into and out of the world, constituting it as its boundaries, but also undermining its coherence. In Chapter 3 these strangers will take an even stranger form, as ghosts and machines. Nature cannot remain itself—it *is* the flickering shapes on the edges of our perception, the strangers who disturb us with their proximity, the machines whose monstrosity inspires revulsion.

We begin with a Hegelian observation that causality, at least in the humanities, works backward. The Renaissance was posited retroactively. We cannot trace its history back to a single origin and then run the story forward. This is even true of those historical moments that name themselves, such as Romanticism and postmodernism. Contemporary art, which makes much of space and environment, retroactively reconfigures all previous art, revealing its ambient qualities. The universality of ambience is itself historical, a retroactive effect of our particular moment. All art can now be assessed for its environmental qualities, and in general, for ambient poetic effects. Consider Caliban's praise of the island in *The Tempest:*

> The isle is full of noises,
> Sounds and sweet airs, that give delight, and hurt not.
> Sometimes a thousand twangling instruments
> Will hum about mine ears; and sometime voices. (III.2.130–133)[5]

Caliban is describing the magic of the island as the presence of Aeolian voices. Prospero the magician himself employs the disembodied Ariel, a spirit of the elements, to produce acousmatic music that "creeps by" Ferdinand "on the waters" (I.2.391), singing a song of how the matter of Ferdinand's dead father is transformed by the medium of the ocean "Into something rich and strange," complete with an echoing chorus of ringing bells and barking dogs: "Ding dong bell," "Bow-wow" (382–384, 386, 401, 403–404).

Still, one cannot dodge the question of origin. Stating that the causality is retroactive from the moment at which environmental qualities become artistic material only pushes the problem back a stage further. How do we account for what we mean by "contemporary"? When did the contemporary emerge in this respect? I date its emergence to the rise of commercial capitalism, and to the rise of consumer society. In particular, the moment at which society began to become reflexive about consumption—when it began properly to recognize that it *was* a consumer society—was decisive. As I have argued elsewhere, the birth of *consumerism* coincided with (and to some extent *was*) the Romantic period.[6] Different European and American societies have had their Romantic moment at different times. But this is of little consequence, since we are talking about socially significant *moments* rather than mechanical, objectified time.

There are legacies of Romanticism in current environmental movements. The trouble is not that these legacies are obscure; rather, there are *too many* connections. The relationships are overdetermined—a sure sign that we are in the warped space of ideology. The Romantic term *culture,* hovering somewhere between nature and nurture, evokes a surrounding world. Furthermore, this "fact" has been imbued with "value"—culture was good, and good for you. "Culture," like "nature" (the terms are intimately related), resembles what Gandhi said of Western civilization: "I think it would be an excellent idea." T. S. Eliot's and Raymond Williams's idea of "culture" as "a whole way of life," while supposedly descriptive rather than normative, has a utopian ring, in a world that is not hale and hearty.[7] Ecology has inherited the languages of "wholeness" and "life."

Moreover, history itself has taken on ambient qualities, and there is a history to be told of how it has done so. Science, politics, ethics, and aesthetics are coming under the sign of the environment. Even postmodernism, held in suspicion by much ecocriticism, might eventually appear as a moment in the process of including the environment in thinking, doing, and making. People may eventually recognize in the Romantic period the beginning of "environmental" ways of understanding and acting. Romantic history emerged, evoking the spirit of the age, the *Zeitgeist,* the flavor of a culture at a particular moment in time. The phenomenological approach to history has had a long run, and has recently developed forms of auditory history and cultural studies that seek to imagine what the "soundscape" of a particular period might have been: ambient history. Phenomenology is a philosophical movement that emerges in Hegel and continues through philosophers of history such as Dilthey, Collingwood, and later incarnations in the twentieth century (Husserl, Heidegger, Merleau-Ponty, even Derrida).[8] The turn to phenomenology—literally, the science of phenomena—attempts to insert the conscious, feeling subject into a *world* with which it interacts.

Just as history (as a sequence of events) has been becoming more global since the early modern period and the rise of capitalism, so history (as writing) has tuned in to the idea of *world:* of a surrounding environment or culture; what German thinking calls *Lebenswelt* or *Umwelt.* Anthropology, newly arisen in the Romantic period, with its synchronistic style of looking at a particular culture without considering historical change, valued societies that appeared static rather than dynamic, prehistoric rather than historical. Such "primitive" societies belonged to a "lost world" where writing, and therefore history (Greek *historia,* which means both historical events and their inscription) was unknown.[9]

The Continual Whirr of Machines: World Literature, World History, World Philosophy

In *The Communist Manifesto,* Marx and Engels state that under the current economic conditions, "National one-sidedness and narrowmindedness become more and more impossible, and from the numerous national and local literatures, there arises a world literature."[10] If this idea is to mean more than people from several countries writing the same thing in the same ways, it must include the idea that writing in general can, under certain circumstances, meditate upon the idea of *world* as such. This capacity to imagine a world is not unconnected to the globalization of specific kinds of misery. It eventually becomes possible to sing a song called "We Are the World," and wince about it, or to see the many levels of painful irony within the phrase "United Nations."

Ecology has reminded us that in fact we *are* the world, if only in the negative. In material historical terms, environmental phenomena participate in dialectical interplay insofar as they bring an awareness of environmental negatives such as global warming, the Asian "brown cloud," and toxic events such as Chernobyl. Such phenomena were already visible in the Romantic period in the form of global epidemics such as yellow fever. Alan Bewell's penetrating ecocritical study *Romanticism and Colonial Disease* shows how such forms inspired writers to make ethical, political, and aesthetic accounts of "miasma," a biological word that had regained the ethical charge given it in classical Greece.[11] Far from needing filling out with some positive "thing" such as "nature" or the ecofeminist/Lovelockian image of Gaia, this negative awareness is just what we need.

Environmental Romanticism argues that globalization has undermined any coherent sense of place. At least, that is an argument within Romantic and ecocritical thinking. Such thinking aims to conserve a piece of the world or subjectivity from the ravages of industrial capitalism and its ideologies. Place, and in particular the local, have become key terms in Romantic ecocriticism's rage, as impotent as it is loud—rhetorical affect is in direct proportion to marginalization. Moreover, this impotent rage is itself an ironic barrier to the kind of genuine (sense of) interrelationship between beings desired, posited, and predicted by ecological thinking. Place and the local, let alone nation, entail subject positions—places from which Romantic ideas of place make sense. For this reason, it is all the more important to consider deeply the idea of place, and in general the Romantic attitude to nature prevalent today.

The fact that metabolic processes create dynamic conditions that change both organism and environment means that nothing in ecosystems remains the same. Materialism puts paid to "nature," itself an early materialist term. Ulrich Beck has observed that the logic of unintended consequences plays out in industrial society such that, despite class differences, risk becomes increasingly democratic. Radiation is ignorant of national boundaries. In a bitter irony, the equality dreamt of in the 1790s has come to pass—we are all (almost) equally at risk from the environment itself. Nationality and class affiliations aside, we share the toxic legacy of Chernobyl. And no matter where in the world capitalism puts its industry, giving rise to the recent illusion of a "post-industrial" landscape, all societies are affected. No wonder ambient poetics has arisen to point out utopias and dystopias that lie just beyond our reckoning. While nature writing claims to break down subject–object dualism in the name of a brighter day, "highly developed nuclear and chemical productive forces" do just the same thing. They "abolish the foundations and categories according to which we have thought and acted to this point, such as space and time, work and leisure time, factory and nation-state, and even the borders between continents." Ironically, this is happening at a moment when sciences of "nature *without* people" make it difficult to imagine how we might address this abolition.[12]

"Modernization" itself, observes Beck, "is becoming *reflexive;* it is becoming its own theme."[13] The Frankfurt School had already given voice to this. Ernst Bloch asserted that "where technology has achieved an apparent victory over the limits of nature . . . the coefficient of known, and, more significantly, unknown danger has increased proportionately."[14] One name for this is postmodernism, but another name is ecology. The melancholy truth of high postmodernism is that all its talk of "space," all the environmental multimedia installations, are just the same as the lowbrow eco-schmalz that high environmental art wants to eschew (the art of *place* rather than *space*). They are identical because, under current economic conditions, not only is there no *place,* but there is also no *space.* Contemporary capitalism seeks to "annihilate space by time"—and then to collapse time itself.[15] When we consider it thus, the postmodern insistence on space is a high-cultural denial, a mystification rather than a theoretical breakthrough, flat-out contradicting objective conditions rather than expressing them.

Henri Lefebvre pioneered the idea that capitalism *produced* certain kinds of space and spatiotemporal relations.[16] Capitalism does not simply construct ideas about space; it creates actually existing, concrete spaces. In the category of spaces unique to capitalism, Rem Koolhaas's "junkspace" is distinctive.[17] Space itself becomes one of the things that capitalism discards in its furious progress, forever revolutionizing itself. Thus, "Junkspace is best enjoyed in a state of postrevolutionary gawking."[18] So we are not just dealing with the kinds of supermodern "non-place" analyzed by Marc Augé, who calls them "immense parentheses."[19] (Note the similarity to De Quincey's trope of *parenthesis,* which the previous chapter noted as a figure of ambience.) Concrete parenthesis is not just a case of vast airports, but also of abandoned airports. Marx describes how capitalism affects not only people, but also tools and buildings:

> Tools, machines, factory buildings and containers are only of use in the
> labour process as long as they keep their original shape, and are ready

each morning to enter into it in the same form. And just as during their lifetime, that is to say during the labour process, they retain their shape independently of the product, so too after their death. The mortal remains of machines, tools, workshops etc., always continue to lead an existence distinct from that of the product they helped to turn out. . . . The instrument suffers the same fate as the man.[20]

"Empty" space—space that capitalism has left relatively undeveloped—is intrinsic to capitalism, since the laws of capital may dictate that a vacant lot is more profitable over a certain span of time than one that has been developed. *Plot* is a potential space, a limbo waiting to generate value. Capitalism moves onto this empty stage, with its phantasmagoric carnival, leaving junkspace in its wake. Consider the idea of a ghost town. The leavings of capitalism have a haunting quality, if there is not enough political will, or hard money, to relate to them.[21] But even when things get fixed up nicely, a certain erasure and silence is evident, a heaviness like Levinas's *there is,* or a Raymond Chandleresque sense of atmosphere as *clue.* Yves Klein's International Klein Blue, hanging in galleries around the world as slabs of pigment made of precious stone suspended in a commercial medium on canvas, is a perfect metaphor for, and not so metaphorical embodiment of, the utopian face of abstract value, a space that "bathes" us in potential paradise.[22] Before and after the work of capital, there persists a curious silence and absence marked by traces of misery and oppression.

As Marx puts it, in a pithy sentence that accounts for pastoral poetry and even nature writing and ecocriticism: "First the labourers are driven from the land, and then the sheep arrive."[23] Capitalism modernizes agricultural space. The way the land appears unoccupied is *not* a relic of an ancient prehistoric past, but a function of modernity: "The last great process of expropriation of the agricultural population from the soil is, finally, the so-called 'clearing of estates', i.e. the sweeping of human beings off them."[24] Works such as Oliver Goldsmith's "The Deserted Village" mark this process. The earth, air, and waters are so much potential space, as frontiers of progress; in the wake of progress, they are so much junkspace. Koolhaas: "Air, water, wood: All are enhanced to produce . . . a parallel Walden, a new rainforest. Landscape has become Junkspace, foliage as spoilage: Trees are tortured, lawns cover human manipulations like thick pelts . . . sprinklers water according to mathematical timetables."[25]

Capitalist thinking, and capitalist machinery, actively "disappear" the workers who operate it. From the commoditized atmosphere in a restaurant to the more general sense of "aroundness," ambience is a symptom of automation. More and more processes of production are performed directly by machines. The human being is progressively side-lined, as anyone who has operated a photocopier will affirm. Humans "man" the machines: more than ever, human beingness is now revealed as a product of mechanical processes.[26] The section title comes from Deleuze and Guattari's perverse ecomimetic hymn to machines:

> While taking a stroll outdoors, on the other hand, he is in the mountains, amid falling snowflakes, with other gods or without any gods at all, without a family, without a father or mother, with nature. "What does my father want? Can he offer me more than that? Impossible. Leave me in peace." Everything is a machine. Celestial machines, the stars or rainbows in the sky, alpine machines—all of them connected to those of his body. The continual whirr of machines.[27]

Automation affected art. Repetition builds itself into the process of artistic production, both externally, as mechanical reproduction (and consumption) generates thousands of iterated copies, and work processes are stereotyped; and internally, as repetitive forms begin to become the content of art, as in minimalist music. The DJ performs a role not unlike a worker on a production line. An incomplete object passes into the DJ's hand, a recording of beats and chords, evoking a sonic state of suspension without resolution. The recordings are often produced and packaged anonymously. The DJ "mixes" this object with another object, the record currently playing in the club, and puts the previous record back in his or her crate. Although some DJs have created superstar cults, the notion of the disco or house DJ is that of an anonymous worker in a "sound factory," generating libidinal pulses in a space of dancing, producing ambience, in the same way as fairgrounds provide machines for enjoyment rather than work.[28] Work your body. In a further extension of automation, dance music specifically designated as ambient, becomes a weekend within the weekend, a space of leisure within the larger leisure space of the rave. The use of machines in music generated new forms of subjectivity that do not rely upon an illusion of depth, but nevertheless evoke the tenderness of the human being: for instance the tremblings and stutterings of an Elvis at the microphone.[29]

Ambience is a symptom of capitalist alienation—not just the existential *feel* of capitalist society, though that certainly comes into it, as environmental writing shows, with its struggle against what it sees as the spiritual depletion of modernity. Marx described how capitalist alien-

ation is fundamentally how human labor power and labor time get fac-
tored out of the process of value generation, even though they are intrinsic to it. Capitalism *encrypts* labor. Capitalist ideology "knows very
well" that labor produces value. This is an open secret, as Adam Smith
and Ricardo plainly demonstrate. But the objective system by which
capitalism bestows a value on its products acts as if this were not the
case.[30] It is ironic that a clothing store that operates using sweatshop
labor from other countries is called Gap. In this model of globalization,
labor is what gets "outsourced" and vanishes almost without trace.
Marx shows how capitalism performs this operation on a much deeper
level, in every monetary transaction, an operation elegantly evoked by
the word *gap*.

Labor is on the "inside" of capital, and it even appears that way on
the "outside," in the commodity form. But there is an invisible gap between inside and outside. The commodity form has a skeleton in its
closet, a skeleton that the detective fiction of *Capital* uncovers through
painstaking work. Commodities behave as if they sprang from
nowhere, from some wheel of fortune in outer space. Capitalist poetics
in the commercial eighteenth century imagines commodities flowing
spontaneously toward the consumer, if not from outer space, then from
the old-school version—the Spice Islands.

There are at least two ways of looking at ideology. The first is that it
is a set of conditions that rule our subjectivity—a set of beliefs, or more
strongly, a series of unconscious, "hardwired" fantasies. The other way
is as part of objective social conditions. Ideology resides "out there"
rather than "in here," which is one reason why it is so difficult to get a
mental grasp on it—it does not belong to the realm of the mind. Ideology resides in the "mouthfeel" of a McDonald's hamburger; the way
men hold open doors for women; and so on. It doesn't matter whether
we believe in these forms and practices very much. Indeed, they maintain an even stronger grip when we have a postmodern, cynical or
ironic attitude toward them. This is certainly the case with the disappearing process that capitalism carries out on labor. This idea of ideology as externalized was what Marx was after in his theory of capital.

Something has been hidden in full view. This is the force of Amiri
Baraka's "Something in the Way of Things," a paranoiac, surrealist
glimpse of something that cannot quite be seen, something found along
the way that also gets in the way, playing on the two senses of "in the
way."[31] The disappearing of the worker is active. The worker's body is
imagined as a system of movements without a subject: "[the black-

smith] can strike so many blows per day, walk so many steps, breathe so many breaths, produce so much work, and live an average, say, of fifty years; he is made to strike so many more blows, to walk so many more steps, to breathe so many more breaths per day, and to increase altogether a fourth of his life."[32] Engels notes that to the untrained eye, the streets of an industrial town appear curiously empty: "the members of the money aristocracy can take the shortest road through the middle of all the labouring districts to their places of business, without ever seeing that they are in the midst of the grimy misery that lurks to the right and the left."[33]

Although ambience is strictly untenable as a concept, it is valid and pervasive as a social form. Ideology shapes the actual physical world. The Lake District, a British national park, would not have existed if it had not been for Wordsworthian Romanticism and such seminal texts as Wordsworth's *Guide to the Lakes*.[34] Frederick Law Olmsted, one of those responsible for establishing the national park system in the United States, constructed places such as Central Park in New York City. But to get to grips with the disappearing worker, think only of the common lawn—so much ecocriticism does not, because its gaze is fixed on higher, steeper, more distant things.

The suburban garden lawn's flat, almost opaque surface—so like high abstract expressionism—obscures in plain view the work that goes into it.[35] Just like the lawn, but for a more limited audience, abstract expressionism turned the dissolution of lyrical distance into a profitable enterprise.[36] The lawn expresses the disappearing of the worker that resulted in picturesque landscape, the production of distance, of simulated fusions of tameness and wildness, and fascinating points of view.[37] In the early modern period lawns were used for sport, as relief from smoke and other people, and as power on display. Modern American lawns emerged in the Romantic period.[38] Their lack of fences distinguished them from English ones. Thomas Jefferson's design for Monticello was for a seamless "vista flowing from the mansion through the lawned garden fringed by trees to the foothills of the Blue Ridge Mountains."[39] In a fitting minimalism, the Jeffersonian precinct of the University of Virginia, from which Monticello itself is visible thirty miles away, is simply called "The Lawn." Monticello was a republican refuge from political vicissitudes, the martial struggle of public life. The green floor cloth in the entrance simply elided the boundary between the outside lawn and the indoor carpet. The lawn creates ambience, a fantasy space that fuses inside and outside—all lawns are carpets.

Monticello's open lawn, however, also hid a plantation full of slaves, and was designed explicitly to exclude the sight of slaves from the front view. Side paths prevented them from being seen in their traffic to and from the house. Monticello's Web site persists in describing activity without actors, a feature of the hiding of labor through the construction of empty space:

> During Jefferson's time, Mulberry Row would have been humming with activity, with over thirty people at work in its shops and yards. While linens boiled in the wash house and milkpans clattered in the dairy, the hammers of fourteen nailmakers rang on anvils near the roaring forge of the blacksmith. Wood chips and shavings were scattered by the axes and planes of the carpenters and joiners, and two sawyers worked a pit saw slowly through a cherry log. Mule-drawn carts rattled up and down this plantation "street" bringing barrels of water, firewood for the kitchens, and charcoal for the forges. As daylight faded, the shops grew silent and the dwellings on Mulberry Row were animated by the return of Monticello's workers, both black and white.[40]

Work just "happens" in a middle voice, as if part of a background. The eventual appearance of labor and race requires a dimensional disorientation from Monticello to Mulberry Row. For Thorstein Veblen lawns must not appear like a working farm: "The vulgar suggestion of thrift, which is nearly inseparable from the cow, is a standing objection to the decorative use of this animal."[41] The lawnmower relieved the need for the "indecorous" presence of animal labor.[42] Distortion (anamorphosis) is a consistent feature of lawn representation. The chapter of Rachel Carson's *Silent Spring* that deals most directly with lawns is entitled "And No Birds Sing": an allusion to John Keats's "La Belle Dame sans Merci."[43] In Keats's fine instance of Romantic *noir* an idealized femme fatale appears to her hapless courtly lover as a "sidelong" distortion. The opening and closing refrains depict the lover's depression in a bleak *terra nullius* in which "no birds sing" (4), an environment drained of psychic significance. Carson implies that the toxic quick fix will lead to a literal drainage of the environment.

Groups of workers on the same project do not need to inhabit the same space, let alone a place invested with subjective warmth: "Only a few parts of the watch pass through several hands; and all these *membra disjecta* come together for the first time in the hand that binds them into one mechanical whole. This external relation between the finished product and its various and diverse elements makes it a matter of chance . . . whether the specialized workers are brought together in one workshop or not."[44] Marx views machines and automation as absolutely alienating:

> "If," dreamed Aristotle, the greatest thinker of antiquity, "if every tool, when summoned, or even by intelligent anticipation, could do the work that befits it, just as the creations of Deadalus moved of themselves, or the tripods of Hephaestus went of their own accord to their sacred work, if the weavers' shuttles were to weave of themselves, then there would be no need either of apprentices for the master craftsmen, or of slaves for the lords." And Antipater, a Greek poet of the time of Cicero, hailed the water-wheel for grinding corn, that most basic form of all productive machinery, as the liberator of female slaves and the restorer of the golden age. Oh those heathens! They understood nothing of political economy and Christianity . . . They did not, for example, comprehend that machinery is the surest means of lengthening the working day.[45]

Humans become "an appendage of flesh on a machine of iron."[46] In the production process, as in the commodity form, humans are essential but also cast aside, literally squeezed into the tiniest possible space: "Dr. Letheby, Consulting Physician of the Board of Health, declared: 'The minimum of air for each adult ought to be in a sleeping room 300, and in a dwelling room 500 cubic feet.' "[47] The use of numbers is chilling. This is an age of sheer quantity—"facts," as Dickens's *Hard Times* unforgettably puts it.[48] It is ripe, therefore, for ambient poetics, whose exploitation of tone is a matter of quantity rather than quality, and absence rather than presence, generating the aesthetic equivalent of junkspace.

The immiseration of the worker is in parallel with ecological devastation, as Marx observes:

> All progress in capitalist agriculture is a progress in the art, not only of robbing the worker, but of robbing the soil; all progress in increasing the fertility of the soil for a given time is a progress towards ruining the more long-lasting sources of that fertility. The more a country proceeds from large-scale industry as the background of its development, as in the case of the United States, the more rapid is this process of destruction. Capitalist production, therefore, only develops the techniques and the degree of combination of the social process of production by simultaneously undermining the original sources of all wealth—the soil and the worker.[49]

Ecological criticism, especially the spiritual kind, castigates capitalism and industrialism for being materialistic. But capitalism holds no respect for matter, despite the ruthless demystification it imposes on the world. In truth it looks much more like an idealism gone mad. Nevertheless, it is the society of pure space, of "disappearing" the worker, and encrypting labor, rather than some feudal or earlier idyll, that enables genuine cooperation, as we shall explore in the next chapter.

Being Environmental

In such an age, subjectivity and the environment, both marginalized and exploited, frequently find themselves brought together in conceptions of other possible worlds. There are several reasons for dating the rise of environmental art to capitalism and consumerism. They are encoded into the language and ideology of ecomimesis, and of ecocriticism in general. When we widen our view, there emerge continuities in the discourses of ecology like layers of color in a slice of rock. Romantic artistic and philosophical practices and theories are preserved within contemporary ecological languages and beliefs. The primary instances are views of the critical aspect of art. This oppositional quality can take many forms. It can be avant-garde, attacking society and aesthetic norms head on. It can be salvational, promising a quasi-religious transcendence or escape from social and aesthetic dilemmas and sufferings. Whatever form it takes, art since Romanticism comes with an explicit or implicit manifesto attached to it. Art has an edge not fully absorbed into the social matrix. It stands awkwardly outside it, either trying to supplement it with something lacking in society, or trying to suggest another way of being.

A common view is that Romantic culture rejected the fantasy of capitalist enjoyment. Romanticist ecocriticism, for example, assumes that it is recapitulating the resistance of Romantic poetry to the technologies of capitalism. But the reverse was the case. What if we widened the lens to encompass an expanded view that did not take the *oikos* of ecology in the sense of home or dwelling as its center? In the Romantic period, capitalism moved from its colonialist to its imperialist phase. Intense war, plunder, and slavery spread over the earth. Monocultures appeared: unfeasible ecosystems where business produces only one crop.[50] Ireland was the test case, its potatoes transplanted from South America. In the resulting Potato Famine, countless people died or emigrated to America. Language blanketed places from Kingston, Jamaica, to Calicut, India, as "spice islands," "the Indies." This alone indicates how Europe was thinking. English, Portuguese, and French psychic and political maps of the world included open, empty places (empty of society or Western social norms), soaked with desire, producing goods spontaneously. Poetry caught wind of the coordination of imperialism and ecological destruction.

Nevertheless, you did not have to oppose capitalism to have environmental awareness. Global commerce itself gave rise to poetry that celebrated the global. We think of globalization as new, but it is only the most recent form of social processes that existed in the Romantic period. Powerfully depicted in Coleridge's *Ancient Mariner,* empty wilderness spaces owe something to imperial geography and the "because it's there" attitude of Everest climbers: imperialism in the abstract, the attempt to grasp the pure space, the intangible spacious*ness* of the environment.[51] David Simpson has argued that the empty, Antarctic wilderness toward which the Mariner voyages is an aesthetic (Romantic) version of the imperialist conquest and objectification of the world.[52] In our time this objectification has reached the limit of life-forms themselves. Rainforests are ransacked for biotechnology, and the insides of life-forms provide new products such as patented genomes in what ecofeminist Vandana Shiva describes as another wave of colonization.[53] In the language of the exhilarating rush to the new genetic frontier it is not hard to detect the strains of the Romantic voyage. Bill Clinton compared the first coding of the human genome with the travels of Lewis and Clark across the frontiers of America.[54]

The very form of alienation, the commodity, gave the first inklings of global environmental awareness in a poetic mode I have elsewhere described as "the poetics of spice." In this early form of advertising language, global flows of trade are represented as flows of spicy odor toward the nose of the consumer, in a form of ekphrasis (vivid description) that is very often deeply ambient. Ambience has become a way of describing value, the kind of thing you pay an interior designer a lot of money to achieve. Good restaurants have it—often without a qualifying adjective, just as they can have "class." The poetics of spice creates an embodied space, not nothingness, not caught up in the logic of negative and positive. This embodied space resembles what is meant by "environment" or "ecosystem." The naturalized ecopoetics of Romantic-period writers, including Wordsworth, Coleridge, Charlotte Smith (especially in *Beachy Head*), and Landon, ironically creates spaces similar to those perfumed by a cloud of incense in a church or temple. It is an atmosphere, a realm in which events have room to happen, a thick, embodied, heightened atmosphere, neither full nor empty. There is a sense of potential: something is "about" to happen, but there is no label or concept for this yet. Presence and absence, past and future events, discursive thoughts and memory traces, are contained within this space. This "thick" space is strictly impossible, but it is a compelling fantasy.

Private property aided ecological awareness, however strange that may sound. In eighteenth-century Britain, Enclosure privatized land held in common, obliterating feudal and communal relationships with the earth. Some ecological movements have since been trying to get it back, materially and symbolically. In returning to Romanticism, ecocriticism highlights the yearning for a bygone life of feudal hierarchy. Primitivist environmentalisms crave a lost golden age of interconnectedness with the environment. They look to pre-feudal, sometimes prehistoric, pasts to discover forms of primitive communism. In contrast, futurist environmentalisms are based on the notion that the golden age has not yet happened. They acknowledge that despite the medievalist glamour, most people never had much of a relationship with their land under a feudal hierarchy. These environmentalisms are also distinctively Romantic, in the tradition of William Blake and the Shelleys.

Capitalism compressed time and space. In culture, space became potent, while place, and the sense of place, became potent in its absence. That place has become endangered, like a species on the edge of extinction, is what Heidegger means when he talks about the way in which modern culture knows nothing about *nearness,* despite the preponderance of cell phones and the Internet.[55] Conversely, alternative forms of place and space appeared. In environmental and other forms of "militant particularism," such as the Zapatista movement in Mexico, the ideology of place has become more trenchant, while utopian forms of space are generated alongside capitalist space, such as the "thick space" of ambient poetics. Let us investigate the ways in which the culture and philosophy that derived from Romanticism deal with the realities of capitalism, industry, and science. We will concentrate on the ideas of *world, state, system, field,* and *body,* and in particular, ideas of organicism and holism. As these ideas are caught up in notions of the aesthetic, the aesthetic will become our focus.

World

Geography has recently provided ways of talking about interactions between space and place in a materialist, no-nonsense way. Franco Moretti has proposed that in order to study "world literature" properly, we need a more scientific, quantitative way of reading, "distant reading" (it is not clear why we cannot also search for signs of the global in the small print). Moretti applies this technique in mapping the ways in which a very significant novel, *Our Village* by Mary Russell Mitford, distributes places and space.[56] He could also have analyzed time. *Our Village* is a vivid example of late-Romantic ambience, a narrative of stasis and suspension in which cyclic techniques render the rhythms of an English village measured against the abstract time of urbanization and factories. Reading *Our Village* recovers a sense of *Gemeinschaft*, of rich, satisfying human interactions in a world of significance. On the other hand, this sense of world emerges against the background of mechanical, industrial *Gesellschaft,* and partakes of it, since the novel was serialized and mechanically reproduced. Participating in the time of the novel meant waiting for the next installment, and this is a textual village that provides an aesthetic, distanced intimacy. During the Napoleonic Wars, before the village novels of the nineteenth century appeared, the Ordnance Survey had mapped Britain according to rigorous principles. Localism was already a construction in relation to a more general view.

Our Village tries to encapsulate the *feel* of a social milieu. Likewise, phenomenological history endeavors to render the experience of the past. There is something ecological in the history of "soundscapes," a symptom of a wish to recover a vivid sense of place—what did England *sound like* in Shakespeare's age?[57] Perhaps because it is more physically involving than vision (sound waves vibrate air, which vibrates the body), sonic history tries for a more vivid rendering of place than traditional history. Auditory history has sometimes joined with actual place-based environmental politics, for example, in the American West, where campaigns to ban military aircraft and snowmobiles from the national parks' land and air is aided by accounts of what the Rockies sounded like a century ago before the internal combustion engine.

Sonic history is actually the symptom of a radical *loss* of place—if we had such a thing at all. It aestheticizes place, as the suffix "scape" warns us. A landscape is a *painting*. A soundscape has been framed. It implies a distance. There is a sonic equivalent of a frame or a pane of glass separating the historians from the time they are evoking. The re-mark is in play, differentiating between what is inside and what is outside the soundscape, and between what counts as "sound" and what counts as "noise." It would be less seductive, after all, to call the sound world a "noise-scape." After the fact, the clip-clopping of horses becomes charged with significances that it did not have at the time—even if it did, such significances would already be caught in the paradoxes of the echo.

"Environmental" or "soundscape" recordings of the 1970s prefig-ured soundscape history, with records of birdsong and especially the sounds of whales. The "Save the Whale" campaign gained enormous help from such albums as *Songs of the Humpback Whale* and *Deep Voices*.[58] These recordings are *medial*. They draw attention to animals as inhabitants of the earth, conveying a sense of the environment in general: animals become part of the weather. Because we cannot under-stand what the animals are saying, even whether they are saying any-thing at all, we become aware of the communication medium. The opacity *is* the environmental quality. As soon as we can figure out what the whales are singing, their messages will be in the foreground rather than in the background. Ambient poetics is about making the imper-ceptible perceptible, while retaining the form of its imperceptibility—to make the invisible visible, the inaudible audible. On one of the tracks of *Deep Voices*, a blue whale is sped up to within the range of human hearing. We cannot understand it, but we can hear it.

This brings to mind the found object, the action painting, the free im-provisation. Ambient art wants to make the unknown known, like sci-ence. But it also wishes to retain the flavor of the unknown, a certain mystifying opacity—otherwise ambient art would in fact be science. What is the difference between ambient art, say, setting up some sub-sonic microphones to record the sound of standing waves of air pres-sure over the Atlantic as they affect the atmosphere in a city room, as Felix Hess did, and sheer scientific experiment, data collection, or mon-itoring?[59] On the other hand, this "unknown" is already accounted for. Ambient art predicts, or sets up the parameters for, certain kinds of un-known. We cannot control the whale sounds, but we know that we will be getting whale sounds and not, say, the sounds of a flying saucer, if we dip a microphone into the ocean. In both cases—preserving the un-known as a reflex of artistry as opposed to science; "knowing" the un-known in advance, in some sense—ambient art misses the genuine unknown, which would consist of radical nonidentity.

The idea of an aesthetic history is close to that of national identity as an embodied thing. Nationalism has always appealed to the sensory world, generating a specific national tone. Like nature, Englishness seems mysteriously more than the sum of its parts. It appears alongside monarchs, checks and balances, strawberries and bluebells, irreducible to them yet caught up in them. Organicism, that peculiarly English form of nature ideology, paints society as a nonsystemic heap of classes, beliefs, and practices, as ramshackle and spontaneous as a pile of compost. This is a rich, compelling, and finally authoritarian fantasy—there's no arguing with it. Many environmentalist values (complexity is good, the world cannot be totalized though it is a whole) are slices of Romantic organicism exemplified in Edmund Burke's reactionary prose. But environmentalism need not be organicist, not even in the Romantic period. *Frankenstein* shows how organicism fails. Incapable of loving his creature spontaneously, Frankenstein would benefit from a more rational and planned social structure that treated all social actors as equal participants with equal rights.

Nationalism, a quintessentially Romantic ideology, continues to motivate environmental art seeking to re-enchant the world. The nation-state remains a real yet fantastic thing. As the idea of world *(Welt)* became popular in German Romantic idealism, so the nation-state was imagined as a surrounding environment.[60] The idea of the nation as "homeland," as in American Homeland Security or the German *Heimat,* demanded a poetic rendering as an ambient realm of swaying corn, shining seas, or stately forests. Nature appeared sublime, "there" and yet fundamentally beyond representation, stretching beyond the horizon and back into the distant, even pre-human past. It was a suitable objective correlative for the *je ne sais quoi* of nationalist fantasy. Walter Scott's invention of historical novels, realist fictions generating an entire world in a bubble of past-tense narrative, did as much for environmental nationalism as explicitly Romantic criticisms of modern society and technology. Can progressive art rescue the aesthetics of environmental ambience from its ideological frame? Or is the thick, embodied space of nationalist representation hopelessly saturated with ideological content?

The Shire in J. R. R. Tolkien's *The Lord of the Rings* depicts the world-bubble as an organic village. Tolkien narrates the victory of the suburbanite, the "little person," embedded in a tamed yet natural-seeming environment. Nestled into the horizon as they are in their burrows, the wider world of global politics is blissfully unavailable to them. Tolkien's work embodies a key nationalist fantasy, a sense of "world" as real, tangible yet indeterminate, evoking a metonymic chain of images—an anamorphic form. *The Lord of the Rings* establishes not only entire languages, histories, and mythologies, but also a surrounding world. If ever there was evidence of the persistence of Romanticism, this is it.

In Heidegger's supremely environmental philosophy, the surrounding ambience created by Tolkien's narrative is called *Umwelt.*[61] This is the deep ontological sense in which things are "around"—they may come in handy, but whether they do or not, we have a care for them.[62] It is a thoroughly environmental idea. Things are oriented in relation to other things: "The house has its sunny side and its shady side."[63] Others (elves, dwarves, men) care for their surroundings differently. The strangeness of Middle-earth, its permeation with others and their worlds, is summed up in the metaphor of the road, which becomes an emblem for narrative. The road comes right up to your front door. To step into it is to cross a threshold between inside and outside. There is a sense that the story, and the world it describes, could go "ever on and on" like the road in Bilbo Baggins's song.[64] But wherever we go in this world, however strange or threatening our journey, it will always be familiar, insofar as it has all been planned in advance, mapped out, accounted for. This planning is not quite as narrowly rational as a modern factory. Still, the recent film of *The Lord of the Rings,* with its built-in commentaries on the special edition DVD about the craftsmanship and industrial processes that went into making it, reveals something true about the book. This *Umwelt* is a function of holistic, total design, total creation: Wagnerian *Gesamtkunstwerk* with a how-to booklet thrown in. The holistic world that "goes ever on and on" is exciting and involved, but in the end, it is just a gigantic version of the ready-made commodity. This is ironic, since one of the themes of the work is the resistance to industrialism and specifically to commodity fetishism, in the form of the hypnotic ring itself.

What gets lost in this elaborate attempt to craft a piece of kitsch that could assuage the ravages of industrialism? Like some nature writing and ecocriticism, Tolkien's *Umwelt* edits out significant aspects of Romantic literature pertaining to hesitation, irony, and ambiguity, even and especially in Wordsworth. Consider Schlegel's idea of Romantic irony. It manifests in narratives in which the narrator becomes the protagonist, unnervingly aware that the world he or she has constructed is a fiction.[65] Must ecological and ecocritical worlds be absolutely self-contained, utterly sincere—and how Romantic is that? Irony involves distancing and displacement, a moving from place to place, or even from homey place into lonely space. Early ecological science developed terms resonant with the idea of home, such as *niche,* a word derived from a place that houses a statue.[66] Science itself can be Tolkienesque. Where does that leave migrating birds, hominids, pilgrims, gypsies, and Jews?

The question of animals—sometimes I wonder whether it is *the* question—radically disrupts any idea of a single, independent, solid environment.[67] Each animal, perhaps, has its own environment, as German scientists such as Jacob von Uexküll wanted to establish in the early twentieth century, profoundly influencing Heidegger.[68] Even if this is not true (if it were, it would multiply the problem of "the" environment exponentially), the idea of "our" environment becomes especially tricky when it starts to slither, swim, and lurch toward us. The beings known as animals hover at the corner of the separation of inside and outside generated by the idea of world as a self-contained system. Strangely enough, thinking in terms of "world" often excludes animals—beings who actually live there. For Edmund Husserl, animals are like deaf people, "abnormal."[69] For Heidegger, animals lack of a sense of world *(Weltarm)*.[70] Or, more precisely, their sense of world *is* this lack.[71] In contrast, some ecological thinking wants to forget about the differences between humans and other animals, real or imagined, as soon as possible. This inverted speciesism celebrates "the more than human world" (Abram). For Percy Shelley, animals lose their cruelty just as humans begin to live a more pacifist existence. In his vegetarian ecotopia they end up "sport[ing] around [man's] dwelling" (*The Daemon of the World*, 2.444). For Rilke or Levertov, post-Romantic poets keen to establish an environmental poetics, animals have an access to the "open" that is denied to humans, either entirely or as a result of bad training.[72] It all depends how up close and personal you want to get. Levinas strove to exclude animals from his idea of contact with the "face" of the other as the basis of ethics. But he was haunted by the face of a dog who had looked at him, perhaps with kindness, in a Nazi prison camp.[73] For Tolkien, dwarves, elves, hobbits, and talking eagles are welcome others, but swarthy "southern" or "eastern" men are not.[74] Some of those who refused to evacuate New Orleans in the wake of hurricane Katrina did so because they were not allowed to take their pets and would not abandon them. This may be a matter of moral feeling rather than stubborn primitivism.

The Nazis ferociously opposed animal cruelty but thought nothing of exterminating threatening human others. Animals bring up the ways in which humans develop intolerances to strangeness and to the stranger. We must become like animals (ecocentrism), or vice versa (anthropocentrism). We are back with the quantum state we discovered in Chapter 1. There is no way of maintaining the strangeness of things without coming down on one side or the other. What of the *arrival* ("human" or "animal" or other) your worldview was not expecting? I use the word *arrival* in the sense Derrida means when he speaks of a "pure hospitality" as one that "opens or is in advance open to someone who is neither expected nor invited, to whomever arrives as an absolutely foreign visitor, as a new arrival, nonidentifiable and unforeseeable, in short, wholly other"; "without at least the thought of this pure and unconditional hospitality . . . we would not even have the idea of the other, of the alterity of the other, that is, of someone who enters into our lives without having been invited. We would not even have the idea of love or of 'living together' *(vivre ensemble)* with the other in a way that is not a part of some totality or 'ensemble.' "[75] This genuinely "other other" appears to be held up at the border of the world as nestling horizon. Just as ambient poetics undermines the environmentalism that uses it to establish itself, so strangers undermine the very *Umwelt* that uses them to establish its boundaries. Far from healing the rift between humans and others, thinking since the Romantic period keeps opening it up in all sorts of ways. This is despite the fact that radical linguistic theory of the age posited language as deriving from animal cries.[76] Onomatopoeia is ecomimesis in miniature. Despite the recent attempt to categorize the bonobo chimpanzee as a species of *Homo,* a seemingly endless series of hominids and humanoids stands between humans and animals. And no one has yet categorized humans as a species of *Pan paniscus.*

If we knew what to do with animals and their kin, we could take a break from the painful exertions of consciousness. We could shout "We are the world!" and it would be true. Of course, we would not be able to watch ourselves on video as we dissolved into oneness with the stranger. And so ecological writing keeps beating itself against the glass of the other, like a fly. The constant dinging of the impact—in which the strange other, as soon as it enters into proximity, becomes an inert or threatening *thing*—indicates a loss of irony. The only way to remain close to the strangers without killing them (turning them into yourself or into an inanimate object) is to maintain a sense of irony. If irony and movement are not part of environmentalism, strangers are in danger of disappearing, exclusion, ostracism, or worse.

Schlegel determined that irony was democratic. All truth claims are fragmentary, and the more you know, the more you realize that your own perspective is shot through with fragmentariness, negativity, and hesitation. You start to tolerate other ways of life.[77] But is toleration enough, as Derrida asked? You might end up not with a sense of the other as other, but with a sense of sheer "I," a blank space or black hole, transcending all possible positions—a state of "quiescence and feebleness—which does not like to act or to touch anything for fear of surrendering its inward harmony . . . the source of morbid saintliness and yearning."[78] This is Hegel's view of the "beautiful soul," as we shall see, and it has much to tell us about environmentalism. When it becomes a way of being, irony ironically ceases to be irony. Instead of establishing an aestheticized distance toward everything, irony must forge intimate relationships with strangers. We will be grappling with this intimacy in Chapter 3. For now, let us continue to steer ourselves through different possible forms of environmental immersion.

State

While we are on the subject of self-containment, and the irony that punctures it, we should clarify the Romantic idea of holism. As well as being a major ecological ideology, holism constitutes the "feel" of nationalism—"we" are interconnected in a whole greater than the sum of its parts. The struggle between individualism and holism offers an attenuated choice between absolute liberty and absolute authority—in other words, the dilemma called America. Americans are caught between the constitution and a militarized state, between placards and pepper spray. There is something of this in the way in which models of nature give to organisms with one hand, while taking with another. Organisms are politically all-important, and yet they are easily sacrificed for the sake of the greater whole. The ideological supports of American capitalism have gradually shifted away from individualism toward corporatism. Holism is not as oppositional as some environmentalists claim. State terror takes an interest in ecological catastrophe. Far from writing it off with the reactionaries as "junk science," the Pentagon has published documents on the geopolitical effects of global warming.[79] Paul Virilio has even suggested that ecological catastrophe is an excellent simulation of total global war. Hurricane Katrina, which devastated New Orleans, provides a perfect example. President Bush appointed Homeland Security, an umbrella department covering military, intelligence, and counterterrorism, to oversee the cleanup operation. Popular resistance, and military might, could both be considered in ambient terms. The war theorist Clausewitz imagines the Spanish resistance to Napoleon as "something fluid and vaporous which condensed *nowhere* into a solid body."[80]

We have seen how De Quincey's theory of consumerist reading now looks a lot like a theory of environmental poetics. His experiments with opiated prose generate an understanding of tone, a plateau of intensity. Art and philosophy have become interested in the ways in which certain states are indeed static—tonally undifferentiated and consistent. It may surprise some that Romanticism, far from supporting sheer temporality, developed a static poetics of environments suspended in time. Wordsworth's idea of the *spot of time,* whose name alone suggests this suspension, is a traumatically vivid experience that punctures the regular rhythms of consciousness, a moment when something outside the habitual world breaks through. The mind is jerked out of its normal medium, like a fish out of water.

Heidegger's idea of thinking as *dwelling* has a static quality. Walter Benjamin's ideas of *dialectics at a standstill* and *phantasmagoria* are static. The musical perceptions of John Cage, celebrating a notion of quietness, evoke a communitarian suburban or libertarian form of quiet that is also static in a political sense—there is no chance of progress, just an endless application of laws. Quiet is a meaningful, continuous absence of noise, often with strict legal definitions.[81] Static art and static philosophy arose as the nation-state, and beyond its borders, the environment gradually "dissolved" into view. Can progressive ecological thinking rescue the ecological Thing, fantasy object of the nation-state, and always somewhat in excess of nationalism, from the place of its birth? Ecological reality, produced in part by the industrializing processes of nation-states themselves, has eclipsed national boundaries. Only an ecological language opposed to the phantasmagorical positivities of nation-speak is anywhere near legitimate, and only if it does not prove to be just another "new and improved" version of the same thing.

System

It is better for environmentalism to think in terms of *collectivism* rather than *holism.* A collective does not imply an organic whole that is greater than the sum of its parts. Indeed, ecology without nature rules out holism. Is ecological collectivism entirely unknown to us yet, as Bruno Latour has suggested? Or are there models that do not suffer from the vices of holism? Perhaps the notion of *system* is less chewy, less substantial? After all, reactionary substantialism in the Romantic period protested against systematic theory—Holbach's *Système de la Nature,* for instance, a radical atheist's textbook.[82] Nature has been tightened up by the idea of ecosystem. *Ecosystem,* coined by Roy Clapham and Arthur Tansley in the early 1930s, updated the idea of ecology (Ernst Haeckel [1834–1919] was the first to use the term).

Ecology derived from the Enlightenment view of the *economy of nature*. This economy is an organization to the mutual cost and benefit of its participants. But ecology had begun to appear rather fuzzy and even spiritual, a superorganism composed of all organisms. Despite its connotations of the theoretical, at least to reactionary ears, the idea of environment as a system rules out critical anomalies. The ecosytsem becomes an immersive, impersonal matrix. Unfortunately for ideas of an ecological politics that would liberate us from the modern state, this is the systems thinking adopted by the RAND corporation, the sort of thing that inspired Marcuse's Romantic-ecological critique of one-dimensional man.[83] Systems theory is holism without the sticky wetness, a cybernetic version of the ecological imaginary.[84]

System has the virtue of seeming less Romantic and misty than *world*. But it merely updates Romanticism for an age of cybernetics. Deep ecology, the most Romantic of all ecological forms of politics, is curiously enough the one most devoted to systems thinking. System can generate its own forms of mysticism. Arne Naess's seminal philosophy of deep ecology is based on an idea of the encounter of a (little /s/) self with a (big /S/) Self: "Organisms and milieux are not two things—if a mouse were lifted into absolute vacuum, it would no longer be a mouse. Organisms presuppose milieux. Similarly, a person is a part of nature to the extent that he or she is a relational junction within the total field. The process of identification is a process in which the relations which define the junction expand to comprise more and more. The 'self' grows towards the 'Self'."[85] It sounds like secular science, with its talk of organisms and fields. But Naess's idea is a version of Hinduism. Through systemic organization, and in contemplating the system, the "self" *(atman)* realizes itself as the "Self" *(Brahman)*. But the argument is puzzling. In a vacuum the mouse would remain a mouse. It would just be a dead mouse. There is a slip between the sentences. If they are to survive, organisms require milieux. To argue in this way, to reformulate the self as a "relational junction," is to push the issue of identity back a stage further, but not to get rid of it. And it is unclear how a "relational junction" gets rid of the dualism that Naess sees as the problem. The logic is still that something must relate to something else. The "total field" continues the idea of environment as different from these relational junctions, the background to their foreground, however much the ideas of field and totality strive to submerge difference.

Naess's figuration relies on highly nonorganic language, more reminiscent of electromagnetism and cybernetics, if not cyberpunk, than trees and roots. Naess reduces the self to a (zero-dimensional) point in a field, as David Harvey rightly puts it in his reading of this passage. Naess's position actually resembles nothing so much as the Cartesian reduction itself, the limitation of identity to a dot of doubt. Like Pascal's before him, Naess's prose ironically experientially renders what it *feels like* to inhabit a Cartesian universe: "The eternal silence of these infinite spaces fills me with dread."[86] As Blanchot observed, anti-Cartesians such as Pascal end up being Cartesian, "For it is based upon the self that Descartes founds objectivity."[87]

Field

Phenomenology developed the term *field* to refer to the perceptual aspect of what it called "intersubjectivity." While it has a pastoral ring, it surely derives from nineteenth-century natural philosophy, with its positing, for the first time, of "fields" of energy. The idea of *field* usefully dispenses with conventional notions of particles. The field concept is the first to amalgamate particles and energy under a single heading—Einstein would eventually show that they were convertible into each other. The third definition of *field* is "Area of operation or observation," a sense retained from Middle English; its first use in physics was not until 1845.[88] Michael Faraday (1791–1867) had discovered magnetic fields, and suggested that electrical and magnetic fields "are *real* physical 'stuff.'"[89] William Rowan Hamilton (1805–1865) summarized a body of work in Newtonian physics that had been emerging throughout the eighteenth century, by such scientists as Laplace and Liouville. Hamilton developed equations that enabled one to study the momentum of particles changing over time, thus defining a vector field in what came to be known as "phase space." James Clark Maxwell (1831–1879) generated proper field equations to describe the behavior of electromagnetic fields (rather than Hamilton's equations, strictly for particles).

A field is an array of vectors, down which specific particles are aligned: think of the way iron filings arrange themselves in the field around a magnet. Naess would have been better off talking about vectors than relational junctions; at least he would have achieved a sense of movement. Husserl claims that phenomenology is not metaphysical, because "it proceeds within the limits of pure 'intuition,' or rather of pure sense-explication based on a fulfilling givenness of the sense itself."[90] This is life lived on the pulses, though Husserl's prose gives the dizzying sensation of establishing everything from the point of view of a transcendental subject cut off (or bracketed off, in his terminology) from the usual world. But the idea of field is already on the side of the object, rather than of the subject—unless we want to reduce the subject to a vector (or to a point), in which case we will not have reconciled subject and object, or collapsed the difference between them, so much as turned everything into an object. Fields are physical—somewhat ironically for phenomenology, which is busy redrafting or attacking Descartes, who himself claimed that there could be no such thing as empty space and that the body (as extension) *was* space.[91] Descartes has been the bugbear of ecological thinking ever since.[92] Michel Serres: "We must . . . change direction and abandon the heading imposed by Descartes' philosophy."[93]

Husserl is hampered by his admission that he must seek a Cartesian way out of Descartes. Husserl is honest enough to confess that "one might almost call transcendental phenomenology a neo-Cartesianism, even though it is obliged—and precisely by its radical development of Cartesian motifs—to reject nearly all the well-known doctrinal content of the Cartesian philosophy."[94] Trying to get over or around Descartes involves, as Husserl admits, using a Cartesian method, consisting partly in fictional devices that in themselves cast suspicion upon the idea of a genuine, independent, and unique "I."[95] As David Simpson puts it: "to [follow Descartes] without careful thought would involve accepting his personal maxims as authoritative, in direct contradiction to the spirit of the method of self-discovery; this is the theoretical implication."[96]

At the very moment at which it requires certainty, ecomimesis guarantees an overdose of doubt. Even as it hemorrhages irony, it builds up a tremendous ironic resonance. One sense of field is of a flat surface, notably the undecorated ground of a picture, a flag, or a coin.[97] The field is the margin, the blank part of the page, or, more recently, a placeholder for data in a database. The rich, spatial quality of field in phenomenology is simply the holographic hallucination of reading or scanning, turned into a philosophic system. Like those optical illusions made of millions of dots that reveal a three-dimensional picture when we look at them askew, phenomenological prose wants to conjure up a sense of a surrounding world that will jump off the page. Aside from its strict use in physics, field is all over the place.

Body

The play of the re-mark devastates "new and improved" fusions of subject and object, such as the idea of intersubjectivity, which seek to do away with the dilemma of specifying the boundary between inside and outside. It becomes impossible to distinguish between the intersubjective field and "the Body," which pushes further the intermixing of subject and object, without really resolving the contradiction, since "the Body" is a manifold of psychic and physical ("psychophysical") events. If we are disabled, either by a physical disability or a change in the medium of perception, reality will appear differently. Husserl's dilemma gives rise to his use of chiasmus, as the dog of his argument chases its tail: "Each thing of my experience belong to my 'environment,' and that means first of all that *my Body* is part of it precisely as body."[98]

I am he as you are he as you are me and we are all together—in which case, why bother using "my" and "I" at all? Inspired by phenomenology, some ecological writing aspires to the notion that the ecosystem makes available an idea of intersubjectivity, an entanglement of minds with other minds and perhaps nonmental or inanimate things. Reframing subject–object dualism in a "better" way, as a dualism of subjectivity/intersubjectivity, is a "new and improved" variant of the same dualism. Phenomenological talk of "*the* Body" feels like Romantic wishful thinking. There is a way of firmly establishing the reality of the intersubjective field; unless, that is, we claim that what we are really talking about is a specific physical field—in which case it would be better to talk of interobjectivity rather than intersubjectivity. The subject perishes before it is even born. Phenomenological rhetoric comes off at once as a delicate, intense, highly subjective contemplation; and as a reduction of the subject to a set of scientific processes. For David Abram (more about him soon), encountering a crow becomes a thrilling moment of interspecies contact—and a Cartesian experiment in which we necessarily distinguish between the *I* who is narrating and the *I* who is experiencing the crow, the *I* that becomes an object in an experiment that we cannot satisfactorily separate from a thought-experiment conjured up on the page . . . and so on.[99]

Edward Casey argues that place reappeared by way of the body, something that has troubled Western philosophy since Descartes. In spite of his general view of space as a transcendental category, Kant did employ an idea of physical, experiential directionality, defying his more general aim to do away with situatedness.[100] Place shrank to the immediate space of "the body." It became possible to conceive of a small region that was not abstract and empty. Some philosophy wants the body to ride in like the cavalry and save it from Western dualism. "*The* body" is an in-between state that is a function of "world and field" thinking. The body becomes the site of a revised aesthetics. One of the defining characteristics of environmental writing is how little attention it pays to the fact that only some bodies have arms and legs; only some bodies are sighted or can hear. There is no such thing as *the* body, if by that we mean something unmarked by gender, race, or physical ability. Environmental writing is keen to embrace other species, but not always so interested in exploring the environments of "disabled" members of the human species. It is an ethics of hale-and-hearty refreshment, an extra-nourishing aesthetic with added vitamins; but if gender, race, and capabilities coordinate the body, then so must they coordinate place and the environment, since according to phenomenology, the body and place are in a chiasmic relationship with one another. To reach out into a shared world is not to transcend one's physicality but to become conscious of its determinacy.[101]

The more you think about the body, the more the category of nature starts to dissolve. The argument in Chapter 1 about the car (when I retrofit it, does it remain the same?) affects the way in which we have come to think of the body as a solution to our woes. The body is the umbrella under which terms such as *nuance* and *rhizome* find shelter. If I add to or take away from this body (a prosthetic device here, an amputation there), is it still *the* (same) body? This "body" is a special version of metaphysics. It is literally not "beyond" (meta) the physical realm. But it is conveniently mysterious and compelling, and other terms gravitate towards it. Its "in between-ness" is just as peculiar, on reflection, as the "beyond-ness" of the metaphysical. We need a word like *mesophysical* to register this strangeness. It would help to explain how marginal spaces such as wetlands have recently come in for the same praise as the body. For Rod Giblett, Thoreau finds wetlands "the perfect place to still the senses, and the limbs, and allow the swamp to write on the body, not as a *tabula rasa,* but as a responsive surface."[102] Mud, mud, glorious mud. The body is also the name in post-structuralist thinking for all that gets traditionally left out of the aesthetic, which started off with the body but ended up transcending it. It is extraordinary that post-structuralism, a discourse that claims so vehemently to be against grand narratives, should have produced *the* body.

In the Romantic period the aesthetic stood between reason and passion, subject and object, fact and value. Nowadays, that task falls to the body. The body is the aesthetic, with all the disgusting things that the aesthetic normally edits out put back in. The body is the anti-aesthetic, and its virtue (or vice) is that it is both entirely different from, and just an alternative version of, the aesthetic. Thus, experimental noise music "puts back in" elements that used to be excluded from the artwork: the sound of the space in which the music was recorded; the bodies of the instruments and the musicians; the presence of "noise" that alerts us to the fact that we are listening to a physical medium, and so on.

The body stands in for what we think we've lost, a little world, a floating island. But it is easy to deconstruct this body: where does it start and stop? Is a tennis racket an "extension" of my body? What about the tennis ball? The tennis court? When does this body stop being "my" body? Freud called the telephone a "prosthetic" ear. Donna Haraway has written persuasively and influentially that cybernetics and prosthetics have reconfigured our sense of human being.[103] How about when we subtract things from the body? Is it still my body when I lose the hand, the arm? Melanie Klein's idea of "partial objects," or even Winnicott's softer notion of "transitional objects" undermine our prejudices about the integrity of the object. Once we have admitted that there are such things as partial objects, all objects become contaminated with the idea of partiality. Is bodily integrity an adequate or desirable court of appeal?

This is a matter of real urgency. Environmentalism worries that we are disconnected from the world. But what if one of the problems were *this idea itself*? Science backs up sheer speculation: "the" body is a palimpsest of symbiotic organisms, such as energy-producing bacteria that have become the mitochondria in each individual cell.[104] Industrial society has produced what Latour calls "quasi-objects" such as asbestos, radioactivity, and dioxins, which have truly opened the body to its environment, albeit in the negative. Quasi-objects have undermined the classical difference between humanity and nature.[105] Thus, there is nothing "in between" either. Quasi-objects do lie "between" classical conceptions of subject and object, nature and society, claims Latour; he goes so far as to call them "rhizomes."[106] Rhizomes are at best as untenable as "linear," "hierarchical" forms. But in lying between categories quasi-objects have a net negative effect on metaphysics rather than a positive one. We *are* the world, unfortunately. One solution to the paradoxes of the body is thus to turn it into the environment itself, reconceived as a kind of inverted deity, a form of natural supernaturalism. Merleau-Ponty started to describe "the Flesh," a suggestive term for what David Abram evokes as "the mysterious tissue or matrix that underlies and gives rise to both the perceiver and the perceived as interdependent aspects of its own spontaneous activity."[107] This combination of a world of "one" (monism) and a world of "two" (the dualism of perceiver and perceived) inevitably suffers from the problems that beset both views. The idea of "flesh" or "fleshliness"—viewing the body without a holistic structure, without center or edge—is an aesthetic one, and thus subject to the paradoxes we have explored.

The problems that beset the idea of the body also affect ideas of the environment. Ecological rhetoric tends to imagine nature as a closed system in which everything is ultimately recycled, like the Romantic idea of the aesthetic object as an organic whole. Just as Georges Bataille suggested a "general economy" that is wider than a normative "restricted economy," or closed system, so we can posit a "general ecology."[108] Bataille implicitly includes ecology in thinking about economics: "Should we not, given the constant development of economic forces, pose the *general* problems that are linked to the movement of energy on the globe?"[109] Why stop there? Since asteroids keep crashing down, perhaps laden with the building blocks of life, why does an ecological view have to stop at the edge of the biosphere? And what *is* this edge, since the sun is a key component "in" the biosphere itself? Environmentalism, inheriting economic ideas from the long eighteenth century, runs the risk of being a rebranded version of regular economics. Paul Hawken's "natural capitalism" takes account of a wider view, without changing the basic model.[110] All attempts to account for phenomena marginalized and exploited by economic "progress" are fraught with difficulty, from the Zeitgeist to the body, from world to system. Since it looks like capitalism is about to use an ecological rhetoric of scarcity to justify future developments, it is vital that we recognize that there are serious problems with imagining an ecological view based on limits, even at the level of abstraction we have been exploring. And we need to notice that scarcity and limitation are not the only ecological concepts on the block. What if the problem were in fact one of a badly distributed and reified *surplus?*

None of the substitutes for environment or ambience is sufficient. Coming up with a new term will never help, because the overarching metaphor is flawed, for reasons already given. So much for the ecological *object.* Now let us consider the context for ambience in another way, by examining how *subjectivity* is oriented toward it.

Beautiful Souls: Romantic Consumerism and Environmentalism

In 1988, Prime Minister Thatcher "greened" herself, proclaiming something like "The first thing we have to do is get this country really, really *tidy.*" It was the tidiness of that "tidy" that grated; as if ecology were about rearranging the furniture. Thatcher, like Hitler, was thinking in terms of living rooms; Hitler proposed that the destiny of Germany was to increase and purify its *Lebensraum* ("living room"). The 1980s had witnessed one of the least tidy critiques of modernity in the transgressive form of the Greenham Common women, who camped outside a proposed cruise missile base in the United Kingdom and practically created an alternative society.[111] Thatcher was not reacting directly to the Greenham women, whom she dismissed as dangerously marginal, witch-like figures (ironically some *did* consider themselves witches). Thatcher was reacting to a growing pile of "environmentally friendly" products. Green consumerism made it possible to be both pro-capitalist and green, repeating the Romantic struggle between rebelling and selling out.

Thatcherite "tidiness" included processing the world's nuclear waste at Sellafield, a concern so lucrative that British Nuclear Fuels now has an interest in the "cleanup" at Rocky Flats nuclear bomb trigger factory near Boulder, Colorado. Rocky Flats was renamed, temporarily, an "environmental protection site"—which meant removing enough plutonium to accord with "safe" levels for the establishment of an open-space wilderness reserve; not safe enough for suburban houses, but safe enough, apparently, for microbes that will eventually enter the groundwater. Against such crass co-opting of green politics, a Romantic scream is entirely justifiable, a rage against the machine of modern life. Allen Ginsberg's "Plutonian Ode," commemorating an action on the rail tracks toward Rocky Flats, is a gigantic scream, a paratactic list deriving from Romantic experiments with expansive lineation by William Blake and Walt Whitman.[112]

And yet—and this is a big "and yet"—Romanticism *is* consumerism; consumerism is Romanticism. Notice the word "consume*rism*," not "consuming": a particular style of consuming that arose from the growth of consumer society throughout the long eighteenth century.[113] One can take this notion too far. Other forces were in play: the rise in the price of meat, for example, meant that working-class food actually deteriorated. In the seventeenth century the high cost of bread was not vitally important to the lower classes: they lived on other sorts of cheap food and occupied the land. By the Romantic period they could hardly afford meat, while tea and white bread had become necessities. Nevertheless, even the working class had its versions of consumerism, which developed in the Romantic period. Consider the politicized demand for fine white bread and even working-class versions of vegetarianism: a self-reflexive "choice" of certain kinds of food that, in other circumstances, they *had* to eat.[114] So consumerism is not entirely a middle-class or bourgeois affair.

By the Romantic period, it became possible to *be* (or if you prefer, to *act*) consumerist. Consumerism is a reflexive mode of consumption. It is about how one appears *as* a certain type of consumer. One doesn't just eat carrots, one styles oneself as a carrot eater. This idea can be taken a notch further. There is such a thing as *reflexive* consumerism.[115] In modern society we are all potential reflexive consumerists, a type that in the Romantic period was restricted to a certain avant-garde faction (Baudelaire, De Quincey). The reflexive consumer is interested in what it feels like to experience a certain form of consumerism—window-shopping in the shopping mall of subjectivity—"Kantian" aesthetic consumption without "purpose" or purchase.[116] The *flâneur* (French "stroller," "loafer") was born. There is a certain sense in which we are now all *flâneurs* whether we like it or not. Objective social forms (television advertising, the Internet, malls) have made it impossible not to be a reflexive consumerist.

To be a consumerist, you don't have to consume anything, just contemplate the *idea* of consuming. Consumerism raised to the highest power is free-floating identity, or identity in process. This is a specifically *Romantic consumerism*.[117] Transformative experiences are valued, such as those derived from drugs, or from intense experiences, such as Wordsworth's "spots of time," traumas that nudge the self out of its circularity and force it to circulate around something new. The (necessarily) external event becomes the piece of grit that helps to generate the pearl of revised selfhood. The title of Emily Jenkins's *Tongue First* suggests the approach of the reflexive consumerist, or bohemian, in the nineteenth-century phraseology.[118] The idea is to dive into new forms of subjectivity by consuming a previously avoided substance (in Jenkins's case, heroin), or acting different roles. This dive is vicarious. There is always a lifeline, in the form of a certain ironic or cynical distance toward the role being played.

This is the quintessentially Romantic poetic voice. Though he is usually labeled as getting his experiences artificially, De Quincey has as much to tell us about environmental writing as Wordsworth, who is commonly labeled as "natural" by comparison. Since the Romantic period, capitalism has become adept in selling this paradoxical identity—a sort of freely chosen narcissistic state—back to people.[119] *All* consumer objects approach this luxury status, whether we think of them as luxuries or as necessities.[120] What Freud called the oceanic feeling—the

feeling, supposedly derived from early infancy or intrauterine experience, of being immersed in a medium even to the extent of a loss of distinct identity—has become one of the supreme capitalist products.[121]
Ambience is the form that this environmental consciousness assumes.
The oceanic state was of great interest to Romantic poets such as
Shelley, who wrote in his essay "On Life" that children "less habitually
distinguished all that we saw and felt, from ourselves." Some adults
who find themselves still capable of accessing this "state called reverie
feel as if their nature were dissolved into the surrounding universe, or
as if the surrounding universe were absorbed into their being."[122] The
New Age language of a future state of humankind, in which the oceanic
has been reintegrated into everyday experience, is one of the most sophisticated—refined and paradoxical, even to the point of being critical—forms of the commodity. The recent Gnostic spirituality around
the Internet (when we are all wired our bodies will dissolve into the
ether!), and the development of techno dance music and massive outdoor raves, are two manifestations of an *objectified subjectivity* that is
trying to be "environmental." On a more mundane level, the free-
floating "window-shopping" model of identity is a social version of the
"in between" state we examined as an aesthetic event in the Chapter 1.
Pierre Bourdieu has named this reflexive consumerism a *Kantian* form
of consumption, that is, an aesthetic one, in which the purpose is to
have no purpose. Romantic consumerism is practically a tautology.

Identity as dissolution and change becomes a paradox. There remains the part of us that is stable, "sitting back, relaxing and taking it
all in." A fusion of identity and nonidentity is strictly impossible. But
ideology behaves as if it were the only way to be, turning all consumers
into teenagers, that category invented by advertising in the age of authoritarian anti-communism. In this light, the liquid subjectivity that
Keats's idea of the "camelion poet" suggests is really a "new and improved" version of subjectivity in general, mired in the same paradoxes
and dilemmas as what Keats calls the "egotistical sublime."[123] Keats
proposes that the true poet's identity is metamorphic. It can dissolve
into the world, shifting its shape to match its environment. For the
"camelion poet," identity *is* ecomimesis. Instead of sitting back at one
remove from the consumer object, one tries to *become* it, to slide into
its intrinsically slippery, objectal form. No sooner does the subject turn
into the object, in this fantasy, than the object naturally starts to behave
like a subject. Keats makes this very literal. He describes claret creeping
around inside one's stomach like Aladdin stepping silently around the
enchanted underground garden of jewels in the *Arabian Nights*.[124] This

image provides the inverted form of the Romantic consumerist idea that "you are what you eat," a phrase coined by both the gastronome Brillat-Savarin and the philosopher Ludwig Feuerbach.[125] For Keats, you eat what you are. Although it does make peace with the fact that we are all consumerists, the "camelion poet" does not resolve the inner tension of the subject–object dualism.

Romantic consumerism produced subjective states that eventually became technically reproducible commodities. But it also influenced the construction and maintenance of actually existing environments. Consider how Wordsworth's Lake District became the National Trust's Lake District, or the American wilderness, places you go to on holiday from an administered world. Environments were caught in the logic of Romantic consumerism. Wilderness can only exist as a reserve of unexploited capital, as constant tensions and struggles make evident. It is an abstraction. I mean this much more strongly than Jack Turner, for whom wilderness is an abstraction that must be filled in with concrete aesthetic details.[126] Such details tend only to increase the level of abstraction. Wilderness embodies freedom from determination, the bedrock of capitalist ideology. It is always "over there," behind the shop window of distanced, aesthetic experience; even when you are "in" it, as the elegiac frenzy of much nature writing demonstrates. "Respect" for the environment entails a certain aesthetic rather than purely ethical reaction, which involves the distance that Kant says is essential for maintaining the sublime object:

> In order to get the full emotional effect from the magnitude of the pyramids one must neither get too close to them nor stay too far away. For if one stays too far away, then the apprehended parts (the stones on top of one another) are presented only obscurely, and hence their presentation has no effect on the subject's aesthetic judgment; and if one gets too close, then the eye needs some time to complete the apprehension from the base to the peak, but during that time some of the earlier parts are invariably extinguished in the imagination before it has apprehended the later ones, and hence the comprehension is never complete.[127]

As far as wilderness goes, this distance is not an empirical one, but a social and psychological one that persists even when you are in a wilderness. If you came too close, say, by actually living in one, then it would no longer be a wilderness. The stranger ruins my existential supping on wild vastness. Sartre observes that the simple presence of others acts as an "internal hemorrhage" in being, undermining the self's ability to consume the scene whole.[128] Exclusion and violence is the only way in which quietness and solitude can be guaranteed. Sartre's scene of encounter is an innocent-seeming suburban lawn. But as we have seen, lawns, with the communitarian rules they marshal (no stepping on the grass), are spaces of erased violence, pages rubbed out to look spacious and blank. They are just a horizontal, mass-produced version of the wildernesses people visit to find peace and quiet and a sense of abstract nature. Lawns are a type of "instant distance"—just lay down the sod and sit back contemplatively.

Wildernesses embody both "soft," "shallow" Romanticism—a provisional getaway from the mechanical or total administered hurly-burly—and, in "deep" terms, a radical alternative. Wilderness is a fusion of Puritan utopianism about the immanence of God in newly settled America and the lineage of pantheism running through such writers as Wordsworth and Emerson.[129] Wilderness therefore expresses various kinds of negative: fingers wagging, strongly or weakly, at modern society. To the extent that wilderness spaces and the laws that created them persist, we are still living, literally, within the Romantic period. It is strange to discover a secret passage between bottles of detergent and mountain ranges. But there is one, and it is called Romantic consumerism. Green consumerism is only one kind of environmental consumerism. Environmentalisms *in general* are consumerist.

Literature about the environment takes on various roles within consumerism. One function is to soothe the pains and stresses of industrial society, as national parks assuage our weekday world. Ecocriticism revives the idea that poetry is a balm for hurt minds and even bodies, an idea born in John Stuart Mill's recuperative reading of Wordsworth, to cure him of crass utilitarianism, the dominant ideology of the nineteenth century.[130] This idea of literature as good medicine became the dominant mode of paternalistic arguments for the establishment of English literature studies themselves.[131] George Sampson asserted that if the lower classes were not given a spiritual version of the collectivity they sought in communism, a "common share in the immaterial," they would soon be likely to demand the real thing.[132] Ecological discourse is also about collectivity: how to share this earth with other humans, animals, plants, and inanimate things. Much ecocriticism images itself as politically situated neither to the left nor to the right, nor exactly in the middle, but transcending left and right, deeper than politics as usual (as in "deep ecology").

In doing so, ecological writing (including criticism) fills a gap in normative forms of consumerism. It does not fall out of consumerism altogether. It provides a "new and improved" version of it—however little those invested in such literature and criticism may like it. Then there are more critical forms, such as the advocacy of animal rights, ecofeminisms, environmental justice criticism. These are all, in different ways, forms of refusal, the negation of current ways of consuming the world and the advocacy of something else, whether that something else is spelled out or not. Such critiques themselves risk becoming new and improved kinds of consumerism, just as, in miniature, ecomimesis turns out to be a rebranded rendering of the aesthetic—which has itself always maintained a relationship, either antagonistic or supportive, with consumerism.

Charles Baudelaire plays with the poetics of spice in "Correspondences." The ambience of a forest becomes penetrable and yet mysterious, spacious and yet opaque, gesturing toward and withholding meaningfulness, through the play of sound and scents:

> As long-drawn echoes heard far-off and dim
>   Mingle to one deep sound and fade away;
>   Vast as the night and brilliant as the day,
> Colour and sound and perfume speak to him. (5–8)[133]

The "decadence" of this poem relative to the supposed nature-worship of Romanticism lies in its dovetailing of nature with artifice. Columns become trees; trees become sticks of incense; natural perfume becomes commodified ambience. This dovetailing is a feature already latent in Romanticism. It is not only latent, however. The mystical relation to the commodity form that Benjamin noted in Baudelaire's play with the character of the *flâneur* or dandy was enabled by Romantic consumerism. It is Romantic consumerism that makes of the forest a shop window—and allows the ambience of a shop window to be experienced as the temple of nature.

In "Sounds," a chapter in *Walden,* Thoreau investigates his utopian dwelling as a soundscape. "I realized," he writes, "what the Orientals meant by contemplation." This effect is given an explicitly literary typographical metaphor: "I love a broad margin to my life." For Thoreau this broad margin contains historical traces. The sound of a train brings to mind other places (where has the train come from, where is it going?) and other times and, in general, the idea of commerce. This is far from the myth of the hermit enclosed in a self-sufficient Nature, the myth that Thoreau embodies for so many. Yet the entirety of this experience reflects upon a single subject, Thoreau, the Romantic consumerist: "I *feel more like* a citizen of the world at the sight of the palm-leaf which will cover so many flaxen New England heads the next summer, the Manilla hemp and cocoa-nut husks." The sonic intervention of the train is not an interruption of the meditative state, but a welcome note of variety in the perceptual milieu.[134]

Objectified subjectivity becomes the content and form of art. It even becomes the manner in which we criticize it: the critic as artist, as Oscar Wilde put it. Since Schlegel, theory itself could become art. This kind of theory has a particular affiliation with Romanticism. As a loose affiliation of post-structuralist ideas, theory *itself* becomes an aesthetic pose, evoking an idea of "listening" quizzically, quasi-contemplatively; talking about Zen, referencing meditation while not actually going to the trouble of doing any, with all the irritation and pain it might cause. In his recent book on sound art, David Toop digs the ambience of his breakfast table.[135] Styles of leisure are legitimated by being underwritten by a tame version of theory, whose radical questioning has been blunted into a soft exclamation mark.

Theory always had a harder bite than this. To be a consumerist is not simply to be caught in the stuff-your-face logic of capitalism, but to have the potential to resist and challenge it. One could use one's refusal to consume certain things in certain ways as modes of critiquing modern society. Without doubt, there are those green Romantic consumerists who have gone so far as to not consider themselves consumerists at all. A deep ecologist such as Julia Butterfly Hill will surely protest that she is not a consumerist, and activists in the Earth First! group would be shocked to find that their tactics derive from consumerism. When *Adbusters,* the American fashion magazine for the tortured anti-consumerist, proclaims itself a journal of "the mental environment," it is promising something beyond consumerism. But this promise typifies the paradox of the Romantic avant-garde. If we could just get the aesthetic *form* right, we could crack reality, open it up, and change it. With its brilliant parodies of advertising spectacle, the *Adbusters* approach is simply greener-than-thou consumerism, out-consumerism-ing other consumerists. Surely this is why deep ecology names itself in opposition to "shallow ecology." Those shallow ecologists are just daytrippers, from the deep point of view.

One available consumerist role is the refusal exemplified by the *abstainer,* the *boycotter.* This role reflects upon the idea of what it means to be a consumer altogether. The sugar boycott and vegetarianism in the Romantic period typify a style we would now recognize as ecological.[136] The same forms confront today's "green" consumers as confronted the earlier Romantic consumers. Will buying organic food really save the planet? Romantic consumerism at once broadened and narrowed the idea of choice. The sense that we have a "choice," giving rise to utopian desires, indicates social deadlock as well as possibility.

There is nothing intrinsically wrong with avant-garde consumerist forms. Like art, they embody what Adorno—a great Romantic in his engagement with Hegel—describes as a negative knowledge of reality.[137] This negativity is negative not in the sense of "bad," but in terms of a dialectical moment of negation. Romantic consumerism embodies what has been negated, left out, excluded, or elided. It shows just how far one would need to go to really change things. Boycotting and protesting are ironical, reflexive forms of consumerism. By refusing to buy certain products, by questioning oppressive social forms such as corporations or globalization, they point toward possibilities of changing the current state of affairs, without actually changing it. They are a cry of the heart in a heartless world, a spanner in the works (Dave Foreman's term for green direct action is "monkeywrenching").[138] They thus have not only a practical, but also a religious aspect. Many religious practitioners are involved in environmental movements: nuns who hammered on Colorado's nuclear missile silos, the "Church of Deep Ecology" in Minneapolis. The nuns did not change the missiles into flowers, but they did draw attention to these weapons of mass destruction lurking almost literally in people's backyards.

We may usefully understand the process of green consumerism via Hegel's dialectic of the *beautiful soul*, a moment in his history of different kinds of consciousness.[139] The beautiful soul appears at a certain historical moment, which Hegel identifies with Romanticism. It is a persona of the "unhappy consciousness" that separates humanity and nature. In strict chronological terms the beautiful soul appears after the Enlightenment and the French Revolutionary Terror. Hegel models it after a string of literary and aesthetic texts from Shaftesbury (the figure of the virtuoso) to Novalis and Schiller (the *schöne Seele*).[140] But the beautiful soul is highly relevant to the ecological view. Ruskin complained that one of the horrors of modern life was its ugliness. Leopold's *Sand County Almanac* is devoted to an aesthetics of wilderness appreciation. Even certain positions in animal rights have an aesthetic component. The disgust associated with animal eating in vegetarianism is partly aesthetic.

Many interpret the beautiful soul as existing in a realm of pure nonaction, as a form of quietism. What, then, of "monkeywrenching" and other forms of ecological activism? Both quietism and activism are two sides of the same beautiful coin. The beautiful soul fuses the aesthetic and the moral. The aestheticization has a moral dimension, the result of an achieved distance. The beautiful soul maintains a split between self and world, an irresolvable chasm created by the call of conscience—"consciousness raising," as an activist might put it. Yet the beautiful soul also yearns to close the gap. Hegel is an elegant choice of theorist for ecological consciousness. Convinced that all other forms of philosophy, especially those of the "orient," were insufficient, Hegel himself suffered from a classic case of beautiful soul syndrome.

The title of a popular ecological book in the late 1980s, by David Icke, the erstwhile deputy secretary of the British Green Party, says it all: *It Doesn't Have to Be Like This*.[141] (Since then, Icke has embraced a more extreme refusal, to the point of paranoia.) Modern art and green consumerism have this refusal stamped on them. Just how deep the stamp goes is the issue. Integrity and hypocrisy, keeping the faith and selling out, become the ways to calibrate commitment. This is ironic, since the ultimate hypocrite, claims Hegel, is the beautiful soul itself, which cannot see that the evil it condemns is intrinsic to its existence—indeed, its very form as pure subjectivity *is* this evil. The chasm cannot be fully bridged; not, at any rate, without compromising the beauty of the soul itself.[142]

Beautiful soul syndrome did not know that it was in trouble in the thinking of Hegel himself. He and Coleridge both wished for the subject to be reconciled to the object, but on the subject's terms. The wish for reconciliation reached a crisis in the self-abnegating, quasi-Buddhist view of Schopenhauer, and the self-affirming strategies of Nietzsche's superman. Schopenhauer imaged peace as a disappearance of the egotistical will, a state of oceanic calm that dissolves everything else into nothingness (a common misinterpretation of Buddhist *shunyata,* emptiness).[143] Schopenhauer held the view that "to those whom the will has turned and denied itself, this very real world of ours with all its suns and galaxies, is—nothing."[144] Such a state is glimpsed in the aesthetic, which soothes the mind to a state of tranquil dissolution. Schopenhauer puts this in environmental terms, describing an aesthetic state "when, delivered from the fierce pressure of the will, we emerge . . . from the heavy atmosphere of the earth."[145] Music helps this state the best, since it is the most shapeless art form; Schopenhauer comes close to a theory of ambience. Even if it helps an individual to salvation, this view (utopian? atopian?) is not too helpful for us poor saps in a world that will still be all too obviously around "the day after tomorrow," as the title of a film about global warming puts it.[146] Schopenhauer's ascetic aesthetics appeals to a self that still maintains that there is a crack between itself and the world—otherwise how would it ever "emerge" from its "heavy atmosphere"?

Nietzsche's solution was quite different. He advocated a process of constant overcoming, very much like critique, with its similarly endless quality. But this overcoming is still a style of subjectivity. Furthermore, it has little time for darkness, weakness, or the negative. Malcolm Bull has shown how any and every attempt to get beyond Nietzsche risks ending up simply reaffirming him, since his is the philosophy of winners rather than losers. An ecological approach would surely identify with the losers, whom Bull calls the "subhuman," rather than the superman.[147] Difficult as it is, this identification would involve a radical de-aestheticization, since for Nietzsche, the aesthetic is the ultimate form of justification and victory. The un-hip, even dangerous, identification with the apparently less-than-human, creates a "philistine ecology" in which it is possible to generate rights for apes, for instance.[148]

The landscape on the other side of the chasm between subject and object turns out to be the beautiful soul in inverted form. We could call it "beautiful Nature." It suffers from the same ailments as the beautiful soul: it is opaque, exclusionary, absolutely right and proper. Despite their apparent immersiveness, all the models for the environment in this chapter are examples of beautiful Nature. The beautiful soul beats its heart against a solid wall. Nature remains a reified object, "over there." As Marx, that erstwhile Romantic poet and Hegelian, maintains about his university experience, "the kingdom of poetry glittered opposite me like a distant fairy palace and all my creations dissolved into nothingness."[149] Marx superbly embodies the idea of an ambient world, albeit one to which he has no access, since it is an aesthetic thing, distanced from him. The Romantic environment twinkles and glitters like Bambi's blinking eyes. We could think of a thousand ecological examples of what Marx meant. But the name of many of them, in America, is Thoreau. The choice for engagement appears as a strong tension between, and blending of, quietism and activism. Thoreau practiced both—he was prepared to go to prison and advocated nonviolent resistance, and he wrote about the importance of contemplating the natural world.

At its extreme, beautiful soul syndrome can lead to fascism. The composer Richard Wagner dramatized his life as resistance to the inexorably commercial capitalist aspect of the music business. In part this consisted in anti-Semitism.[150] The core of Wagner's "beautiful" resistance was a fantasy object of hate around which he generated all kinds of biological essentialist (racist) thoughts. But beautiful soul syndrome can also lead to hippiedom: if we think hard enough, the rain will stop, as the man said at the Woodstock festival in 1969. Likewise, there are fascist and New Age versions of environmentalism. The neo-Nazi American Eric Rudolph was arrested in the summer of 2003. Against the backdrop of the War on Terror, it was paradoxical that he was romanticized in the mainstream media. (I am at pains to stress that my argument in general does not equate environmentalism with terrorism.) In the press, Rudolph became a Thoreauvian forest dweller, an isolated crank feeding on cans of tuna left him in the back gardens of sympathetic town residents, resisting the incursions of "big government" in the form of the FBI, a dramatic version of the Romantic bard holding out against the encroachments of big reason. In this respect he had better luck than Islamic terrorists of the sort who destroyed the World Trade Center in 2001, whom the media had not anointed with inwardness or subjectivity, or indeed than left environmental activist groups, which the government has targeted as so-called terrorists since 9/11. Rudolph was alleged to have bombed two abortion clinics and the Olympic Games in 1996. He referred to the television as the "electric Jew." Far from being isolated, he had participated in extreme right-wing survivalist and white supremacist terror groups.

Rudolph is a classic example of the persistence of the beautiful soul in the modern age. The disconnection between felt life and objective reality at the heart of Rudolph's ideological stance was reproduced by the split between the objective features of Rudolph's case and the way in which the media subjectivized, romanticized, and lionized him. An editorial in the *New York Times* skillfully wrote the kind of ecological rhapsody suitable to the construction of the beautiful soul: as outside, so within.[151] Here we witness the construction of an inner landscape, celebrated in nature writing and ecological literary criticism as a benign simulation of the external world.[152]

Rudolph manages to be a quietist and a terrorist all at once, occupying both positions available to the beautiful soul. Rudolph's sin, in the eyes of society, was to take its misogynist, racist and homophobic injunctions too seriously; a paradox from his anti-government viewpoint that makes sense if we consider him as a fantasy figure in a larger ideological framework. By romanticizing him, the media performed for the government the helpful task of reinserting him into the ideological matrix. We are compelled by the image of the Thoreauvian loner, but forbidden to take what he did too seriously, that is, in fact, with adequate seriousness. We are involved, but distant.

The beautiful soul is ecological subjectivity. Ambience is really an externalized form of the beautiful soul. Without doubt, the discovery of the beautiful soul as the form of ecological consumerism is the most important concept in this book. The beautiful soul holds choices within itself in a state like quantum superposition. Physics refers to this as state U, before measurement (if "before" makes sense in describing an unmeasurable state), as opposed to R, the moment at which a particle is measured.[153] Hegel describes a superposition of ethical possibilities in the beautiful soul:

> Contrasted with the simplicity of pure consciousness, with the absolute *other* or *implicit* manifoldness, [the beautiful soul's] reality is a plurality of circumstances which breaks up and spreads out endlessly in all directions, backwards into their conditions, sideways into their connections, forwards in their consequences. The conscientious mind is aware of this nature of the thing and of its relation to it, and knows that, in the case in which it acts, it does not possess that full acquaintance with *all* the attendant circumstances which is required, and that its pretence of conscientiously weighting all the circumstances is vain. However, this acquaintance with, and weighing of, all the circumstances are not altogether lacking; but they exist only as a *moment,* as something which is only for *others;* and this *incomplete* knowledge is held by the conscientious mind to be sufficient and complete, because it is its *own* knowledge.[154]

Ethical space opens up and "spreads out endlessly in all directions"—ethical ambience. The beautiful soul maintains a critical position about everything except for its own position. In this state, "Refined into this purity, consciousness exists in its poorest form, and the poverty which constitutes its sole possession is itself a vanishing." The beautiful soul floats in an oceanic "submergence of consciousness within itself."[155] In the syndrome of the beautiful soul *immersion* is reduced to *emulsion.* Beautiful ecological souls hope that by circulating ambient rhetoric enough, the olive oil of subjectivity will blend with the vinegar of the objective world. This emulsion is itself a symptom of the ideological division of nature and history. "New and improved" versions of beautiful soul syndrome establish conditions in which the subject is stretched throughout the world, coating every molecule of objectivity. By no means does this get rid of the problems of identity and subjectivity.

Ambience moves between a positive concept that refuses limited models of localization or subjectification, and one that underpins various naive environmentalisms. Likewise, there is a virtue in the state of the beautiful soul. Like an intense form of religion, beautiful soul syndrome shows us how far we would have to go in order to change things utterly. The problem resides not so much in the beautiful soul's noble ideas, but in the form of its relationship to them. The beautiful soul distinguishes between theory and practice so sharply that reflection and hesitation are seen as inane cloud-castle building, and "pure" action becomes solidly material and absolutely, guilt-inducingly vital. Or it comes to the same conclusion in reverse: reflection becomes ethereal transcendence, action a rather grimy thing that other, less enlightened people do. The notion of *praxis,* in contrast, is that reflection can be a form of action; and that action—such as a nonviolent protest—can be theoretical, reflexive. Ecocritique inverts beautiful soul syndrome. If ideology relies upon enjoyment as well as disguised truth claims, one could adopt a paradoxical strategy toward ideology's fantasy spaces, images, and objects. Instead of spitting them out, or refusing to inhabit them, one could instead identify, overidentify, or inhabit them differently, like the Latinos/as who have begun to transform cities such as Los Angeles.

Current environmentalist literary criticism is drastically limited. Ecocriticism is another version of Romanticism's rage against the machine, a refusal to engage the present moment. Like imperialism, ecocriticism produces a vision of the text as a pristine wilderness of pure meaning. Some are beginning to theorize ways in which pure celebration of the pristine wilderness is only one facet of an ecological-political spectrum of responses. Although among ecocritics themselves there has persisted the survival mentality of the small group, turning ecocriticism into eco-ideology, ecocriticism now has greater potential to become a contested field: a healthy symptom of "arrival" or legitimation.

Ecocriticism wavers between the "apolitical" or quasi-political ersatz religion of a call to care for the world, and the New Left inclusion of race, gender, and environment in socialist thinking. Both have significant ties to Romanticism. While capitalist ideology had been formulated by Adam Smith in 1776, out of Romanticism there emerged, eventually, figures such as Marx and William Morris. Some right-tending ecocriticism, in its return to Romanticism, regresses to a historical state in which the socialist and communist developments had *not yet happened.* The regression is redoubled in championing an anti-modern, medievalist form of Romanticism. Regression can assume the form of rousing environmental rhetorics seeking to convey a *sense* of the empirical in an aesthetic of the touchy-feely, combined with a motivational sense that ecocriticism is good for us.

Regression is not entirely "wrong"; it is a symptom of social malaise. As Adorno remarks, "So long as progress, deformed by utilitarianism, does violence to the surface of the earth, it will be impossible—in spite of all proof to the contrary—completely to counter the perception that what antedates the trend is in its backwardness better and more humane."[156] Both empiricism and its experiential equivalent, specialized components of capitalist ideology itself, act as correctives to "tarrying with the negative" and seeing the shadow side of things. If ecological criticism is to progress—beyond the idea of progress itself as the domination of nature, that is—it must engage negativity fully rather than formulate suppressants against perceiving it.

The real problem is not the debate between postmodernism and ecocriticism, which sounds like two sides of the same warped record. The trouble is that as intoxicants go, clichéd post-structuralist relativism, even chic nihilism, is no match for something more religious: it is indeed religion's inverted form. Believing in nothing, while strictly untenable, is still a form of belief. Both sides miss seeing that it is not so much technology and language that are the issue as oppression and suffering. Both bypass earthly conditions: one by canceling it, the other by preserving the mere idea of it, in however compelling and squidgy a form.

Reality Writing

From wilderness writing to apocalypticism, environmental discourse wants to go beyond intellectuality to a realm of instantly compelling facts. Empiricism is the name of the thinking that tries to be no-thinking.[157] Empiricism assumes that facts speak for themselves, that things come with a built-in bar code of truthfulness. Some satisfying, almost physical beep will guarantee that we are on the right track. This beep is the clicking sound of Dr. Johnson's boot kicking the stone in refutation of Berkeley's idealism ("I refute it *thus*").[158] There is something of this factical brutalism in environmental rhetoric. A clicking sound is not a refutation. This dangerous misapprehension about the relationship between mind and world has recently met with attention from within neo-Kantian philosophy.[159] The "Myth of the Given" is that the space of factical things can put a stop to thinking, while it is evident that "there must be a standing willingness to refashion concepts and conceptions [of things outside thought] if this is what reflection demands."[160]

The beep or click of empirical immediacy has a yearning quality, a feel of "if only." Since the click is only a click, the impression of a reverberation, it suffers from the poetics of ambience, which remains inconsistent with the goal of ecomimesis. The aggression of kicking a stone philosophically carries within it its own impotence. It is the same with environmental culture, which has inherited the discourse of sentimental empiricism from the proto-ecological language of the eighteenth century, such as vegetarianism. The more in-your-face the aesthetic gesture gets, the more distant it becomes. Nature writing is Romantic insofar as it tries to "get back to nature," and knows that this possibility is forever excluded. "As soon as the artifact wants to prompt the illusion of the natural, it founders."[161] Adorno puts it well, though in fact his claim that nature poetry is now anachronistic needs strengthening. It was always anachronistic:

> Today immediacy of aesthetic comportment is exclusively an immediate relationship to the universally mediated. That today any walk in the woods, unless elaborate plans have been made to seek out the most remote forests, is accompanied by the sound of jet engines overhead not only destroys the actuality of nature as, for instance, an object of poetic celebration. It affects the mimetic impulse. Nature poetry is anachronistic not only as a subject: Its truth content has vanished. This may help clarify the anorganic aspect of Beckett's as well as Celan's poetry. It yearns neither for nature nor for industry; it is precisely the integration of the latter that leads to poetization, which was already a dimension of impressionism, and contributes its part to making peace with an unpeaceful world. Art, as an anticipatory form of reason, is no longer able—if it ever was—to embody pristine nature or the industry that has scorched it; the impossibility of both is probably the hidden law of aesthetic nonrepresentationalism. The images of the postindustrial world are those of a corpse; they want to avert atomic war by banning it, just as forty years ago surrealism sought to save Paris through the image of cows grazing in the streets, the same cows after which the people of bombed-out Berlin rebaptized *Kurfürstendamm* as *Kudamm*.[162]

The ambient sound of jet engines "destroys the actuality of nature as . . . an object of poetic celebration." Nature writing often excludes this negative ambience. When it does include it, it distinguishes it from the positive ambient of rustling trees or quiet ripples on a lake. It goes without saying that modernity is full of these sounds, both large and small. Jack Gladney becomes obsessed with the crackling of plastic in his refrigerator, in Don DeLillo's appropriately named *White Noise*.[163] Once heard, never forgotten. The "bad" ambience haunts the "good" one. Even a vast mountain forest shrinks in the memory of the cars and roads we used to reach it. If embeddedness in the world is a good in itself, what if this world were, in the words of the Devil in Peter Cook and Dudley Moore's film *Bedazzled,* full of "Wimpy Burgers . . . concrete runways, motorways, aircraft . . . plastic flowers . . . supersonic bangs"?[164] Nature writing tries to be "immediate"—to do without the processes of language and the artful construction of illusions. It wants to maintain the impression of directness. But this can only be a supreme illusion, ironically, in a world in which one can find Coke cans in Antarctica. The immediacy that nature writing values is itself as reified as a Coke can.

Nature writing partly militates *against* ecology rather than for it. By setting up nature as an object "over there"—a pristine wilderness beyond all trace of human contact—it re-establishes the very separation it seeks to abolish. We could address this problem by considering the role of subjectivity in nature writing. What kinds of subject position does nature writing evoke? Instead of looking at the trees, look at the person who looks at the trees.

In sitcoms, canned laughter relieves the audience of the obligation of laughing. Nature writing relieves us of the obligation to encounter nonidentity, sometimes called "nature," the "more-than-human," the "nonhuman." Like a daytime chat show, its mode is one of avoidance rather than escapism. The aesthetic, artful, contrived quality of writing is downplayed. Nature writing seems to be a sheer rendering of the real, just as "reality TV" appears to be real (and we all know very well that it is not). Nature writing is a kind of "reality writing" (and we all know very well that it is not). There is something similar to this in Hegel's lectures on aesthetics. Art "relieves" us of the "power of sensuousness" by remaining within a sensuous realm: professional grievers at funerals relieve one of one's inner state. Hegel carries on by criticizing an injunction to merge with nature: "we may often hear those favourite phrases about man's duty being to remain in oneness with nature, but such oneness in abstraction is simply and solely coarseness."[165]

The daytime chat show is designed for the person sitting at home. Does nature writing have a similar target? Even when someone appears on a chat show, there is a certain pretense involved. Someone sitting on a sofa on the other side of the television greets people, who also come and sit on the sofa for a while. Distancing, the "couch potato" syndrome, appears to be on both sides of the television screen. The same goes for nature writing. The narrator struggles within nature, and yet all the while views him- or herself from a contemplative distance. Heidegger was not actually a peasant living in the Black Forest. A white male nature writer in the wilderness may be "going native" to some extent, but he is also usefully distancing this wilderness, even from himself, even in his own act of narration.

Louis Althusser suggests that ideology works by "hailing" or *interpellating* a certain subject.[166] When a magazine in the supermarket seems to call out to *you* ("Are you one of those people who . . . ? Take our quiz and find out."), it is interpellating us. Ideology can mean (strongly held) beliefs and ideas. But it can also refer to the idea that we ourselves exist, prior to or above or beyond the elements of our experience, such as ideas. One idea—that the mind is like a supermarket and that our consciousness floats, with free choice, among various ideas that can be selected at will, like so many different bottles of shampoo, or magazines—is itself *the* ideology of consumer capitalism. Significantly, Althusser suggests, if only poetically, that ideology is a *dimension* of existence—we exist "within" it.[167] A more engaged ecological criticism would acknowledge *this* environment—one we are caught in even as we judge it.

Instead of confronting the reader with an intrinsically unreliable first-person narrator (who really trusts someone else who calls him or herself "I" anyway?), Levertov's "To the Reader" hails us: "As you read . . . and as you read . . . and as you read." (1, 4, 7). This hailing encourages a certain relationship with the content (the images in the poem). It is trivially true that nature writing suffers from selectivity. Yes, it seldom mentions jet engines or nuclear fallout, at least not as an intrinsic part of the ambient world. "To the Reader" does not mention that as you are reading this, Islamic people are being tortured. New historicist readings indict poems for not being explicit about certain forms of misery. Why didn't Wordsworth directly mention the homeless people in "Tintern Abbey"?[168] This selectivity is indeed a matter for consideration. Ecocritique should certainly deal with the *kinds* of fantasy object that ecomimesis sets before us. But in another sense, the specific content is really just a fantasy bait, with which the ideological matrix captures its real object—us.

Moreover, the "we" captured here are specifically, if ambiguously, located. "As I write" or "As you read" puts us in front of a text, a location for which it is tempting to imagine a domestic rather than outdoor setting, for historically precise reasons having to do with the development of reading as a private, silent act. We are in a state of privacy, yet able to access the outside world—we see it reflected in the text, or out of a window, or in a mirror. Despite the simulation of immediacy, ecomimesis, especially in phenomenological prose (both "artistic" and "philosophical"), establishes an *interior* space as much as an *exterior* one, a space furthermore furnished with reading materials, windows, or mirrors. Adorno is on the mark when he reveals this aspect of Kierkegaard's writing, situated as it is in a bourgeois interior, often a living room.[169] Geoffrey Hartman's words about Wordsworthian nature as an "outdoor room" for thinking (see Chapter 1) make it feel more like a study or a drawing room. Descartes himself, from whom phenomenology deviates and to whom it returns, describes his situation by a fire (see Chapter 3). Heidegger in his Black Forest cottage is, to some extent, simply a variant of this wider situatedness rhetoric. And what could be more interior than Sartre's lawn, really an outdoor extension of the carpet? The basic interior would be the tent, or the recreational vehicle—or the text itself, standing in for an interiorized privacy. It creeps up on you in "Grantchester Meadows," a song by Pink Floyd, masters of ambient psychedelic kitsch:

> In the lazy water meadow I lay me down
> All around me golden sun flakes settle on the ground
> Basking in the sunshine of a bygone afternoon
> Bringing sounds of yesterday into this city room. (9–12©)[170]

This is a medial song. The lyrics enact the contact. The "sounds of yesterday" are literally the recorded sounds on the LP coming through the speakers in your "room." The song, surrounded by renderings of rippling water and wading birds, ends with the sound effect of a fly buzzing around a room and being loudly swatted. With this rendering, and the phatic verse, the song puts us in our proper place(s): sitting indoors, attending to or hallucinating a real or imagined (how can we tell?) soundscape.

The fact that the "as I write" / "as you read" / "as you listen" occurs at the end rather than at the beginning helps us to understand something about the illusory immediacy of ecomimesis. Simulative effects do *not* make us believe completely in nature "out or over there." They also enable us to establish the appropriate cynical—ideological—*distance* toward immediacy. We can experience (pain), but in comfort. And this is a tenet of Romantic consumerism. I am struck by how much Roger Waters's lyrics resemble those of another doubly situated poem, Coleridge's "Kubla Khan." "And a river of green is sliding unseen beneath the trees / Laughing as it passes through the endless summer making for the sea" (7–8, 23–24©) is surely a revision of "Where ALPH, the sacred river, ran / Through caverns measureless to man / Down to a sunless sea" (3–5). Coleridge's well-known note performs the work of distancing by situating precisely the poem as a "psychological curiosity," a record of an opium dream in "a lonely farmhouse between Porlock and Linton, on the Exmoor confines of Somerset and Devonshire."[171] Try as it might to render naked, direct, natural experience, ecomimesis gathers to itself a host of associations between drugs, writing, intoxication, and reminiscence.

Let us look very closely at this weird combination of vividness and distancing, naturalness and artifice, remembering and recording, attuning and hallucinating. David Abram's *The Spell of the Sensuous* is a remarkable and popular study of phenomenology as a way of creating a fresh, ecological sense of identity. It contains many passages of rich ecomimesis. At the very end, Abram pulls out all the stops:

> In contrast to the apparently unlimited, global character of the technologically mediated world, the sensuous world—the world of our direct, unmediated interactions—is always local. The sensuous world is the particular ground on which we walk, the air we breathe. For myself as I write this, it is the moist earth of a half-logged island off the northwest coat of North America. It is this dark and stone-rich soil feeding the roots of cedars and spruces, and of the alders that rise in front of the cabin, their last leaves dangling form the branches before being flung into the sky by the early winter storms. And it is the salty air that pours in through the loose windows, spiced with cedar and seaweed, and sometimes a hint of diesel fumes from a boat headed south tugging a giant raft of clear-cut tree trunks. Sometimes, as well, there is the very faint, fishy scent of otter scat. Each day a group of otters slips out of the green waters onto the nearby rocks at high tide, one or two adults and three smaller, sleek bodies, at least one of them dragging a half-alive fish between its teeth. The otters, too, breathe this wild air, and when the storm winds batter the island, they stretch their necks into the invisible surge, drinking large drafts from the tumult.
>
> In the interior of this island, in the depths of the forest, things are quieter. Huge and towering powers stand there, unperturbed by the winds, their crusty bark fissured with splitting seams and crossed by lines of ants, inchworms, and beetles of varied shapes and hues. A single woodpecker is thwacking a trunk somewhere, the percussive rhythm reaching my ears without any echo, absorbed by the mosses and the needles heavy with water drops that have taken hours to slide down the trunks from the upper canopy (each drop lodging itself in successive cracks and crevasses, gathering weight from subsequent drips, then slipping down, past lichens

and tiny spiders, to the next protruding ridge of branch). Fallen firs and hemlocks, and an old spruce tree tunneled by termites, lie dank and rotting in the ferns, the jumbled branches of the spruce blocking the faint deer trail that I follow.[172]

This writing attempts to generate a fantasy-environment that sits beside the steps of the writer's argument, not so much illustrating them as providing a compelling yet inevitably inconsistent sequence of images that aesthetically reinforce that argument. The imagery itself is ambient, indicating that which surrounds the narrator; what surrounds, by a metaphorical extension, the page we are holding. The world is so dense, so full of real "stuff," that it literally has no echo, we are told. This is an ecological version of Cage's anechoic chamber, which showed him that there was no such thing as silence.[173] This fantasy world depends on the technology of silent reading, a synesthetic process, as Celeste Langan has argued, which Abram values as a path toward ecological awareness.[174]

The fantasy is an *exemplum:* the figurative adumbration of an argument. It raises the question of whether *exemplum* is part of that argument, or strictly an illustration of it: a question of where you come down on the division, or not, between rhetoric and logic. Ekphrasis erases the trace of writing. Writing is absorbed into reading, whose metaphorical analogue is perceiving (or "tracking" as Abram puts it), an absorption that turns the outer world into a (reading) room of solitude, but also, in a chiasmus, opens the introverted space of reading up to the supposedly healthy breeze of the outside.[175] The narrator is not describing but channeling, an Aeolian harp. On the one hand, the narrator is entirely absorbed in the environment. He or she is an object among others, a set of sensing devices. As we have seen, it is more appropriate to talk of *interobjectivity* rather than *intersubjectivity* (Abram's favorite concept). And yet there is another, ghostly quality: that of *experiencing* the sensitivity of the sensory apparatus, or *appreciating* it—much like how, in the televised coverage of the second Iraq War, the "embedded" reporters and news anchors appreciated the capabilities of their imaging machines.

The dualism of subject and object reproduces itself, though the ekphrasis seeks to burst it through an outpouring of language. This happens despite how the Aeolian poetics of ambience insists upon a materialist, physicalist, or at any rate monist continuity of thought and thing—that I am picking up good vibrations. (I sometimes think that California embodies Spinoza down to the level where the board meets the surf.) If only we could tune in to the environment properly, then we

could become more ecological—isn't this the idea? Criticism should relate the poem to its real and figurative environments, just as ecological
analysis should follow the waste down the toilet and out into the sewer
and the ocean. In which case, why not reduce all poems to mere happenings, collections of things? Why even go that far? Why not just describe things in the world already? There is plenty of metonymy to go
around. There is a black hole at the middle of the galaxy that is emit-
ting a B-flat, if we had big enough ears (really big ones) with which to
hear it. That is a terrifying thought, in the Burkean sense—sheer magnitude overwhelms us with its authority.[176] Ultimately, the physicalist
view of the sublime upon which Aeolian poetics depends is authoritarian. On the other hand, what about the other universe *right here,* the
universe of (other) subject(s)? Environmental poetics ignores the sheer
chasm between you and me. Kant says that this chasm finds its analogy
in a sublime conceived differently from Burke's. In this sublime, the notion of infinity exceeds any number or magnitude, no matter how vast,
and thus terrifies-inspires us with the power of our mind, not of an
overwhelming physicality.

Ecomimetic ekphrasis sits in an oblique relation to the text. In its
very form, then, it is ambient: it appears alongside the argument.
Somehow the argument is not rich enough to sustain nature by itself.
We need this oblique, anamorphic reference point, a memento naturae,
just as the distorted skull in Hans Holbein's painting *The Ambassadors*
is a memento mori. This oblique relation is dramatically different from
the direct, vivid, and exorbitant quality of the rhetoric itself. The ecological argument requires something stronger. The point is not to convince through reason, but to impart a heavy dose of a certain subject
position to the reader. If only writing could become a chamber without
echoes, a thicket of description so full of vivid language that it sounded
directly in our mind, without any reminder of loss. A Romantic
yearning sounds in the compelling empirical beeps of Abram's prose.

Ecomimesis does consciously what Hegel expresses accidentally in
his lectures on aesthetics. Nature appears by the side of his argument,
ironically evoking the ambient world that surrounds genuine art:

> The birds' variegated plumage shines unseen, and their song dies away
> unheard, the *Cereus* which blossoms only for a night withers without
> having been admired in the wilds of southern forests, and these forests,
> jungles of the most beautiful and luxuriant vegetation, with the most
> odorous and aromatic perfumes, perish and decay no less unenjoyed. The
> work of art has not such a naïve self-centered being, but is essentially a

question, an address to the responsive heart, an appeal to affections and to minds.[177]

In contrast with Abram, Hegel declares that there is a world beyond the text that language *cannot* reach. It is empirically real, but we are deaf to it—an ironically material version of the proverbial Berkleyan tree, falling without ears to hear it. But this world *does* appeal to our affection! An apophasis sublimely renders the very things that the argument claims, at another level, remain unperceived, a common trope in an era that has produced untrodden ways, unfrequented lanes, and paths not taken.[178] Through the negative Hegel arrives at the same place as the positive Abram. Hegel's language is plaintive and plangent. It evokes the natural world as a dying, and a dying-away, of which we are hardly conscious. The "self-centered" being that Hegel attributes to this dying world is strikingly similar to the infamous "I = I," the self-absorbed, self-negating subject that, for instance, is the product of Buddhism, which Hegel thinks of as the religion of "being within self" *(Insich-sein)*.[179] And this "I = I" is also the beautiful soul.[180] Hegel's notion of pure consciousness without content is an apt theorization of some of the aesthetic phenomena of the Romantic period.[181] The world of dying that Hegel hauntingly describes is an inside-out version of this interiority. Of course, when the "I" begins to reflect on "I," all kinds of echoes and afterimages appear that trouble Hegel's idea that meditative awareness is a form of blank nothingness.

There is an implied ecomimetic "As I write" at work in this passage. It splits the reader's awareness between the moment of reading and the moment that the writing is evoking. As a formal decoration that nevertheless evokes a concrete world, Hegel's ecomimesis undoes the very distinction between ultimately irrelevant decorativeness and essential substance that the argument tries to enforce. Unheard melodies are sweeter: Hegel's formulation is very close to his critique of the exact opposite tendency, that which in Romantic art pipes ditties of no tone: "In [Romantic art] the inner, so pushed to the extreme, is an expression without any externality at all; it is invisible and is as it were a perception of itself alone, or a musical sound as such without objectivity and shape, or a hovering over the waters, or a ringing tone over a world which in and on its heterogeneous phenomena can only accept and remirror a reflection of the inwardness of soul."[182] The ultimate "beautiful" but unheard entity is the soul itself. It is not surprising that Hegel's dialectic of the beautiful soul also contains this language: "In this transparent purity of its moments, an unhappy, so-called 'beautiful soul,' its light dies away within it, and it vanishes like a shapeless vapour that dissolves into thin air."[183] The beautiful soul is the truth of the compelling environment. It is a tit for tat. The more we have of *that*—the writhing writing of a palpable yet evanescent nature—the more we have of *this*—the one who is compelled, who shines with fascination, who is possessed with vision.

In seeking to be non-art, ecomimesis becomes poetical, a kitsch embodiment of the artistic aura itself. Extreme externality (so "out there" that it's apparently beyond art) and extreme internality (so inward that there's no substantial embodiment) wind up in the same place. Adorno dialectically inverts the idea that nature writing leads to environmental art: "Many works of contemporary music and painting, in spite of the absence of representational objectivity and expression, would rightly be subsumed by the concept of a second naturalism."[184] While it pretends to rub our noses in the natural world, ecomimesis is caught in the logic of reification.

Abram's "As I write" is the opening ecomimetic gesture. "As" could mean not only "while," but also "just as": just as I am writing, in the very same way in which I am writing, in/as my writing itself, these natural phenomena are inscribed. The process of writing is in excess of its ideological effect. Here is the sinthome, the inconsistent kernel of meaningless enjoyment that provides the compelling, yet slippery, heart of an ideological system: slippery, because inconsistent. The metonymic list will never succeed in hemming in its intrinsic heterogeneity, despite the supposed integration of the images under the rubric of the natural. The dizzyingly additive quality of the images makes us forget where we came from at the start of the paragraph, and where we are going—how do we end up at otter scat? But just as "out of joint" is the metaphorical slash of the "as I write." Since the "as" slides between analogy, temporality, and strict semantic continuity, and since this sliding *must* take place for the passage to seduce us to visualize a fantasy world, "As I write" breaches the consistency of the ecomimesis even as it broaches it.

Ecomimesis attempts to carve out a strong sense of place, a radical embeddedness in the landscape—I use "landscape" with all the aesthetic weight of that word. The metonymic list threatens to go on and on forever. It suggests, in its quantity, Kant's mathematical sublime: an infinite series that gives us a sense of the infinite capacity of our mind, in the very failure to count to infinity. The intent is to reflect back the authenticity and capacity of the narrator—they're *there*. "Romantic ecology" sets itself against Hartman's view that the world is merely the sounding board for Romantic subjectivity.[185] But it is in danger of collapsing back into Hartman's notion of Romanticism.

The heaping of phrase upon phrase has two unintended consequences. At the level of form, the richness of the pile teeters on the brink of poverty. If *every* phrase is in fact metaphorical for "nature," then each one is equally bereft of positive value. Each phrase is just a placeholder for a phenomenon that never arrives, can never be seen directly but only glimpsed obliquely, in anamorphosis, like the goddess Diana. The anamorphosis regarding the ecomimetic occasion *(occasio)* is repeated at the semantic level. We could speculate that nature and its analogue, the local, the sense of place *is this negativity.* It disappears when you try to look at it. This also goes for labor, including the labor of reading. When you are involved in something fully, it dissolves—though not into the stupidity praised by Heidegger. As soon as the narrator drags the background into the foreground, it loses its coherence. But such a dialectical speculation is not one that the narrator wishes us to make.

As far as the level of content goes, the image is of being embedded within a horizon, which establishes the *ersatz* primitivism of ecological writing in general. The cumulative effect of the figures is self-defeating, for the more embedded the narrator becomes, the less convincing he or she is as a spokesperson for the totality that he or she is trying to evoke—an all-encompassing intersubjective field, "an intertwined matrix of sensations and perceptions."[186] The narrator gets lost in his or her own system. Note the Old English alliterative quality of Abram's language: "faint, fishy scent," "drinking large drafts," "cracks and crevasses," "tunneled by termites." Like that other embedder, Tolkien, Abram wants English to return to its mythical, localist, pre-Norman past.

A magnetic field shimmers into view, an ambient impression of naturalness, a perceptual dimension incarnated like Merleau-Ponty's "Flesh," surrounding and sustaining the narrator and the reader. In the same way as the "embedded" reporters in Iraq gave their audiences nothing but ambient descriptions ("I hear the sound of gunfire around me"), the narrator promises the intersubjective force field, but delivers nothing but a list of perceptual events. If the fine writing is supposed to be a "touchstone" for the ecological, in an Arnoldian sense, then in this very quality it betrays itself. One touchstone is as good as another (one infrared shot of bullets flying is as good as another). Just as the narrator is a conductor, so the rhapsody, as touchstone, is a magnet, but only for other pieces of charged writing.

All this is in the name of noticing that we are subject to air pollution, which is the subject of the chapter in which this piece of ecomimesis appears: *parturient montes, nascitur ridiculus mus*. The less logically convincing ecomimesis is, the more convincing it is aesthetically: there is no reason for this proliferation of sentences about scat. But nature as totality *is* paradoxically a "decentered," "organic," "not-all" set that is made of contingent, nontotalizable parts. The list of contingent perceptions, we must recall, is *for* someone.

"As I write": the narrator becomes an Aeolian harp, a conduit. The narrator is plugged directly into the world, receiving its reality like paper receiving ink: ecorhapsody. This condition is more like being a worker in a factory (or a machine in one) than it is like being an artisan or a boss. The worker receives an unfinished, fragmentary product and does what he or she can to complete it. Given the division of labor, he or she is a temporary stage in the onward flow of commodity parts and a necessary tool in the machine that creates value. Abram, however, also marshals the realm of leisure. The reference point is the Romantic consumerist. The sense of freedom and autonomy marked by the birth of the consumerist in the Romantic period works even better with trees than with commodities. They are the objective correlative of inutility, of free time, which has a utopian edge. The narrator luxuriates in the ability to look up from one's work, as the gesture of describing what's outside and around "as I write" enacts. The breathless excitement of the passage, taken as an extended metaphor for a statement like "I've got legs! I can see!" is in direct proportion to the alienation and commodification that gave rise to such a Romantic outpouring in the first place. Only a very privileged person would make such a big deal out of having eyes and ears, of being able to walk, read, write. There are hints that nature is best accessed by the able-bodied, or at least, those with sharp, undistracted organs of perception. The ultimate riposte to Heidegger in the Black Forest is that no self-respecting peasant would talk like that.[187] To be ignorant is one thing; to be self-stupefying is quite another: "The peasant woman wears her shoes in the field. Only here are they what they are. They are all the more genuinely so, the less the peasant woman thinks about the shoes while she is at work, or looks at them at all, or is even aware of them. She stands and walks in them. That is how shoes actually serve."[188] Heidegger himself surpasses Abram, in his positing of place *as* question, *as in* question. Although the way he puts it, as we shall see, resembles entranced wondering rather than biting critique, Abram provides mere positivity, a series of exclamations as brittle as they are hyperbolic.

In the case of the Iraq War, the embedded reporter is really a version of the couch potato conveniently lodged *inside* the television screen. In Abram the narrator establishes the appropriate aesthetic *distance* for the reader, even in the midst, and even in the very inscription of, intense, close-up detail. Ecomimesis aims to rupture the aesthetic distance, to break down the subject–object dualism, to convince us that we belong to this world. But the end result is to reinforce the aesthetic distance, the very dimension in which the subject–object dualism persists. Since de-distancing has been reified, distance returns even more strongly, in surround-sound, with panoramic intensity. The strange, interactive passivity (Žižek calls it "interpassivity") is reminiscent of what Freud says about masochism. Masochism is the looping of enjoyment through an other. An environment is being evoked, just as, for Freud, the masochistic fantasy is that "a child is being beaten."[189]

Ecomimesis works very hard at immersing the subject in the object, only to sit back and contemplate its handiwork. It reproduces with a vengeance the Cartesian opposition between *res cogitans* and *res extensa*. This very dualism is the bugbear of eco-phenomenological rhapsody,[190] including its *locus classicus,* Heidegger's description of the "aroundness" of being in the world *(Umwelt)*.[191] Phenomenology claims to surpass Descartes, if only rhetorically, in evoking a world or an intersubjective field. But in many ways it offers a sense of what Cartesianism "feels like." It thus falls into the dilemma of Pascal and, later, of phenomenology in general. This is a stupendous problem for environmental thinking and art, whether it is kitsch or avant-garde. In the next chapter we will delve more deeply into this strange turn of events. It turns out that Descartes, of all people, does ecomimesis.

The Beautiful Soul and Nonviolence

Let us take "As I write" at face value for a moment, and explore the fantasy it conjures up. We have established a correlation between "As I write" and the injunction to leave the scene of reading. Wordsworth's command in "The Tables Turned," "Up, up! My friend, and quit your books" (1) conveys a highly paradoxical message. It takes the form of the impossible superego injunction, the same one that appears on the sides of Coca-Cola bottles: "Enjoy!" There is no explicitly didactic content here. The didacticism lies in the injunction to enjoy. In general, the ego finds this injunction impossible to fulfill. It is harder than straightforward prohibition: there is nothing to struggle against. "Enjoy!" is the current form of consumerist ideology. At the very moment at which didacticism becomes suspect (the Romantic period), a form of writing appears that transmits a command far more potent than any explicit set of instructions. We are now in the realm of modern advertising, where the injunction is attached to an image of idiotic enjoyment. Like Platonic mimesis, ecomimesis tries to differentiate itself from *bad* mimesis, from mimesis as drug or poison. But in this very differentiation, it refines itself as a consumer drug par excellence, generating all kinds of hallucinatory enjoyment.[192]

Alongside the hale-and-hearty rhetoric, there is an uncanny ghost. This ghost speaks a language that sounds more like passive consumerism: "Why bother intellectualizing . . . just sit back and let Nature wash all over you." Just sample "One impulse from a vernal wood" ("The Tables Turned," 21) instead of working hard at forming an idea. Implicitly, there's something wrong with you if you don't. There is an injunction against what Freud called *introversion,* a contemplative state decried as a queer form of inwardness. Wordsworth was no Nazi, but forms of totalitarianism have tended to espouse "extraversion" and denounce introversion as autoerotic withdrawal.[193] In this sense at least, we should be wary of claims that Wordsworth helped the English to avoid Nazism.[194] Relishing nature is not too far away from the modern religion of sport. Nature writing often presupposes a body in possession of all the "proper" limbs and faculties. But aside from its masculinist and ablist qualities—even when it does not exhibit such tendencies—nature writing exhorts the reader to snap out of it, to stop what he or she is doing (which is—but this is no time to argue!) and go and do something more healthy instead. The outdoors crew are legion, so just one quotation will suffice, from an essay on Shelley by Aaron Dunckel: "It is one of the truly salutary aspects of ecological criticism that it insists on an 'outside' to the text." This outside enables us to question "cultural solipsism."[195]

It is not hard to detect in the terms *introversion* and *extraversion* the metaphysical opposition of inside and outside. Outside is normal; inside is pathological. "Up! Up!" really means "Outside! Outside!" "Genuine" contact with whatever the truth of the "natural world" ought to be found indoors as much as outside, in introversion as much as extraversion, in contemplation that is itself not hale and hearty but may suffer from a constant breakdown of its supporting structures—in other words, in critique. But as we have seen, one form of consumerism is being swapped for another. Do you want to be a couch potato with a remote, or a couch potato with a pair of field glasses?

We could go even deeper. Ideology can split introversion itself into a healthy, outward-turning kind, full of splendid insights, and an unhealthy, inward-turning, negative one. Contemplation is always in danger of being mobilized in an aggressive manner. For Marcuse, "Marxist literary criticism often displays scorn for 'inwardness' . . . this attitude is not too remote from the scorn of the capitalists for an unprofitable dimension of life."[196] Ironically, nature as a healthy exteriority is far from what Marcuse calls libido and Wordsworth calls "impulse." Ecological inwardness might not be vigorous and aggressive. It might be all too aware of its aches and pains, its difference from clean oneness with nature. Only then would it remain true to the idea of peace hidden, to the point of disappearance, in the assertion of hearty oneness. I am reminded of a CEO who said he was leaving his job to "focus on his battle with cancer."

We are about to reach a startling conclusion. If our advice to the beautiful soul is "get over it," "Get up! Get up!"—then we are far from transcending the erotophobia, the fear of and fascination with a feminized state, that we glimpse in the injunction to stop contemplating and breathe the fresh air. Hegel's disparagement of Buddhism, which for him embodied the "I = I" of the Fichtean beautiful soul, had to do with a phobic reaction to what he had read about the education of incarnate lamas. Hegel lingers over the "feminine" education of the young lama "in a kind of prison" of "quiet and solitude," living "chiefly on vegetables" and "revolt[ing] from killing any animal, even a louse."[197] The prison of quiet and solitude is only the objective form of the view of nothingness, which *The Philosophy of Religion* imagines as an oroboric, self-swallowing man.[198] Such a man "does not hold the Spiritual Essence as his peculiar property, but is regarded as partaking in it only in order to exhibit it to others," in a spirit not unlike that of French or American republicanism.[199] The culture of the lama uncannily echoes the Europe of absolute freedom and terror, while simultaneously retaining a monarchical structure, an unsynthesized parody of the very state for which Hegel himself argued.

Kicking the beautiful soul in the pants will never work. Indeed, the beautiful soul thrives on alternatives that are just two sides of the same coin: "Don't just sit there, do something!" is merely the inverse of

"Don't just do something, sit there!" A more thorough investigation of the very things that preoccupy the beautiful soul (violence, nonviolence, action, contemplation) is in order. While we are on the subject of Buddhism, consider the following hilarious example from a talk by a Tibetan lama, the Venerable Chögyam Trungpa, Rinpoche. It concerns a high Romantic, theistic sense of immanence at the heart of a certain flavor of nature. Writing outside the dominant Western traditions, Trungpa notices how materialism and spiritualism are joined at the hip:

> The theistic tradition talks about meditation and contemplation as a fantastic thing to do. The popular notion of God is that he created the world: the woods were made by God, the castle ruins were created by God, and the ocean was made by God. So we could swim and meditate or we could lie on the beach made by God and have a fantastic time. Such theistic nature worship has become a problem. We have so many holiday makers, so many nature worshipers, so many hunters.
>
> In Scotland, at the Samye Ling meditation center, where I was teaching, there was a very friendly neighbor from Birmingham, an industrial town, who always came up there on weekends to have a nice time. Occasionally he would drop into our meditation hall and sit with us, and he would say: "Well, it's nice you people are meditating, but I feel much better if I walk out in the woods with my gun and shoot animals. I feel very meditative walking through the woods and listening to the sharp, subtle sounds of animals jumping forth, and I can shoot at them. I feel I am doing something worthwhile at the same time. I can bring back venison, cook it, and feed my family. I feel good about that."
>
> . . . We are not particularly seeking enlightenment or the simple experience of tranquility—we are trying to get over our deception.[200]

Ecological contemplation can provide fuel for a possessive, predatory grasp of the world. The humor in this passage derives from the hunter's "and"—"and I can shoot at them." It resides in the casualness with which the hunter links his admiration for nature with his capacity to use it for target practice. This way of appreciating the natural world has a poetic lineage traceable through such works as Alexander Pope's "Windsor Forest." In that poem, the forest is seen as through the sights of a gun. It is admired as so much potential weaponry, as raw materials for battle ships.[201] There remains a subtle hint of this even in the literature of the empty wilderness. Although it has no potential for capital— although, more precisely, it has been politically and poetically cordoned off from capitalism—still, it has a *potential* for this potential, as George Bush's administration knows. It thus sets up a more or less sublimated version of the catascopic gaze of the hunter with his gun in

"Windsor Forest." We possess the wilderness aesthetically—after the aesthetics of Kant, that is. Like an object of value in a shop window as seen by a window shopper, we consume the wilderness in a purposively nonpurposive way. Horkheimer and Adorno claim that that secret link between the inward and the environment is divulged in the lyric, whose "pure subjectivity . . . testifies to . . . the suffering in an existence alien to the subject, as well as to the love of this existence."[202]

The beautiful soul, with its sermon of "beautiful Nature," is preaching to the choir. We always already have to be on the beautiful souls' side, seeing it their way. But how do we go beyond that? We must move gingerly, nonviolently. The first sections of this chapter concluded that numerous ideas about nature are inadequate, ideological constructions created in an age of machines and capitalism. We then saw how the ecological subject position was identical with consumerism. And then we found out that any attempt to tear off this skin would only reproduce existing conditions. Like Alice at the Looking Glass House, we are stuck, especially when we try to get away. Let us see if we can get any smarter, stuck as we are.

Imagining Ecology without Nature

I am here, sitting by the fire, wearing a dressing gown,
holding this page in my hand.

—DESCARTES, *MEDITATIONS*

Chapter 2 could leave us in a state of cynicism. On some days, environmentalist writing seems like patching up the void with duct tape. So
many solutions seem either out of date or inadequate in their attempt to
generate different ways of making us feel about the state we are in,
without changing it. But all cultural forms lag behind processes of production. Environmental art and politics are no exception. Moreover,
certain radical or avant-garde practices have come more up to date with
the current moment. The Paris Communes were experiments in the production of social space, documented by poets such as Rimbaud. The
revolutionary space mobilized the floating world of the *flâneurs* and
their psychic disposition of boredom, opening up desires for utopian
"free space" that sounds much like the wilderness.[1] The Situationists in
1960s Paris and other experimenters in "psychic geography" have
struggled to keep abreast of the productive forces.

Remaining in cynicism is a habit of the beautiful soul. Our choice is
false if it has been reduced to one between hypocrisy and cynicism, between wholeheartedly getting into environmental rhetoric and cynically
distancing ourselves from it. In both cases, we would be writing litur-
gies for the beautiful soul. Although it is "realistic" to be cynical rather
than hypocritical, we do not wish to reinforce the current state of affairs. Our answer to the ruthless ransacking of nature, and of the idea
of nature, must be yes, we admit to the reality of the situation. And no,
we refuse to submit to it.

Instead of serving up lashings of guilt and redemption, might ecological criticism not engage the ideological forms of the environment, from capitalist imagery to the very ecocriticism that opposes capitalism? Ecocritique could establish collective forms of identity that included other species and their worlds, real and possible. It would subvert fixating images of "world" that inhibit humans from grasping their place in an already historical nature. Subverting fixation is the radical goal of the Romantic wish to explore the shadow lands. The hesitations of a Wordsworth, the unreliable narrators of a Mary Shelley—the whole panoply of irony and linguistic play is not marginal, but central to Romanticism. Subversion of identity fixations is what Alain Badiou calls a truth process, a rigorous and relentless distinction of the subject from its identifications.[2] It is valid both to say that subjectivity is profoundly Romantic, and to claim that we haven't attained it yet. Indeed, an ecological collective to come would definitely not look like the nature-nation construct with its fascist-tending ideal of work and wholeness. It would be more like Jean-Luc Nancy's society of "unworking," and in this sense, the "unintention" and openness of ambient art hold out a promise of an almost unimaginable kind of being together.[3]

The environment was born at exactly the moment when it became a problem. The word *environment* still haunts us, because in a society that took care of its surroundings in a more comprehensive sense, our idea of environment would have withered away. The very word *environmentalism* is evidence of wishful thinking. Society would be so involved in taking care of "it" that it would no longer be a case of some "thing" that surrounds us, that environs us and differs from us. Humans may yet return the idea of the "thing" to its older sense of *meeting place*.[4] In a society that fully acknowledged that we were always already involved in our world, there would be no need to point it out.

At the Looking Glass House

The more strenuously we try to exit the Looking Glass House of the beautiful soul, the more we end up back at square one. If we leave the beautiful soul bleeding in the street, have we really transcended it? Instead of trying to fight it, that is, to burst its bounds on its own terms, a more subtle, nonviolent, judo-like approach is in order. There is a rich vein of thinking on how to get out of beautiful soul syndrome.[5] Forgiveness is the key. But as Derrida has shown, forgiveness is an infinitely rich, difficult, and complex subject.[6] It has to do with acknowledging the gap between, the difference between, ideas and signs, between selves, and the gap between beautiful soul and "beautiful Nature." Ecology wants to go from dualism to monism, but not so fast! Rather than seeking some false oneness, acknowledging the gap is a paradoxical way of having greater fidelity to things. We will be exploring this later under the heading of "dark ecology."

To think in terms of either crude action or pure ideas is to remain within the prison of the beautiful soul. Oppositional consciousness is blessed and cursed with beautiful soul syndrome.[7] *Ecology without Nature* certainly suffers from it. The world of nature writing shimmers "over there" while we remain here safe (or stuck) in our critical mode. We cannot remain on the fence. But the possibilities are restricted: there is a strong gravitational pull toward the "new and improved" world of commodified solutions to a commodified world. The siren song of the beautiful soul exerts a fascination that could falsely induce one to think that one had transcended it. There is something of the "I can't go on . . . I'll go on" quality found in Adorno and Beckett about this part of our investigation.

The shape of this chapter is twofold. In the first few sections, I will consider some possibilities for a critical ecomimesis. Ambience may have a liberating potential. It is a candidate for what Benjamin called a "dialectical image," a form that looks both toward oppression and toward liberation, like the two-headed god Janus. On the one hand, ambient rhetoric provokes thought about fundamental metaphysical categories, such as inside and outside. On the other hand, if ambience becomes a resting place, a better version of the aesthetic dimension, then it has abandoned its liberating potential. If we find no resting place in ambience, no new religion or territory upon which to pin our flag, then ambience has helped to liberate radical thinking.

Our analysis needs to return to Romanticism, for Romantic experiments had already surpassed the conundrum of how embedding yourself in reality can also produce the opposite, a sublime aesthetic distancing. This is the problem that haunts David Abram's utopian prose. The self-defeating routine of puncturing the aesthetic veil, only to have it grow back even stronger, is why some Romantic writers, in their different ways, experiment with ecomimesis. They open up the rendered environment to the breeze of the cosmic, the historical, the political. Moreover, they turn the anti-aesthetic of ecomimesis around on itself. This is only possible because of the intrinsic playfulness and reversibility of language, and because of the inherent qualities of the perception dimension that, as we shall discover, makes *perception* diverge from the *aesthetic* (too often its analogue). The first sections consider two ways of solving the problems of ambience. First, I will investigate the possibility of dissolving the solidity of perception, either through juxtaposition, or through a redefinition of the aesthetic dimension itself. Second, the idea of *place* subtending the aesthetic will be deconstructed.

As Heidegger, Merleau-Ponty, and Derrida remarked in their very different ways, perception contains nonidentity like a carpet contains holes, or as a text is shot through with nothingness. We cannot see ahead, what we see behind us is only a surmise, and what we see in front of us is fleeting and illusory. The specter of a trickster nature, which is precisely what these theories of perception generate, is surprisingly what Abram finally wards off in his evocation of a monist spirit that rolls through all things. And ironically this trickster is available through the study of deconstruction, so our way out of the beautiful soul may seem like going further into it.

In the remaining sections of this chapter, I show how the idea of place is not single, independent, and solid. This leads to developing a new way of doing ecological criticism, which I call *dark ecology*. Dark ecology acknowledges that there is no way out of the paradoxes outlined in this book. Far from remaining natural, ecocriticism must admit that it is contingent and queer. I conclude by asserting that ecocritique, far from being hostile to deep ecology, is a form of "really deep ecology."

Juxtaposition as Ecocritique

Ecomimesis is above all a practice of juxtaposition. Avant-garde art values juxtaposition as collage, montage, bricolage, or rhizomics. But it all very much depends upon what is being juxtaposed with what. If it is to be properly critical, montage must juxtapose the contents with the frame. Why? Simply to juxtapose contents without bringing form and subject position into the mix would leave things as they are. As we have seen, just adding items to a list (such as adding polluting factories to a list of things in "nature") will not entirely do. The most extreme example of "contents" would be the writhing quality of writing. The most extreme example of "frame" would be the ideological matrix that makes things meaningful in the first place. Ambient art gestures toward this (dialectical) juxtaposition of writing with the ideological matrix. By presenting objects without a frame (clumps of "stuff" in a gallery, for instance) or frames without an object (white canvases, empty frames, and so on), ambient art questions the gap between contents and frame.

To juxtapose contents and frame, one must preserve the gap between them, even though ambient rhetoric screams (quietly) that the gap has been abolished. There is a gap between the particular and the general. If there were no gap then infinity would be merely another number—just an extremely high one. But infinity is radically beyond number; otherwise we fall back into the problem of "bad infinity"—an infinity that is ultimately countable. The frame is not just another element. Ambient art plays with what "counts" as either frame or contents, through the play of the re-mark. The re-mark establishes (and questions) the differences between, for example, graphic mark/sign, noise/sound, noise/silence, foreground/background. To reiterate Chapter 1, there is *nothing* in between; literally nothing, not even space, since space is also subject to these distinctions. Something is *either* a noise *or* it is sound. (The ideological fantasy of ecomimesis and especially ambience, *seems* to suggest that something could be both.)

In the universe according to quantum mechanics, things can be either particles or waves, but not both simultaneously. It is not even appropriate to say that "energy" can be either a particle or a wave. There is nothing behind these in the standard model that can be either, or worse, both at once. Similarly, contemporary neuroscience argues that experience comes in discrete quanta that are then blended to appear continuous. Perception may well be made up of moments rather than continua, as the theoretical exploration in Chapter 1 suggested.[8] Despite the fact that many green thinkers have relied on it, almost as a form of automated philosophy (the ontology of physics does it for you! Relax!), the Standard (Quantum) Model does not abolish subject–object dualism.[9] If anything, quantum theory demonstrates the persistence of this conundrum.

The aesthetic dimension is frequently posited as existing between subject and object; so do ecological dimensions. Consider the idea of "mesocosm," developed in studies of food webs by Gary Polis.[10] The mesocosm—a "medium-sized ecosystem"—functions in ecological science in experiments whose conditions simulate real life as closely as possible. Mesocosms exist between microcosm and macrocosm. Practically speaking, mesocosms may be beneficial scientific concepts. Magically, all animals and plants, and ultimately everything else, might find a place in them (or it?). The mesocosm swallows everything. Phenomena become equally meaningful, and thus meaningless, like a 1:1

map of reality. One reason why studying ambient poetics subverts aestheticization is that the re-mark signals a difference that is irreducible—it is not made out of anything smaller or more general. Either that, or everything is "between" and there is no definition. You will never find a thing between noise and sound, or between noise and silence. The re-mark is a quantum event. There is nothing between background and foreground. And there is nothing between frame and contents. Radical juxtaposition plays with the frame and its contents in such a way as to challenge both dualism (their absolute difference) and monism (their absolute identity). Dialectics is shorthand for a play back and forth between contents and frame.

Ekphrasis suspends time, generating a steady state in which the frequency and duration of the form floats wildly away from the frequency and duration of the content. Abram's hyperekphrasis means to transport us to this world—a bubble in the onward flow of the argument, a little island of fantasy. Indeed, there are bubbles within bubbles in the passage quoted in Chapter 2—we get from the present of enunciation "As I write" to the deer tracks the narrator "follows" by the end, via a paragraph break that forces the reader to step further into the fantasy world by tracking the text with his or her descending eyes. Recalling that Abram compares writing with following tracks, we should not be surprised that the narrative-within-a-narrative that is the second paragraph ends with the image of following tracks rather than writing.[11] Even the narrator's act of inscription itself has become attentiveness to the divine other, an attunement, a *Stimmung*. Everything is automated, and everything is seen from the outside and exoticized, in the very gesture of embedding us in a deep, dark inside.

The prose seems to stand up and arrest our progress through the argument's propositions. The passage is coordinated with the tissue of the surrounding text. In an invagination where form plays the opposite role from content, the passage's content surrounds the content of the argument (as I write the world goes on around me), just as the actual text is embedded with it (the reader must pause to take in an inset narrative). But what if a writer were to present this ekphrastic suspension on its own, to decontextualize it, like those modern artists who present lumps of something or other in a gallery without a frame around it?

One approach would be isolating the fantasy object of ecomimesis, leaving it high and dry. It is what Leigh Hunt tries in "A Now, Descriptive of a Hot Day."[12] Hunt's essay is an instance of Cockney ecomimesis—a suburban picture of suspended time interrupted not at the beginning, but at the end, by the notion that the writer is embedded in the scene. The inversion of the order, so that the metonymic exorbitancy comes first, and the "as I write" comes last, undermines naturalization. The last glimpse of the scene is of the author's pen, which waves away the fantasy's compelling quality in a reverse sleight of hand as we realize that the subject of the enunciated is also the subject of enunciation. The narrator takes responsibility for the fantasy—instead of using it as a treasure trove of his beautiful soul, he undermines the distance toward it that maintains the objectification and *vraisemblable* of the narrative world. The mixed-media art of David Robertson likewise juxtaposes everyday texts such as a deck of cards or a newspaper with existential-religious musings and quantum theory, as it takes the reader on a nonholistic ecological tour.[13]

The privileged attention of Abram's narrator is also the fortunate position of the framing narrator of Wordsworth's *The Ruined Cottage*. Wordsworth embeds a narrator—the Pedlar and his tale of Margaret and her husband who went to war and never came back—within another narration. The apparently simple act of double framing induces a sense of hesitation. Can we trust where the frame stops and where the next one starts, what is inside the frame, how truthful it is? The aesthetic, and aestheticizing, frame undermines the necessarily comfortable aesthetic distance with which to accept the poem as a soothing aesthetic-moral lesson. Wordsworth destabilizes the supposed neutrality of the medium in which we glimpse events. The introductory verse paragraph contains instructions on how to read the rest of the poem:

> 'Twas summer and the sun was mounted high;
> Along the south the uplands feebly glared
> Through a pale steam, and all the northern downs,
> In clearer air ascending, shewed far off
> Their surfaces with shadows dappled o'er
> Of deep embattled clouds: far as the sight
> Could reach those many shadows lay in spots
> Determined and unmoved, with steady beams
> Of clear and pleasant sunshine interposed;
> Pleasant to him who on the soft cool moss
> Extends his careless limbs beside the root
> Of some huge oak whose aged branches make
> A twilight of their own, a dewy shade
> Where the wren warbles while the dreaming man,
> Half-conscious of that soothing melody,
> With side-long eye looks out upon the scene,

By those impending branches made more soft,
More soft and distant. Other lot was mine. (1–18)[14]

The lines juxtapose a panoramic view with a more specific one. Details alert us to the idea that we are being let in on a clue. The sun "was mounted" (1)—like the word "sun," itself mounted high on the page. At first, the shadows "lie" on the surface of the land like the words on the page (7), loosely associated in the most open form available to Wordsworth (blank verse). The imagery is pale and minimalist, inviting our closer scrutiny at the very moment at which it seems to offer a relaxing ease. The repetition of "pleasant" (9–10) creates a tiny ripple on a smooth surface, to which our suspicion is drawn. We find ourselves embedded in the poem, via the semicolon (9) that hesitates before we find ourselves placed ("Pleasant to him," 10). This virtual reader, the "dreaming man," both is and is not the reader. Wordsworth is careful not to identify us absolutely with this figure. We are involved in the scene, yet critically so—our view seems to oscillate between a particular point of view within it, and a more general view outside it. This oscillation repeats itself on the very inside itself. The man "looks out" with "side-long eye"—he views the scene anamorphically, from an unexpected vantage point.

By the time we arrive at the quiescence of "more soft,/More soft and distant" (17–18), the scene has become far from an aesthetic blur. We want to peer into the softness, we are disturbed by the distance. All this takes place before we are pulled up short, anyway, by "Other lot was mine" (18). The very beauty of the exorbitant growth around the cottage—like the endless lines of blank verse silent before us on the page—haunts us with the possibility of pain and with the history of other places, other times that impinge intensely on this one. Instead of embedding the narrator in an othered war, *The Ruined Cottage* embeds the war in our experience of reading. In its very tranquility, it is one of the most powerful antiwar poems ever written.

Writing during another moment of oppressive imperialism, the First World War, Edward Thomas juxtaposes content and frame:

Tall nettles cover up, as they have done
These many springs, the rusty harrow, the plough
Long worn out, and the roller made of stone:
Only the elm butt tops the nettles now.

This corner of the farmyard I like most:
As well as any bloom upon a flower

> I like the dust on the nettles, never lost
> Except to prove the sweetness of a shower.[15]

It would be easy to say that the quietism and minimalism evoke the absent presence of Edwardian Englishness, an internal distance toward the pomp and circumstance of state affairs that only serves to throw that state into greater relief. The "corner," the neglected and unlovely plants (a Wordsworthian de-aestheticization), the "dust on the nettles"—in all these images *nature* seems very close to *nation*. This is miniaturized wildness, not the open frontier of manifest destiny, but a little corner of unreconstructed wilderness; even of atavism, a Romantic backsliding into a world before the domination of nature, figured by the rusting farm tools. As surely as do Heidegger's peasant shoes, these broken pieces of abandoned equipment open up the environment, cultural, meteorological, agricultural, and biological.

If tropes are flowers ("the flowers of rhetoric") then the tall nettles are wild tropes: ecomimesis. The poem holds something in reserve, something Blanchot calls the "interminable" of writing, figured in the nettles. At the end the dust, an image of stasis, is "lost" to the rain's "sweetness," a powerfully weak image, if that is not too oxymoronic. The reserve is barely encapsulated in the most imperceptible of things. But its trace is everywhere, on edges and corners—ambient. Thomas's poem is a quiet resistance to imperial poetics, with its corners of foreign fields that will be forever England. It plays with the idea of *world* like Wilfred Owen, who in "Anthem for Doomed Youth" juxtaposes the screams of war materiel (2–7) with "bugles calling for [the dead] from sad shires" (8), a line that never fails to evoke a visceral reaction as it suddenly reconfigures the viewpoint from No-Man's Land back to the grieving families: "Their flowers the tenderness of silent minds,/And each slow dusk a drawing-down of blinds" (13–14).[16] The shifts and turns are Wordsworthian, as is the writing of W. G. Sebald, whose *On the Natural History of Destruction* positions us in an impossible, almost unspoken point of view, as fictional as it is urgent, inside Dresden and Hamburg as they are being bombed to smithereens at the end of the Second World War.[17]

"To see a World in a Grain of Sand" is to juxtapose the content with the frame in a highly critical manner. Writing "Auguries of Innocence" in a time of almost totalitarian surveillance and paranoia, during a particularly oppressive moment of the Napoleonic Wars, Blake imagines how the tiniest particularity can relate to the grandest generality: "A Robin Red breast in a Cage / Puts all Heaven in a Rage" (5–6); "A dog starvd at his Masters Gate / Predicts the ruin of the State" (9–10).[18] The poem sustains an almost static tone, reading the general in the particular over and over in simple AABB rhyming that only changes by increasing in intensity toward the end (tending toward AAAA). This feels like braking. I am reminded of Benjamin's comment that socialism is not so much a progression as the application of the emergency brake.[19] An augury is a prophecy written in the tea leaves, in the guts of a bird, in the real—ecomimesis. It is knowledge that is somehow imprinted in the real.

A stain on the horizon announces the presence of a significant Beyond. But this Beyond is sick: we can read it in the tea leaves. This is an everyday experience for people living in a time of intense war. Jane Austen's novels are saturated with the presence of the war, which appears every day in the paper on the breakfast table.[20] In this atmosphere, it is a supreme political act to de-objectify the world, which is what happens here, especially in the "AAAA" section. It contains its own negation within itself, its own nonidentity:

> Some to Misery are Born
> Every Morn & every Night
> Some are Born to sweet delight
> Some are Born to sweet delight
> Some are born to Endless Night
> We are led to Believe a Lie
> When we see not Thro the Eye
> Which was Born in a Night to perish in a Night
> When the Soul Slept in Beams of Light
> God Appears & God is Light
> To those poor Souls who dwell in Night
> But does a Human Form Display
> To those who Dwell in Realms of day (120–132)[21]

The evocation of the impermanence of perception ("Which was Born in a Night to perish in a Night") breaks up the rhythm into rapid pyrrhics that undermine the solidity of the basic pulse. Seeing becomes not a view of the Beyond (sick or not) from a local vantage point, for the local has swallowed up everything in the human form divine: a hard-won victory in which the narrator generalizes the passionate militancy of what is "in his face" against the shadow play of state terror. This is ecological politics, and it is no surprise that violence toward animals makes an appearance as Blake enumerates canaries in the coal mine of institutionalized violence. Blake's radical leaps are a surprising form of realism. In contemporary Colorado, the nuclear "missile field" exists amidst real estate. Some people actually have missile silos in their back-yards, complete with soldiers on hair-trigger alert. The state jams up against civil society just like the couplets of Blake's poem.

We have read four war poems that have something to say about to an age of war against life forms. It is almost possible to show how any text could deliver a radical message, not because of the presence of some special property in the text (the literalism of ecomimesis, for example), but because of the *absence* of one. *Almost* possible, not only because it seems like hard work getting certain texts to read this way (*Mein Kampf*, a bus ticket), but because this proposition might presuppose the very radicalism it is "finding" in the text as an object of ideological enjoyment. These problems inhere in Benjamin's montage technique. In his (non)monumental study of the space of consumerism in early nineteenth-century Paris, the *Arcades* project, Benjamin shows how sheer juxtaposition can speak volumes. Benjamin practices a form of environmental criticism—not of bunnies and butterflies, but of the distracting, phantasmagoric spaces produced by modern capital. Yet there is a sense of predetermination, of knowing already what we will find.

The text's non-coincidence with us is what is significant. Likewise, the text of nature—it is the silence of the owls that speaks volumes about the environment in Wordsworth's "There was a Boy." Nevertheless, these radicalizations of ecomimesis hold open the aesthetic dimension even as they seek to abolish aestheticization. In an era when the aesthetic has been commodified, and the commodity has been aestheticized, an empty frame or frameless unformed stuff retains the possibility of other ways of being. At a moment such as ours, radical ecomimesis can only honestly appear as sheer negativity.

Radical Ecological Kitsch

Finding out where your breakfast came from can reveal social patterns on a global geographical scale. When it comes to delineating the environment, simple materialism has a lot going for it. Living beings all exchange substances with their environment(s). Any field of study that takes metabolism as one of its objects is bound to generate straightforward environmental images. This includes the study of food and diet. "Oh! for a beaker full of the warm south" says Keats ("Ode to a Nightingale," 15), depicting the idea of *terroir*, the notion that grapes taste of where you grow them.[22] For all his mysteriousness, Heidegger offers an ambient materialism in his idea of *Umwelt:* "in the ontological doctrine of Being's priority over thought, in the 'transcendence' of Being, the materialist echo reverberates from a vast distance."[23]

Areas such as food studies, emerging by the side of traditional work in the humanities, and sometimes connected to the sciences, are to be encouraged. A direct approach to the object—where did it come from, where is it going?—will help people understand ecological politics, without appealing to abstract nature. But this materialism is prone to monism: reducing the world of two to that of one. Monism is not a good solution to dualism. We still need to establish a subtler sense of what "body," "mass," and "matter" might mean; and for that matter, materialism.[24] Idealism and materialism can both generate flat worlds in which there is no otherness. If ecology without nature has taught us anything, it is that there is a need to acknowledge irreducible otherness, whether in poetics, ethics, or politics.

Ecomimesis wants us to forget or lay aside the subject–object dualism. Ecomimesis aims for immediacy. The less thinking or mediating we do, the better. Lest we scoff, notice that such notions are present in high experimental art, not just in kitsch. One of Alvin Lucier's early experiments involved using electrodes to pick up alpha waves in his brain, which activated various instruments. Or think of action painting, drip painting, happenings.

A beer mug in the shape of a president's head, a tea cup with a swastika on it, a tiny ceramic model of a Bambi-eyed fawn; such objects are mind-bogglingly inconsistent, and, as Clement Greenberg pointed out long ago, can supply the kernel of powerful ideological fantasies, by no means limited to fascism.[25] Ecomimesis evokes a sense of "sheer stuff," of sprouting enjoyment—the sinthome. Sheer stuff, historically, is *for* someone: the name we give to it is kitsch, which is really a way of saying "other people's enjoyment." Though the German etymology is obscure, consider the high-handed dictionary definition: "Art or *objets d' art* characterized by worthless pretentiousness."[26] I use *kitsch* in contradistinction to *camp*. Some people confuse the two. While *camp* refers to an "ironic" (distanced) appropriation of a bygone aesthetic commodity, *kitsch* indicates the unalloyed enjoyment of an object not normally considered aesthetic in a "high" sense. Commodities pass through different phases. Some objects are born camp, some achieve it, and some have camp thrust upon them.[27]

Kitsch is unashamed about its status as a mass-produced commodity. And many works that have been mechanically reproduced would count as kitsch. How many student dorm rooms are adorned with that classic example of ecomimesis, a Monet water lilies painting? How many modern shopping malls feature a deconstructed look, where we can see the pipes? Kitsch exerts a fascinating, idiotic pull. It is often synesthetic, and it has no power except for the love we invest in it. Kitsch is the nearest thing in modern culture to the shamanic ritual object. Kitsch is immersive. It is a labor of love: you have to "get into it." It poses the problem of how the subject relates to the object in a striking manner. Kitsch is based on the idea that nature can be copied, and thus on the notion of ecomimesis.[28] For Adorno, "nature" denotes a phase of existence that is both dominating and dominated: "The song of birds is found beautiful by everyone; no feeling person in whom something of the European tradition survives fails to be moved by the sound of a robin after a rain shower. Yet something frightening lurks in the song of birds precisely because it is not a song but obeys the spell in which it is enmeshed."[29] The copying of nature, on this view, is the domination of nature—but also, in a dialectical twist, a condition of being spellbound by its dominating quality.

Kitsch is the object of disgust.[30] It must fall out of the aesthetic for aesthetic judgment to mean anything. He likes kitsch, your nature writing is distasteful, whereas my ambience is richly ambiguous and full of irony. The journal mode tries to drop out of the aesthetic dimension altogether, to subvert the panoply of aesthetic distinctions, and to regain a purposive aspect that Kant ruled out of the aesthetic proper. There *is* a point to nature writing. It wants to make us love nature. All that prose and all those illustrations in *A Sand County Almanac* are meant to melt our hearts. There is something of the fetish in kitsch. It only maintains the powers invested in it, like a souvenir. Nowadays, what separates high art from kitsch is often just the price of admission to a gallery, not even a recherché one. Through the tiny gestures of the re-mark, high environmental art polices the boundaries between itself and kitsch. Witness the gyrations in *The Wire* magazine, a journal about contemporary avant-garde and pop music. The sleeve notes to Brian Eno's *Ambient 1: Music for Airports* attempts to distinguish "ambient" music from Muzak, which he describes as "familiar tunes arranged and orchestrated in a lightweight and derivative manner":

> Whereas the extant canned music companies proceed from the basis of regulating environments by blanketing their acoustic and atmospheric idiosyncracies, Ambient Music is intended to enhance these. Whereas conventional background music is produced by stripping away all sense of doubt and uncertainty (and thus all genuine interest) from the music, Am-

bient Music retains these qualities. And whereas their intention is to "brighten" the environment by adding stimulus to it (thus supposedly alleviating the tedium of routine tasks and levelling out the natural ups and downs of the body rhythms) Ambient Music is intended to induce calm and a space to think.[31]

Decades beforehand, Jean Cocteau and Erik Satie had already deconstructed the difference Eno struggles to maintain. Powerful computers and music software such as Pro Tools and Reason have reduced or eliminated the distinction between high and low sound art. Minimalism is now a way of decorating suburban kitchens. Bamboo has become popular in British gardens for its sonic properties.

Adorno commented on such experimentation by linking it specifically to a form of "naturalism," produced "in spite of the absence of representational objectivity and expression":

> Crudely physicalistic procedures in the material and calculable relations between parameters helplessly repress aesthetic semblance and thereby reveal the truth of their positedness. The disappearance of this positedness into their autonomous nexus left behind aura as a reflex of human self-objectification. The allergy to aura, from which no art today is able to escape, is inseparable from the eruption of inhumanity. This renewed reification, the regression of artworks to the barbaric literalness of what is aesthetically the case, and phantasmagorical guilt are inextricably intertwined. As soon as the artwork fears for its purity so fanatically that it loses faith in its possibility and begins to display outwardly what cannot become art—canvas and mere tones—it becomes its own enemy, the direct and false continuation of purposeful rationality. This tendency culminates in the *happening*.[32]

High experimental art becomes its opposite—a "second naturalism"—despite itself. Adorno is addressing a consequence he identifies in Benjamin's criticism of the "aura" of high art. In its worry about the aura of lofty and commodified artworks, art tries to de-reify itself, to jump off the canvas and out of the concert hall. But in doing so, it finds that it has reduced itself to an even more reified thing, "the barbaric literalness of what is aesthetically the case." Atmosphere, environment, becomes a specific vibration. We could even measure it with subsonic microphones and speed it up to within the range of human hearing. My own procedures—a literalist view of what tone is, for instance—are hopelessly guilty as charged. Is experimental art already aware that it is kitsch, the naturalism Adorno speaks about? Or is this kitsch quality a retroactive effect? Do some works achieve kitsch while others are just born that way? And can kitsch be radical as kitsch? The liner notes to my copy of Lucier's *I Am Sitting in a Room* suggest that it is high kitsch: "[it] pulls the listener along with a process that, whether understandable nor not, seems perfectly natural, totally fascinating, intensely personal, and poignantly musical."[33]

There seems to be no getting around it. The aesthetic itself is, on this view, just a disavowal of kitsch that is, uncannily, its inner essence.[34] Nature writing is easy to dismiss as lowbrow, bad taste, unhip. But in doing so we simply adopt a speculative distance, a distance that actually maintains the object of desire (or disgust). In this way, new historicism is in danger of re-establishing the very aesthetic dimension that it considers public enemy number one. By holding the art object at a distance—it is locked in a past whose otherness we are obliged to describe carefully; it is contaminated with aesthetic strategies that erase history—its power as an object is magnified, because the aesthetic is indeed that which holds things at a distance. The problem with new historicism is exactly the reverse of what ecocriticism is afraid of. Far from contaminating the beautiful art object, it raises the object's aesthetic power to a level of phobic fascination. All art becomes (someone else's) kitsch.

It would be very easy, and highly ineffective, to denounce nature writing as sheer cheesiness without the "class" of proper (aesthetic) writing. This denunciation would reproduce aesthetic distancing. If ecology is about *collapsing* distances (between human and animal, society and natural environment, subject and object), then how much sense does it make to rely on a strategy of reading that keeps re-establishing (aesthetic) distance? Adorno makes a poignant observation about the hypocrisy of high art:

> The hardly esoteric judgment that paintings of the Matterhorn and purple heather are kitsch has a scope reaching far beyond the displayed subject matter: what is innervated in the response is, unequivocally, that natural beauty cannot be copied. The uneasiness this causes flares up only in the face of extreme crudeness, leaving the tasteful zone of nature imitations all the more secure. The green forest of German impressionism is of no higher dignity than those views of the Königssee painted for hotel lobbies.[35]

Kitsch, says Adorno, is common to both "high" and "low" art forms, such that the "tasteful zone" of the officially sanctioned aesthetic gets a pass. In general, however, Adorno wants to exercise an ecology of cleanliness to filter the "poisonous substance" of kitsch out of art.[36]

This is not to say that we should throw away our copies of *The Norton Anthology of Poetry* and start reading books with embossed covers, as if that would save the earth. Throw away the Turner paintings, dust off the cute porcelain models of cows. I am trying not to say that kitsch is a "new and improved" version of the aesthetic. In rendering nature, nature writing tries to be a "new and improved" version of normal aesthetic forms. But, like Lyotard's "nuance," it just ends up collapsing into the aesthetic. There appears to be no way out. Trying to get out by the roof (high critique such as historicism) commits us to the distancing that re-establishes the aesthetic. And trying to get out via the basement (delving into kitsch) just widens the aesthetic dimension, generating a world of sentimental-sadistic sensations. We are going to have to admit it: we're stuck.

In its attempt to outflank aestheticized ambience (both the ecocritical and postmodern kinds), *Ecology without Nature* itself risks becoming a "super-new, ultra-improved" version of the syndrome it has been exploring all this time, consumerist appreciation for the reified world of nature. In so doing, it would ironically become another form of kitsch. Instead of trying to escape kitsch only to be sucked back into its gravitational field, we should try another approach. This would be the paradoxical one of thoroughly delving into, even identifying with, kitsch, the disgusting-fascinating sinthome of high, cool, critical art theory and theory-art.

Terry Eagleton asks how different literary theories would deal with *Finnegans Wake*.[37] One of the tests I applied consistently to theories under analysis in this study was to ask how they would cope with a snow globe of one of the Elves in *The Lord of the Rings* movies. Is it possible for sentimentalism and critique to exist together? I am not talking about the ironization of kitsch as *camp*, because that would be just another aesthetic pose. For kitsch to be critical, it would have to remain kitsch, and not be hollowed out and worn as a design on a T-shirt. Its sentimental qualities would have to persist, along with its objectal properties.

Could there be such a thing as critical kitsch? Children's stories certainly often count as sparkling kitsch fantasy objects. William Blake wrote children's songs and stories that turn out to be for adults. With its detailed, cartoonish watercolor illustrations, *The Book of Thel* approaches kitsch, although its distinctly non-mass-produced form denies it. Blake tells the story of a young girl who does not know her place in life. She lives a pastoral existence in a blissful idyllic landscape, but is somehow afflicted with melancholy sadness. What is the matter with her? Blake's Thel describes herself in natural terms, but those terms are ingrained with figurative, deceptive properties. These terms are also ambient. In a paratactic list, a plateau of tone that is a perverse ecorhapsody, Thel describes herself as various tricksterish forms of environmental anamorphic shape ("Thel is like . . . a reflection in a glass . . . like music in the air" (1.8–11)). Thel is like the beautiful soul, whose certainty Hegel brilliantly describes as "changed immediately into a sound that dies away."[38] She is all dressed up with nowhere to go.

Those with whom Thel converses—a flower, a cloud, a worm, and a clod of clay—describe themselves as natural: "naturally" interpellated into ideological consistency by the penetrative hailing of God's word. They know who they are, paradoxically, insofar as they take delight in their own insertion into their environments. The cloud falls as rain. In a Hegelian world, even nonidentity can be made into identity. In this "ecologocentric" realm, a restricted economy in which elements of the ecosystem are fed back perfectly into it without excess, Thel is a question mark amidst affirmative exclamations. Ambiguity itself can be aesthetically contained. The clod of clay "ponders" its existence (5.6), but this pondering is elevated to a second power as a Heideggerian rumination upon destiny. At the end Thel encounters her "own" voice as a disembodied sound emanating from her grave, from the earth. The voice asks a series of disturbing rhetorical questions that evoke both the materiality of the body and the deceptiveness of perception. Thel screams and flees "back" to her original state (6.22). Has nothing changed?

The juxtaposition of Thel's and her interlocutors' views is a form of ecocritique. Which side is more "ecological," the creatures', as in the standard reading, or Thel's? Most readers end up telling Thel, in the Midwestern vernacular, to shit or get off the pot. Is the poem an erotic version of a "Barbauldian moral hymn"?[39] Or are Thel's disembodied questions, and the question of her disembodiment, in fact theoretical reflections that productively trouble the still waters of ecologocentric identity? Here is a paradox. To condemn Thel would be to inhabit the very position of the beautiful soul that she so poignantly articulates. "That stupid girl Thel. I myself am reconciled to the world with its cycles of life and death." In the beautiful soul's world there is a place for everything except uncertainty. Thel is a figure for ecocritique.[40] Her melancholia is an ethical act of absolute refusal, a series of *no*'s that finally erupt in a bloodcurdling scream. By operating as a modern trickster, ecocritique is paradoxically closer to nature. But nature by now has been deformed into something deceptive, something queer. Thel is a sentimental figure who is nevertheless critical of her ideological world.

For the *flâneur*, all objects achieve the status of kitsch. Consumerism tends to turn every object into the embodiment of the enjoyment of the other—even when it is the consumer's "own" thing. Benjamin was obsessed with phantasmagoria and the lurid kitsch of the Arcades. Wordsworth's response to the Panoramas in London deserves comparison. Wordsworth was far from simply disgusted with these immersive forms of "casual enjoyment," gigantic depictions of landscapes without aesthetic distance, enveloping viewers up and down a spiral staircase.[41] Wordsworth maintained that art could be as immersive as this, and still permit one to think and reflect. His style bears uncanny similarities to the mass entertainment in Leicester Square. Late Wordsworth poems, in their miniaturized triteness, seem to aim for kitsch from another direction—the small rather than the outlandishly large. They are deceptively simple, often turning out to be little essays in poetics. "This lawn, a carpet all alive" offers a mundane garden lawn for our close-up inspection, destroying the aura of the aesthetic object by bringing it into a proximity in which it dissolves into a dancing field of ambiguous signs. To choose a lawn rather than a mountain range is itself significant—we have established that they are the inverse of one another. But to delve into the lawn in the way Wordsworth manages is extraordinary.[42]

Coleridge's *The Ancient Mariner* suggests an ecological approach that we could call an ethics of kitsch. Kant's position is that pure art is nonconceptual. This nonconceptuality has been the basis of radical aesthetics.[43] Could kitsch, with its affective glow, also have a nonconceptual aspect that is even more radical? It is only at the point of utter exhaustion that the Mariner gives up the notion of imposing conceptuality onto the real. This imposition has been read as falling within the territorializing logic of imperialism (see the discussion of the poem in Chapter 2). Alan Bewell argues that colonialism and imperialism in the Romantic period produced tremendous anxiety about, fascination with, and desire to dominate the earth's life-forms. *The Ancient Mariner* deals a swift blow to the aesthetics of wilderness. The Mariner shoots the albatross; the Death Ship takes his men's souls; he is left "Alone, alone, all, all alone" in a vast, panoramic ocean (4.232); "And a thousand thousand slimy things / Lived on; and so did I" (4.238–239).[44] The Mariner embodies all those conscious beings stricken with continuation of poisoned life. The Mariner's conceptuality is resonant in the sliminess of "a thousand thousand slimy things," a register reused in Sartre's disturbingly phobic *Being and Nothingness*.[45] The slimy things absorb the gaze into a teeming infinity and collectivity (Sartre: "a sly solidarity"). At this very moment, however, the Mariner experiences some relief from the burden of his guilt: "Blue, glossy green, and velvet black, / They coiled and swam" (279–280). The snakes are still slimy, but they are not to be abjected (and subsequently objectified). Their sliminess is not only the revenge of objectivity (Sartre: "the revenge of the In-itself"), but also an invitation to look more carefully, to wonder. The "things" become "snakes." As Stanley Cavell declares, the Mariner "accepts his participation as a being living with whatever is alive."[46] The "whatever" is crucial. Ecology without nature needs the openness of this whatever, probably pronounced with the distracted yet ironic casualness of a Californian high school student. Otherwise the ecological collective to come will be captured by the fantasies of nation building that have haunted the concept of nature.

When the Mariner blesses the snakes "unaware" (4.287), does that mean that he appreciates them aesthetically first? Despite his state of mind, it seems, he blesses what before he found slimy and disgusting. What is the place of the aesthetic here? Is it being transcended, reinforced, or subverted in some other way? I am sucked into a culinary reference, especially as it pertains to Coleridge's Romantic opposition between poetic *hypsilatos* (sublimity, power) and *gluchotes* (sweetness), also used in his antislavery writing on sugar. Sartre declares that the revenge of the In-itself is threatening to the masculine subject: "the sugary death of the For-itself (like that of a wasp which sinks into the jam and drowns in it)."[47] The Mariner's temporary solution to the problem of his guilt and isolation is an immersion in the aesthetic experience of *gluchotes:* a sugary sentimentality whose gaze is down, as opposed to the sublime upward gaze of the masculine mountain-climber. This solution is fresh, given Coleridge's linkage, in the mid-1790s, of sugar with softness, artifice, luxury and cruelty.[48] *The Ancient Mariner* and *Frankenstein* are gothic and tacky. The tacky is the anaesthetic (unaesthetic) property of kitsch: glistening, plasticized, inert, tactile, sticky—compelling our awareness of perception; too bright, too dull, too quiet, too loud, too smelly, not smelly enough—subverting aesthetic propriety. Coleridge respected the tacky; he appreciated the ethics of calling sugar the crystallized blood of slaves.[49] So did Mary Shelley: her monster story undermines the myth of Romantic genius. Both stories are about excessively material stuff, art-matter as pure extension.

The Ancient Mariner is compelled to repeat. We become infected with his tacky "rime"—sound pattern or hoar frost? The hoary, frosty quality of the poem is an allegory for the way the environment changes the object. Is the point to digest his story (moral: don't shoot albatrosses!)? Or is it to infect others? Coleridge models the ultra-slow-motion way of falling in love with your world. "He prayeth well, who loveth well / Both man and bird and beast" (*The Ancient Mariner* 7.612–613). *Love itself* is the true form of prayer, rather than: "you'll get the fast dialup speed to God if you are nice to animals." Being nice *is* the fast dialup. It goes beyond refraining from shooting albatrosses; beyond the "Hermit good" who is already way beyond the church on his "rotted old oak-stump" (7.514, 522). In the same way, *Frankenstein* transgresses advanced republicanism (the doctor is already one of those). Nature is not just an Alpine place where everything is equally splendid and sublime.

The problem of human beingness, declared Sartre and Lacan, is the problem of what to do with one's slime (one's shit): "The slimy is *myself.*"[50] Ultimately, is sliminess not the sacred, the taboo substance of life itself? One word for this is Kristeva's *abject,* the qualities of the world we slough off in order to maintain subjects and objects.[51] Ecological politics is bound up with what to do with pollution, miasma, slime: things that glisten, schlup, and decay. Should radioactive waste from the nuclear bomb factory at Rocky Flats be swept under the Nevada carpet of an objectified world, a salt deposit that was declared in the 1950s to be safe, but in the 1990s had been found to leak (the Waste Isolation Pilot Project, or WIPP)? How about the planned destination for spent fuel rods from reactors, Yucca Mountain in New Mexico? What does one do with the leakiness of the world? Deep green notions such as Nuclear Guardianship (advocated by Joanna Macy) assert that substances like the plutonium whose release of poisoned light takes tens of thousands of years to cease, should be stored above ground in monitored retrievable storage; moreover, that a culture, indeed a spirituality, would have to grow up around the tending of this abject substance.[52]

Nuclear Guardianship politicizes spirituality as not an escape from, but a taking care of, the abject. Beyond its cuteness (a reified version of Kantian beauty), an element in kitsch ecological imagery maintains this abjection, a formless, ambient element, Bataille's *informe.* Milan Kundera says that kitsch holds shit at bay.[53] But (other people's) kitsch *is* shit. The bourgeois subject would rule forever if fascination and horror *always* resulted in spitting out the disgusting object. Ecological art is duty bound to hold the slimy in view. This involves invoking the underside of ecomimesis, the pulsing, shifting qualities of ambient poetics, rather than trying to make pretty or sublime pictures of nature. Instead of trying to melt it away, radical kitsch exploits dualism, the difference between "I" and "slimy things." The view of nature according to the ethics of kitsch has more in common with the standard Cartesian dualism than New Age or Deep Ecology. While in these views, nature is a mysterious harmony, kitsch ecology establishes an existential life substance.[54] *Ecology without Nature* has argued consistently that the phenomenological and existential approaches flesh out, rather than make obsolete, the Cartesian view of nature as an automatic machine, a universe of mechanical reproduction.

Picking up Bad Vibrations: Environment, Aura, Atmosphere

Although environmental writing is historically determined, and although it has been the tool of many a potent ideology, ecomimesis can allow speculation on other, more free and just, states of affairs, if only in the negative. This is far from saying that it could be our salvation or medicine. Ecological criticism wants desperately to market new brands of medicine. The qualities of ecomimesis affect our ideas of what "negative" or "critical" means. If all forms of positive ecological poetry are compromised by setting up an idea of nature "over there," how about trying a negative path? This is also problematic. Claiming that valid ecological art falls short of a nature that necessarily cannot be included within it makes a success of failure—a Romantic solution that makes the earth as impenetrably real, and as distant and intangible, as the modern forces against which it is raging.[55] In Derrida's words, negative theology establishes a *hyperessential* being beyond being itself.[56]

Delving into ambience is about exploring the aesthetic, since aestheticization maintains the beautiful soul—hence its apparent *beauty* (of course Hegel means this ironically). The beautiful soul holds all ideas at a distance. Aestheticism is the art-religion of distance. Collapse the distance, and beautiful soul syndrome is cut at the root. This argument itself entirely runs the risk of beautiful soul syndrome. It could see all positions as flawed, except its own, and remain untouched in perfect, beautiful isolation, safe in the (non)position that is its own resistance to coming down firmly somewhere or other. The collapse of distance would consist in owning up to the contingency of one's own ecological desires.

Benjamin and Adorno raised ambience to a new, potent pitch. The idea of *field* explored in Chapter 2 gains a much more fruitful resonance in Benjamin, who politicizes it: the potential for political action is a field of vectors. The idea of a historical "moment" grasps the importance of momentum. The peculiarly charged atmosphere Benjamin detects in modern cultural forms is what he and Adorno call *force field*—a cluster of apparently unrelated elements that resonates with significance.[57] This *Jetztzeit* or nowness is an intense signifying atmosphere that erupts out of the "homogeneous empty time" of official reality, even when the ideological machinery is running smoothly.[58] All is not lost in a consumerist universe, if only because the junk that surrounds us is so inconsistent. Its inconsistency has the quality of a clue. This clue is the secret of suffering curled up inside the very dimension of the object.

For conservative ecocriticism, the author, the literal content of the text, the referent, are all celebrated unequivocally, as if what "postmodern theorists" needed was a thorough soaking in a midwestern thunderstorm, as the introduction to Karl Kroeber's *Ecological Literary Criticism* puts it.[59] The authority of nature, especially of "place," is uncritically celebrated. A biological basis is sought for social forms: reading Jane Austen becomes an adaptive survival trait.[60] Ecofeminism, apparently the most progressive ecocritical genre, tends toward biological essentialism; though the radical utopianism of 1970s ecofeminism is surely better than the rather watered-down Habermasian version that is now emerging. Coupled with this enforcement of reality is a repetitive claim to be able to spy ecotopia, to be able to see the future—an augury of experience as opposed to innocence. Even ecological apocalypticism has a streak of wishful thinking. At least we can witness the disaster occurring. Is it too much to suggest that we may even take pleasure in it?

Conservative ecocriticism translates ecological crisis into a program for reading the text. The text's significance is conceived as a scarcity that must be conserved. Postmodernism generates a population growth of different and deviant interpretations that must be curbed. Left ecocriticisms have not developed properly yet. There are some skeptical comments on ecocriticism, for instance, in Dana Phillips's *The Truth of Ecology*. But skepticism does not imagine alternatives. Moreover, ecocriticism has either not engaged with, or has positively shunned, "theory"—notably deconstruction. What better time, then, to focus upon Benjamin, who has been claimed variously by deconstruction and Marxism, as a theorist with whom ecocritique could engage productively. Just as Thomas De Quincey, the Romantic consumerist par excellence, is ironically a superb theorist of environmental art, so Benjamin, fascinated with the consumerism that brought De Quincey to prominence, is an ally of ecocritique. Ecocritique needs a figurehead as significant on the left as Heidegger has been on the right. It needs to be able to argue for a progressive view of ecology that does not submit to the atavistic authority of feudalism or "prehistoric" primitivism (New Age animism). It requires, instead, that we be nostalgic for the future, helping people figure out that the ecological "paradise" *has not occurred yet.*

At least two terms Benjamin developed are relevant to the study of aesthetics and atmosphere. An ecological-critical use of Benjamin would develop his key notions of *aura* and *distraction (Zerstreuung).* The tantalizingly brief and very suggestive remarks on aura in Benjamin's writing on technical reproducibility use the analogy (but is it an analogy?) with an (aesthetic) experience of the natural world. The aura is a form of ambience that attaches to works of art, an atmosphere of veneration and value in which they are bathed. The environment evoked in nature writing is itself this aura. Benjamin's definition of aura is, precisely, also a definition of hypostasized Nature (with a capital *n*). The definition is chiastic, evoking nature in describing artifice: "We define the aura . . . as the unique phenomenon of a distance, however close [the object] may be. If, while resting on a summer afternoon, you follow with your eyes a mountain range on the horizon or a branch which casts its shadow over you, you experience the aura of those mountains, of that branch."[61] Benjamin evokes ecological representation. Since we are not living in the mountains, distracted in them by day-to-day tasks, we can be aesthetically captivated by them, as we can by an auratic work of art. The aura is in peril, says Benjamin, because "contemporary masses" wish "to bring things 'closer' spatially and humanly . . . Every day the urge grows stronger to get hold of an object at very close range by way of its likeness, its reproduction."[62] All realms of art are affected. Sampling and recording has done for music what photography did for painting. Chaplin lamented the introduction of sound into cinema, because it decisively altered the audience's distance toward the film, bathing the picture in an aquarium of sound. In particular the role of the acousmatic voice, which we explored in Chapter 1, is startlingly uncanny.[63]

Zerstreuung, on the other hand, de-distances and thus de-aestheticizes the object, dissolving the subject–object dualism upon which depend both aestheticization and the domination of nature. *Zerstreuung* also undermines the capitalist-ideological difference between work and leisure, which attenuates the notion of labor and is a reflection of alienated labor. When people are involved in their work, they experience, and produce, and produce *as* experience, a dissolution of the reified object and, for that matter, the reified subject. Involvement in the world is a negation process, a dissolving. There is no such "thing" as the environment, since, being involved in it already, we are not separate from it. Art as distraction does not obey the normative post-Romantic distinction between art, kitsch, and "schlock"; things are not even kitsch, but decidedly non-auratic, functional-technical objects that are seized and enjoyed and discarded without "respect." I am loath to say that *Zerstreuung* puts back together art and craft, which Romanticism had split apart, for craft now has a Romantic aura all its own; for instance, in the medievalism of a William Morris. A rigorous recycling policy would enable rather than hinder the "disrespectful" tossing away of ecological schlock.

Zerstreuung is the synesthetic mixture of "half-conscious" hearing and soft gazing and "careless" physical absorption of the "dreaming man" in the evocative opening paragraph of Wordsworth's *The Ruined Cottage* (11, 14, 15). *Zerstreuung* invites relaxed but critical awareness. Wordsworth shows us how to look "side-long" (16), how to maintain a critical sense even in the very moment of perceiving things as "soft" and "distant" (17–18)—as auratic and aestheticized. Wordsworth's narrator models for us something that is not so easy to think: an intelligent absorption that inoculates us against the aesthetic moralizing of the awful story of Margaret and her husband which the poem also includes, in its capacious ability to explore all kinds of ways of perceiving war and nature and social conditions. *The Ruined Cottage* is a scream whose very quietness and meditative absorption make it terribly loud. Ambience, as distraction, can indeed function in a powerfully critical way.

Like the meditation described by Trungpa Rinpoche in Chapter 2, *Zerstreuung* is a way of getting over deception, rather than falling more deeply into it. *Zerstreuung* thus contrasts sharply with the meditative bliss (Simpson: "happy situatedness") of Heidegger's peasant woman, a condition that anthropology applied to the "primitive" other.[64] Amazingly, *Zerstreuung* is a fundamental quality of Heidegger's *Dasein,* but Heidegger resists the implications of this distraction, dissemination, or dispersal. *Zerstreuung* does not imply pacifying intellectual productivity or reflexive phenomena such as irony.[65] *Zerstreuung* is the product of contemporary capitalist modes of production and technologies. Yet precisely for this reason it holds a utopian aspect, a quality of nonstupefied absorption in the environment, conceived not as reified nature "over there" outside the city or the factory gates, but "right here"—I put the phrase in quotation marks since we will see the extent to which *here* is both objectively and ontologically *in question*.

The haunting ambience typified in the space of Benjamin's Arcades is a dialectical image. Ever since the Romantic period, ambience, a complex product of automation, private property, collectivity, and new media, has generated ever more virulent forms of aestheticization. The "embedded" reporters in Iraq were virtual couch potatoes passively contemplating the aesthetics of the panoramic, ambient sound of bullets ripping through human flesh. Technology and ideology strive hand in hand to produce forms that unmercifully de-distance the object, only to reify that very de-distancing (reality TV, ambient music in corporate space). The most extreme example would be Adorno's: the "musical accompaniment" that masked the screams in the concentration camps, which he takes as an analogue for the way in which one might try to avoid measuring concepts by the "extremity" that eludes them.[66] But there is another aspect of ambience, one that precisely points out our failure to grasp something. Ambience contains unfulfilled promises of a world without boundaries, a de-aestheticized but nevertheless perceptually vivid world, in which the productive energies of boredom, distraction, irony, and other waste products of capitalism are released. A brief summary of these energies would be the notion of "unworking" *(désœuvrement)* developed in Scott Shershow's reading of Jean-Luc Nancy and Blanchot. One glimpses in radical environmental art the possibility of a radical openness to other beings, without goal.

By connecting what ecocriticism forbids us to connect—consumerism and environmentalism, even the "deep" sorts—we could do fresh ecological criticism, awake to the irony that a national park is as reified as an advertisement for an SUV. Ecocritique should aim not only at globalized capitalism, but also at the "Nature" that gets in the way of looking out for actually existing species, including the human species. In a splendid irony, the theorist of technological development par excellence supplies thinking with resources for ecological critique. Distraction hesitates between a form of politicized consumerism—*flâneurs* against the machine—and a quotidian response to modern sensory input.

Just as the beautiful soul is the subjective form of ambience, so distraction is the subjective form of the collapse of aesthetic distance. There are two types of distraction, and there is a knife-edge of discrimination between them. This makes distraction a very dangerous concept.[67] But distraction is nevertheless something we must explore. Anyway, all aesthetic solutions to the problems posed by the modern world end up reproducing the commodity form.

The first type of distraction is the ignorance born of living in a channel-surfing, easy-clean environment. Ignorance is one of the central ways in which ideology is enforced in the modern world and the United States has pioneered experiments in just how much ignorance people can tolerate. In this state of affairs, escapism proves to be more radical than sheer avoidance. At least art offers the possibility that things might be otherwise. The basic complaint against distraction, asserts Benjamin, is the "commonplace" "that the masses seek distraction whereas art demands concentration from the spectator."[68] This applies to ecology and anti-consumerism. The contemporary "slow movement," an impulse that is more arts-and-crafts than Luddite, which praises the idea of deceleration in "appreciating life," is a contemplative approach that is ultimately aesthetic rather than ethical or political—concentrating rather than being distracted. The aggressive speed of modern technological existence *is* destroying the planet as we knew it. But reclining our aircraft seat to contemplate this is not a good solution. Far from giving us a smoother ride, the deceleration process that is ecocritique makes us notice contradictions and inconsistencies.

The second type of distraction is critical absorption.[69] This form is enabled by two phenomena: synesthesia and the inherent emptiness of the perception dimension. Children's toys are good examples of synesthetic things, evoking a range of responses from eyes, ears, touch, and smell all at once. Food is profoundly synesthetic. It goes in our mouths while we look around the table. The synesthetic manifold makes it impossible to achieve the distance necessary to objectify and aestheticize the object. Far from generating the smoothness of the Wagnerian total work of art, where music, theater, and other media are fused together to create a compelling phantasmagorical sheen, synesthesia makes clear that experience is fragmented and inconsistent. Benjamin's argument about art in our times works its way through the aesthetic dimension all the way to the perceptual level. Aesthetics derives from perception (Greek *aisthanesthai,* "to perceive"). But the history of the aesthetic has been the story of how bodies, and especially nonvisual sense organs, have been relegated and gradually forgotten, if not entirely erased. Benjamin claims that "the tasks which face the human apparatus of perception at the turning points of history cannot be solved by optical means, that is, by contemplation, alone. They are mastered gradually by habit, under the guidance of tactile appropriation." "Reception in a state of distraction" would be more akin to walking through a building than to contemplating a canvas.[70]

Perceptual events only appear in difference to one another. Phenomenology has delineated how perception involves a dynamic relationship with its objects. Current neurophysiology is developing a quantum theory of perception, borrowing the Gestalt idea of the phi phenomenon—the way the mind joins up strobing, flickering images to obtain the illusion of movement. But instead of confirming a holistic world in which object and subject fit each other like a hand in a glove, the reduction of perception to a sequence of dots enables us to demystify it. The perception dimension is effectively devoid of independent, determinate conceptual contents.

In his project for an aesthetics of nature, Gernot Böhme has suggested that "atmosphere" is inherently differential. By moving from one atmosphere to another we become aware of them.[71] This is not rigorous enough. Since atmosphere, as Böhme allows, is a phenomenological thing—since it involves consciousness as well as an object of some kind, which is itself a manifold of bodily sensation and events happening outside the body—then it is inevitably not only spatial but also temporal. A shower of rain is atmospherically different if you stand in it for two hours, as opposed to five minutes. The "same" atmosphere is never the "same" as itself.

This is a matter not of ontological nicety, but of political urgency. The notion of atmosphere needs to expand to include temporality. *Climate* (as in climate change) is a vector field that describes the momentum of the atmosphere—the rate at which the atmosphere keeps changing. A map of atmospheric momentum would exist in a phase space with many dimensions. The neglect of temporality in thinking about the weather is why it is practically impossible to explain to people that global warming might result in pockets of cooling weather.

Even more strictly, atmosphere is subject to the same paradox as identity—it does for the weather what identity does for the idea of self. For something to resemble itself it must be different—otherwise it would just *be* itself and there would be no resemblance. Identity means "being the same as" oneself (Latin *idem*, "the same as"). Since an atmosphere requires a perceiver, just as a text requires a reader, its identity is always a matter of resemblance. The re-mark, which differentiates between what is inside and outside its frame, also appears on the inside of the frame. A cloud of flower scent is only "an" atmosphere (consistent and unique) because an act of framing differentiates itself from the other smells that are pervading the vicinity. In this respect, the ambient stasis we were examining in Chapter 1 is yet another example of an illusion of something lying "in between"—a moving stillness. Even conventional visual art, which is read over time, is not utterly still.

Perception is a process of differentiation. It involves Derridean *différance*, that is, both differing and deferment. There is a quality of "to come" built into hearing, touching, seeing, tasting, smelling. Perception appears utterly direct: this is a red ball; that is a quiet sound. But a process by which objects of sense perceptions differ from each other, like words in a text, underpins this directness. Our capacity to "make things out" is also an ability to hold things in abeyance; we can't tell what something "is" yet; we need to keep looking. Thinking like this retains aesthetics as a basis for ethics, but in a paradoxical way.[72] Curiously, the emptiness of perception guarantees that perceptual events are not just nothing. A certain passion and desire are associated with perception. In the perception dimension, belonging has dissolved into longing.

Unless we are rigorous about perception and the philosophy and politics of distraction, it is likely that distraction will become a political version of the "new and improved" syndrome. We could regard distraction as a special aesthetic appreciation, hovering nicely in between aestheticizing objectification and tuning out altogether. Any critical bite would be lost. This is urgent, since art is now being produced that wants to internalize distraction. Ambient music is music you do not have to listen to front and center. You cannot take in an installation like a painting on a wall. And, at the level of ecology, we are being asked to bathe in the environing ocean of our surroundings as a means to having a better ethical stance toward species and ecosystems. "Automated" critique—sitting back, relaxing, and letting the system do it for you—is just ignorance, the first kind of distraction. At some level, respecting other species and ecosystems involves a choice. This choice is saturated with contingency (it is our choice) and desire (we want something to be otherwise). There is no place outside the sphere of this contingent choice from which to stand and assess the situation—no "nature" outside the problem of global warming that will come and fill us in on how to vote. Ecology has taken us to a place of "no metalanguage," in the strong Lacanian sense. Even the position of knowing *that* cannot exist outside the dilemma we are facing. This is elegantly summed up by Bruno Latour, writing on the 1997 Kyoto meetings to tackle global warming: "Politics has to get to work *without* the transcendence of nature."[73]

To dissolve the aura, then, is rigorously to interrogate the atmosphere given off by ecomimesis. In Romantic, modern, and postmodern hands, ecomimesis is a "new and improved" version of the aesthetic aura. By collapsing the distance, by making us feel "embedded" in a world at our fingertips, it somehow paradoxically returns aura to art with a vengeance. If we get rid of aura too fast, the end result is abstract expressionist eco-schlock that would look good on the wall of a bank. But what would a slow-motion approach to aura look like? We could start by ruthlessly standing up to the intoxicating atmosphere of aura. Seeing it with clear, even utilitarian eyes, lyrical atmosphere is a function of *rhythm:* not just sonic and graphic rhythm (the pulse of marks on the page and sounds in the mouth), but also the rhythm of imagery, the rhythm of concepts. The juxtapositions in Wordsworth and Blake set up complex rhythms between different kinds and levels of framing device. If atmosphere is a function of rhythm then it is literally a *vibe:* a specific frequency and amplitude of vibration. It is a material product rather than a mystical spirit—it is as mystical as a heady perfume or narcotic fumes.

This takes us to a strange point, an intersection between Benjamin, relentless critic of the aura, and Adorno, paradoxical champion of aura. Adorno insists that we not get rid of aura too soon, for precisely the reason that it may return with a vengeance, in an even more commodified, "culinary" form. Strangely, a careful appreciation of aura can open up the *Erschütterung* or "shaking" of the subject, the lyrical "I." In the words of Adorno and Robert Kaufman, this tremor of subjectivity "can break down the hardening of subjectivity . . . [dissolving] 'the subject's petrification in his or her own subjectivity' and hence can allow the subject to catch . . . the slightest glimpse beyond that prison that it [the 'I'] itself is', thus permitting 'the "I," once 'shaken, to perceive its own limitedness and finitude' and so to experience the critical possibility of thinking otherness."[74] In Adorno's words, "The aesthetic shudder . . . cancels the distance held by the subject"—"For a few moments the I becomes aware, in real terms, of the possibility of letting self-preservation fall away."[75]

Adorno probably would have gone crazy at the mere thought of it, but I am suggesting here that the strictly vibrational *rhythm* of atmosphere is the material induction of this shudder. Contra Heidegger, the earth does not stand still in lyric. It does not reveal a world or a destiny.

If it opens, it opens much too much, swallowing us up. This is the very quality that Blanchot calls the "earth" of poetry.[76] Embodied in the sonic and graphic materiality of the text, the earth quakes, setting up a subject quake, a tremor of the "I." What remains after our long delve into the fake otherness of ecomimesis is the fragility of an "I" that we can't quite get rid of, but that at least can be made to vibrate, in such a way that does not strengthen its aggressive resolve (like a hammer or a boot), but that dissolves its form, however momentarily.

Mind the Gap: Place in Question

I take my section title from the signs and audio instructions (intoned in the Queen's English) on the London Underground, to watch the space between the platform and the train. I take it to mean not simply paying attention to gaps (including the clothing store we visited in Chapter 2). "Mind the gap" can also signify that the experiences of *place* and of *mind* are not ones of fullness but of emptiness.

Since the aesthetic is caught in ideas of place, analyzing them would help the critique of the aesthetic beautiful soul. Romantic ecology seeks a place away from the enervating, phantasmagoric illusions of city life, as well as the industry, dirt, and noise. Might one do something perverse and *combine* the fantasy thing of Romantic ecology—the resonant idea of *place*—with the thinking generated by critical consumerism and its ultimate paragon, the urban stroller, the De Quincey, the Baudelaire? It should not be impossible in principle, since nature is already the quintessence of kitsch. But it appears so. It is as if there is a critical discourse of the *country* and a critical discourse of the *city,* to match the other ways in which the country and the city have been kept apart in poetics and ideology. But as David Harvey pleads, ecology must engage with urbanization to have critical relevance in the twenty-first century.[77] Raymond Williams points out with great force that the ultimate wilderness experience is conveyed in Wordsworth's depiction of "a man walking, as if alone, in [city] streets."[78] Having said all that, let us go about this counterintuitively, and take a stroll in the philosophical countryside. It is time to pay another visit to Martin Heidegger.

Casey's *The Fate of Place* tells of how place went from being a fully fledged philosophical concept, wholly different from space, to a nonthing, an empty or arbitrary demarcation, at most a subjective experience rather than a concrete entity. It started with the idea of infinity, promoted in medieval Neoplatonic thinking on the nature of God. The evacuation of place reached its apex in the idea of space as a system of mathematical points (Newton, Descartes, and Locke). The rise of commercial capitalism, with its necessary abstractions of time and space, and the development of technologies such as mapping, transformed objective place into a pie in the sky, at best a dream to which Romantic poetry could longingly aspire. Just as the concept of space colonized the idea of place, so actual capitalism and colonialism turned feudal and pre-feudal places into just more capital, until now, the age of "glocal" shopping outlets, where little fragments of place persist like homeless people huddling against the bleak surfaces of consumerist convenience.

It seems we have lost something. But what if the story were more complicated? What if we had not exactly *lost* something? Surely the loss must at least be recoverable in some way, if ecological politics has any chance of success. What if, delving more deeply, we couldn't *lose* place because we never *had* it in the first place? What if the idea of place as a substantial "thing" with clear boundaries was itself in error? Not that there is *no such thing* as place at all, but that we've been looking for it—in the wrong place?

Rather than wondering how to bridge the unbridgeable gap between the beautiful soul and the world, ecological thinking might pose another kind of question. Indeed, to pose a question is to reveal how our sense of place and what we mean by terms such as *question, aporia,* or *wonder,* are interconnected. What if globalization, via an ironic negative path, revealed that place was never very coherent *in the first place?* Notice the difference here between stating that place as such does not exist at all, and saying that its existence is not as an independent, definable object "over there" somewhere. Place, if anything, is slippery *because* it exists, but not in the way in which, conventionally, mathematical axioms or empirical objects, or, indeed, ideals structurally beyond our reach, exist. Globalization compels us to rethink the idea of place, not in order to discard it, but to strengthen it, and to use it in a more thorough critique of the world that brought about mass hunger, monocultures, nuclear radiation, global warming, mass extinction, pollution, and other harmful ecological phenomena.

Place is caught up in a certain *question.* It takes the form of a questioning, or questioning attitude. Phenomenology has come closest to understanding place as a provisional yet real "thing." Heidegger has most powerfully described place as open and beyond concept. But Heidegger, infamously, solidifies this very openness, turning history into destiny and leaving the way open for an extreme right-wing politics, which can easily assimilate ecological thinking to its ideological ends, precisely because ecological thinking is highly aestheticized. The Nazis passed original laws to protect animals and (German) forests as ends in themselves.[79] Giorgio Agamben observes, succinctly, that this thinking of being as destiny and project is only undermined when we think of humans and animals as connected in a profound inactivity, or *désoeuvrement* (unworking).[80] Here is the utopian side of ambience's imagining of rest and relaxation.

Instead of running away from Heidegger, left scholarship should encounter him all the more rigorously in seeking to demystify place, in the name of a politics and poetics of place. We must put the idea of place into question; hence an ecological criticism that resists the idea that there is a solid metaphysical bedrock (Nature or Life, for instance) beneath which thinking cannot or should not delve. In the rush to embrace an expanded view, the plangent, intense rhetoric of localism, the form of ecological thinking that seems most opposed to globalization and most resistant to modern and postmodern decenterings and deconstructions, must not be allowed to fall into the hands of reactionaries. Instead, the central fixations upon which localism bases its claims must be examined. A left ecology must "get" even further "into" place than bioregionalism and other Romantic localisms.[81] Only then can progressive ecocriticism establish a firm basis for exploring environmental justice issues such as environmental racism, colonialism, and imperialism. This basis is a strong theoretical approach. If we restrict our examination to the citation of ecological "content"—listing what is included and excluded in the thematics of the (literary) text—we hand over aesthetic form, the aesthetic dimension and even theory itself, to the reactionary wing of ecological criticism. The aesthetic, and in a wider sense perception, must form part of the foundation of a thoroughly transnational ecological criticism. If we do not undertake their task, virulent codings of place will keep rearing their ugly heads.

Place need not be a *thing*. It is with the idea of *thing* that Heidegger's meditation on the work of art as a special place begins. Heidegger tries to de-reify the idea of the thing. The work of art tells us something about the nature of the thing. It is an opening, a "place" where phenomena become available to us; a sense of the "thingliness" of things covered over or denied in the notion of the thing as formed matter (a derivation, claims Heidegger, from the status of equipment), or the thing as a perceptual manifold of substance and accidence. Heidegger's reading of the peasant shoes poetically renders the way in which these humble things gather together the entire environment, the social and natural place, of the peasant woman. Heidegger's description opens the shoes to the "earth" (the things that are not worked on by or with human hands), and to the "world" (the historical/cultural dimension in which the shoes are used and gain significance). Similarly, the Greek temple, a product of the "world" of Greek cultural/historical projects, opens the space it inhabits such that we perceive the "earth," the stoniness of the stone, the "breadth" of the sky.[82] In another essay, it is the bridge that makes possible the riverbank as a specific place.[83] Poetry *is* place, for Heidegger. In some deep sense, it actually saves the earth— sets it "free into its own presencing."[84]

Heidegger turns the shoes inside out to reveal the environment in which they come to exist. But why, anachronism aside, did he choose a dirty pair of peasant shoes rather than, say, something like a box-fresh pair of sneakers made in a sweatshop and worn in the projects? The environmentalness of the shoes is a function of modern capitalist society despite Heidegger's best efforts to disguise this fact. There is an ideological flavor to the substance of Heidegger's description. It is a form of Romanticism: countering the displacements of modernity with the politics and poetics of place. The gesture is always aware of its futility. It is a cry of the heart in a heartless world, a declaration that if we just think hard enough, the poisoned rain of modern life will come to a halt. Meyer Shapiro's argument that these are a city dweller's shoes undermines the lyrical heft of the passage, which does appear tied to a heavy investment in the primitive and the feudal. But even on Heidegger's own terms, the shoes are distinctly modern, in their very primitivism.[85]

Romantic environmentalism is a flavor of modern consumerist ideology. It is thoroughly urban, even when it is born in the countryside. The poet who told us how to wander lonely as a cloud also told us for the first time what it felt like to be lonely in a crowd. Wordsworth's descriptions of London are among the most "environmental" of his entire oeuvre.[86] So Heidegger tries to re-establish the idea of place. He goes so far as to state that we could not have space without place: the sureness of place enables us to glimpse the openness of space itself.[87] Heidegger finds an answer to the question of place. This is ironic, since his idea of place is one of the most open and seemingly nonreified ones we could imagine. Indeed, for Heidegger, place is the very opposite of closing or closure. Place is the aperture of Being.[88] Heidegger, however, closes the very idea of openness. Place becomes a component of fascist ideology. The shoes are not randomly chosen. Heidegger could have used a photograph of a dam, but the peasant shoes are the ideological fantasy object of a certain regressive strain in nationalism.

Urban modernity and postmodernity are already included even in pastoral/idyllic evocations of place, both inside and outside the artwork. Edward Thomas's "Adlestrop," which allows us to reflect upon the ambient sounds of the English countryside, is enabled by a train journey. When the "express train" stops "unwontedly" at the eponymous station, when, in other words, the "world" of the train (in Heidegger's language) is interrupted, the passengers are able to sense the earth. The express train necessarily traverses the space between cities. Notice the first wrinkle in the Heideggerian view. The earth actually interrupts the world—Heidegger's term is "jut"—so that the more *world* we have, the more *earth* juts through; thus giving rise to the problem of the ambiguous role of technology.[89] Cities are present in the negative, even in this little Edwardian poem about an overlooked place.

Art simultaneously opens up the earth and carves out a world in that earth. Heidegger tends secretly to side with technology rather than Being, despite his stated intentions. In fact, we could parody his view by declaring the obvious truth that the environment (earth) has become more present precisely because humans have been carving it up and destroying it so effectively. What remains of earth, on this view, is really a ghostly resonance in the artwork itself. Perhaps all the environmental art being produced both in high art and in kitsch (from experimental noise music to Debussy for relaxation), is actually a symptom of the loss of the existing environment as noncultural, nonhistorical *earth*. Heidegger, the philosopher engrossed in deep ecological assaults on modern times, turns out to work for the other side. As Avital Ronell brilliantly demonstrated, the Heideggerian call of conscience, that which reminds us of our earthbound mission, is imagined as an all-too-technological telephone call.[90]

Now consider a further wrinkle. Thomas's poem is an answer to a question, implied in the first word, "Yes" (1). Not necessarily a direct question ("What is Adlestrop?" would be a *Jeopardy*-style question-as-answer), but an invitation to meditate on the place, Adlestrop. Hanging over the poem, and over the place, is the *question*. The poem delves into Adlestrop as the question hangs in the air of thought, its eyes getting wider, just as the sense of hearing in the poem expands outward into space. Place, then, is potentially endless. Even if it is tiny or intimate, it has an inbuilt questioning quality. The objective correlative in the poem for this sense of tentative exploration is the list. We cannot help wanting to expand this list, even as the poem restricts our ability to do so and captures us in a sense of boundary that evokes not just nature but also nation, a sense of home even though the passengers are "away."

"Adlestrop" conjures a metaphysics of place that establishes differences between inside and outside, here and there, even as it seems to erase the boundaries momentarily in its evocation of expanding ambient sound. The poem *knows* this even as it disavows it, and it cannot present *place* as solid without relying on *other* places: the wider county, other counties, the sense of "over there" where the train has come from and where it is going. This otherness is encoded within the poem's very typography. The blankness between the second and third verses cannot be read as "pure" empty space but as a spacing, a stretching of the gap between "name" [the name of the station] and "And willows . . ." that marks the start of ecorhapsody.

The gap enacts the slowing down and expanding perception of the narrator in the railway carriage, who tunes in to the surrounding environment. It is a synesthetic moment in which the "name" dissolves and we notice what lies, and flies, around it. The name becomes placed: literally, it is the station sign, posted in concrete. The "textmark" becomes a landmark.[91] But, as in the optical illusion of faces and candlestick, the reverse is also true. The name is already the space that gets incarnated in the gap between the verses. Its very blankness and opacity is what enables the musing mind to read into and around it. Moving from one station to the next becomes a metaphor for moving from one word to another in a sentence. Landmarks become textual. The poem puts out its ears, meditatively but also scientifically, like a probe newly landed on Mars. Just before it closes upon the metaphysics of land (Oxfordshire and Gloucestershire), "Adlestrop" produces an uncertain, open space, a "vanishing mediator" between ideology (knowing where you are) and science (open to new data); and furthermore, between sheer space—being open—and wondering—the slightest beginnings of an impulse to get metaphysical. We have already lost this vanishing mediator, this speed bump, by the time we figure out that we passed over it. We can be sure that it can never be fully and thoroughly inhabited. Place has been hollowed out from the inside.

Place, even according to this Edwardian miniature, is radically indeterminate—it is intrinsically in question, *is* a question. When I am "here," here includes a sense of "there." *Here* is precisely *not there.* Even if we are not living in a point-based universe, this idea of "there" is intrinsic to "here." It *is* here, in some way, such that *here* is shot through with *there*. Here is not a solid thing. I mean this much more strongly than Heidegger when he claims, "The human being is a creature of distance!"[92] This idea of distance ultimately aestheticizes the idea of *here*. *Here* becomes an object we are gazing at through the glass shop window of aestheticization. Quite the opposite. We are so involved in *here* that it is constantly dissolving and disappearing. It is not where we look for it. *Here is a question*; indeed, *here is question*. Heidegger's word for the dispersal that fractures *Dasein* from within, thrown as it is into the world, into a particular place? *Zerstreuung*.[93]

The environment is that which cannot be indicated directly. We could name it apophatically. It is not-in-the-foreground. It is the background, caught in a relationship with a foreground. As soon as we concentrate on it, it turns into the foreground. In ecological terms, nature becomes bunny rabbits, trees, rivers, and mountains—we lose its environmental quality, though this is what we wanted to convey. We are compelled to rely on ecomimesis, a list that gestures toward infinity. The environment *is* the "what-is-it?", the objectified version of our question. As soon as it becomes an exclamation it has been disappeared. And the list itself is perilous in this regard, because it will necessarily exclude something (cities, pylons, races and classes, genders). Simply adding something to the list that ends in an ellipsis and the word *nature* is wrong from the start.

In sum, *environment is theory*—theory not as answer to a question, or as instruction manual (what is the theory behind that dishwasher?) but as question, and question mark, as *in question*, questioning-ness. The best environmental art is deconstructed from the inside. As theory it retains its fullest existence as questioning—internally fractured by doubt, stronger than English skeptical empiricism (we know the ideological uses of that) or mystical feudalism (we know the ideological uses of *that*). Ecocriticism's concepts and rhetorics of environment must give way to something more theoretical.

We are beginning to see how to sidle out of the Looking Glass House of the beautiful soul. Beautiful soul syndrome is entangled with ambience. How about basing ecological poetics and politics on no-self (and thus on no-nature)? Wherever I look for my self I only encounter a potentially infinite series of alterities: my body, my arm, my ideas, place of birth, parents, history, society . . . The same goes for nature. Wherever we look for it, we encounter just a long metonymic string of bunnies, trees, stars, space, toothbrushes, skyscrapers . . . Of course, where the list ends is telling. But the issue is deeper still. Attempts to found a politics and philosophy on a view of self, however sublimated and radically alternative to a Cartesian view, involve us in an aporia. These "new and improved" versions of identity never entirely get rid of the paradoxes of the idea of self from which they deviate. And yet the ultimate paradox is that wherever we look for the self, we won't find it. That we won't find the self where we look for it is the message of Buddhism and deconstruction, but it is also the message of Lacan's sustained reading of Descartes' cogito.

Lacan develops the cogito, which prejudice construes as utterly rigid, into this outrageously convoluted statement that opens up the possibility of the unconscious, or at any rate, the radically nonidentical quality of mind itself: "I am not wherever I am the plaything of my thought. I think of what I am where I do not think to think."[94] The convolution is eloquent. It speaks to the radical way in which displacement exists at the kernel of the self. It is devastating to the idea that the Cartesian ego is a solid, centered thing. And yet it also undermines the idea that ecological sympathy ripples out from an equally centered self in widening concentric circles. This image has been defended by supporters of Spinoza's monism, and was made popular by the poets Pope and Thomson. The age of sensibility in the later eighteenth century developed the image of widening circles, which eventually found its way into environmental philosophies such as J. Baird Callicott's. Lacan associates his complication of Descartes with the Copernican revolution that displaced the earth as the center of the universe, and the Freudian revolution that discovered the unconscious.

Place as question is *internal* to the very question of self, of that which is located in place. Thus, we return to the epigraph, and Descartes' act of situating himself at the start of the *Meditations*, in a way that should now ironically call to mind any phenomenologist worth his or her ecological salt: "I am here, sitting by the fire, wearing a dressing gown, holding this page in my hand."[95] I venture the provocative, probably heretical and certainly, to many ecological ears, blasphemous, idea that Descartes, the whipping boy of ecological discourse, may have something to tell us about place. Wasn't it Descartes who helped to get us into this mess, with his idea of the skin-encapsulated ego, as so many ecologically minded writers have observed?[96] At least post-structuralists and ecocritics can agree that they hate Descartes.

The *Meditations* climaxes with the cogito, transitioning through a phase of radical doubt. But the text opens in the seemingly innocent scene, where the warm ambience of the fire and the satisfaction to the body that it bestows enable the thinking process to take place. The self depends upon its environment. "I think" depends upon the "I am" of

"I am here, sitting by the fire." Moreover, the very philosophy of the self depends upon this environment, as Descartes starts to subject his innocent situatedness to a series of doubts that hollow out that comfortable place by the fire. "I am here" depends upon a sense of doubt, which leads us to the cogito: I think therefore I am (that is here, sitting by a fire). We are on a Möbius strip whose either side twists about the other. We cannot designate one (either "self" or "place") as ontologically prior.

The Cartesian situation contains a double-take, which Descartes registers by wondering why he shouldn't be dreaming that he is beside a fire—surely a question that any satisfied, comfortable person may ask, relatively unaware of his or her bodily determinacy. The echo effect discussed in Chapter 1 works here. Doubt retroactively corrodes the snugness of situating oneself beside a fire. Alleviated of suffering, the self stops to wonder whether it is dreaming or not. Place is a function of suffering. "This land is my land" is a symptom of injustice. The politics of place, then, is a struggle to achieve a state in which the question of place, the question that is place, can emerge *as* a question. Utopia would thus look more like critique and debate than an affirmation. Ultimately, ecological politics should not be about dissolving the dualism of subject and object. It should be about conquering aggression and violence.

Home is the strangest place. It is strange in its very homeliness, as Freud observed. Indeed, *here* is strange in itself. To see a place in its strangeness is not just to see how it is permeated with otherness. That could collapse into racism: otherness immigrates and I'm ready with my gun. Within a horizon, you can indeed be aware of "another" place over yonder. Appreciating strangeness is seeing the very strangeness of similarity and familiarity. To reintroduce the uncanny into the poetics of the home (*oikos*, ecology, ecomimesis) is a political act. Cozy ecological thinking tries to smooth over the uncanny, which is produced by a gap between being human and being a person—by the very culture which is necessitated ironically because humans emerge from the womb premature, that is, as beings of flesh without a working sense of self.

Freud never directly says why "silence, darkness and solitude" evoke the uncanny, though he does say that *it has been said,* somewhere else—this is itself uncanny.[97] Perhaps beyond "infantile anxiety," silence, darkness, and solitude evoke the difference that *is* identity, whether or not there is someone there just round the corner, whether or not there is a sound one cannot quite hear, a form one cannot quite see. The darkness (an objective correlative for the subject itself, which is a negation process) is a palpable presence. Identity (being the same as yourself) implies difference. Place *is* question.

What Freud says about the fear of the power of a "childlike/primitive" mind (mimetic mind, which mimes reality so perfectly as to *be* and thus to *create* it)—that we fear the suggestion of the omnipotence of thoughts—also sounds like a fear of "civilized" mind! We fear that we can never surmount entirely this magical mind which acts just like a computer, like a thing that thinks—in short, the Cartesian *res cogitans*. The poetic version of this feeling is the delight in the fantastic, in the writerly quality of writing, that it could go on forever spawning image after image—images that evoke reality better than reality does; that writing and language is a *thing* that *thinks on our behalf*. Ecomimesis tries to efface, in the very face of its own "extra-vagance,"[98] this automatic element of writing.[99] This is ironic, because ecological science, with its three-kilometer ice cores and its close reading of the weather, has transformed the environment into a gigantic library, a palimpsest of texts *waiting to be read*. The old metaphor of the book of nature has returned, without an index.

In his study of the uncanny, Freud oscillates between talking about it as the experience of a self and as the experience of a place.[100] What is "in here" and "out there" fold and redouble and entangle and cross over themselves in ways that we have noticed to be ambient. Darkness, silence, and solitude are all good images of ambience, either as empty frame or as unframed thing. The Romantic use of simple (familiar) language, and especially of repetition, introduces a very strong rhythm of the uncanny, like a wave of tone. Strangeness is associated with rhythm because repetition evokes strangeness. Familiarity in poetics is repetition, rhythm; even imagery can have rhythm. A "vibe" or atmosphere is rhythmic: it comes "again and again" when we are "lost in a forest, all alone."[101] Forests are iterations of trees, and hence highly uncanny. Freud's exemplary image of the uncanny is of being lost in one: "when one is lost in a forest in high altitudes, caught, we will suppose, by the mountain mist, and when every endeavor to find the marked or familiar path ends again and again in a return to one and the same spot, recognizable by some particular landmark."[102] The forest is a quintessential image of the text, which is why we say "he can't see the wood for the trees." We are always trying to make forests into wholes.

The rhythm of imagery can invoke something extra, a third thing, De Quincey's *syncope*. The stichomythia in *Macbeth* evokes the space of horror just after Duncan's murder. In "Adlestrop," "and" elides "but"—something is being passed over which returns as a present absence. "Yes" implies a prior conversation, unspoken, and an interruption. "I remember Adlestrop" repeats the title. When we arrive at "The name" this third repetition makes the name familiarly unfamiliar. Even "original" experience is shot through with memory. The reverse form of the poem suggests a premonition—we "remember" Adlestrop before we experience it. Imagery, the textual repetition of the thing, has an uncanny afterlife that suspends the life of the reader.[103] The concentric expanding circles of home and nation at the end are interrupted by the first two stanzas, which render the whole scene strangely (un)familiar. Our very familiarity with Adlestrop has made the cozy concentric circles of the end impossible!

Kenneth Johnston describes Wordsworth's "Home at Grasmere," a poem preoccupied with establishing a sense of place, as a strong form of ecomimesis: "The poem works toward identification with its very moment(s) of composition, toward saying, 'here am I, writing this poem.'"[104] The dilemma of ecomimesis is that you always need a bit more of it. So the more access to unmediated nature we have, the more access to the interminable of writing we have. Wordsworth suggests that there is "Something on every side concealed from view" (486). There is an overdraft facility of nature here (there's more where that came from). But constantly tapping it suggests bankruptcy rather than richness.

Wordsworth talks about "consummating" the marriage of mind and world ("Home at Grasmere," 811). The sexual innuendo is a sophisticated response to the problem of nature. Are we trying to get rid of *duality* in our urge to get rid of *dualism*? If we turn all of nature into subject then we lose its otherness. If we turn it into object then we lose its nonreified quality. If we say nature is "subject plus object" then we mix the unmixable and relapse into the original dualism. And if we say it is neither, then we fall into nihilism. When Wordsworth reduces eros to "fitting and fitted" in the Prospectus part of "Home at Grasmere" (Blake: "You shall not bring me down to believe such fitting & fitted"), he reduces the interaction to one between two pieces of jigsaw puzzle—reducing the world to objects (816–821).[105] The valley loves the narrator: outrageously, the valley *is* God, and so stops being pure nature.

To love *extension*, however, is to love the thingly quality of the other, in the ultimate, Cartesian sense: to respect what is truly other about the other. *As a person*, to be sure; people are indeed bisected by a series of traumatic little pieces of grit that make the pearl of personhood, according to Wordsworth himself. But *not as a human*. So ironically the Cartesian view, which produces an unmixable asymmetry between subject and object, has an enlightened, ecologically progressive aspect that does not even differ all that much from the very shamanism from which enlightenment escapes, since shamanism, to alter only slightly the immortal words of the Coen Brothers' film *The Big Lebowski,* treats objects like people.[106] Indigenous cultures have not much time for nature as imagined in and against modernity. Animism is decidedly not nature worship. For example, according to Keith Basso's study of the Western Apache's use of narrative in the naming of places, there is no difference between a place and the socially reproving and improving stories that the Apache associate with it, and thus, there is no nature. There is no gap between the human and the nonhuman realms. The Apache view is much closer to ecology without nature than conventional ecocriticism. *Place* is indeed a questioning, a "what happened here?"[107] Animism thus turns out to have a lot in common with an ecology to come.

Relationship involves conflict, desire, asymmetry. To love the self *as res,* as thing, is the hard task and perverse act of a genuine "tree hugger." One cannot help anthropomorphism. A completely "flat" approach, one that *never* anthropomorphized and thus kept mind and matter separate altogether, would be worse. Ironically acknowledging the separation and the attempt to bridge it suggests an enlightened Cartesianism, of a kind sketched out by some very powerful arguments in Derrida's writing on forgiveness.[108] On the other hand, *must* we anthropomorphize in order to love? Ecological thinking commonly wants to claim that the inorganic world is alive. This would imply that we should treat animals and plants as ends in themselves and not as means. But the paradox is that maintaining this view denatures nature.

The very small slice of the *Meditations* in which Descartes talks about sitting by a fire opens up deep slits in a metaphysical ecological view. Descartes finds himself in advance accord not with Heidegger, for whom *I am therefore I think,* but with an unfamiliar current of Marxist thinking. In his remarks on Adolph Wagner's economics, Marx explicitly associates production with "consumption": "Men do not in any way begin by 'finding themselves in a theoretical relationship to the things of the external world.' Like every animal, they begin by *eating, drinking . . .* not by 'finding themselves' in a relationship, but by behaving actively, gaining possession of certain things in the external world by their actions, thus satisfying their needs. (They thus begin by production.)"[109] For Marx, place does not exist before we eat and drink and sit by fires. Marx's "production" includes the sensation of eating a nectarine, something that might surprise postmodern readers of Keats, let alone Baudrillard. Eating becomes praxis, a term suggesting the fusion of the theoretical with the practical. In order to be sitting by a fire, you have to satisfy certain needs.

The debate about *environment* and *world*—between humans who are able to contemplate their needs aesthetically (with distance), and animals who make do with whatever is around them—is thus a red herring.[110] Marx's own version is that humans are animals who make their own environments—try telling that to an ant. But the remark on Adolph Wagner is radically suggestive because it eliminates a common distinction between *production* and *consumption*. Is consuming, and more intensely, consumerism, a matter of some "original," "natural" or "animal" state which humans then modify or even spoil by achieving distance? Or is this distance in fact irreducible? A profound, but related, question would be: are animals capable of aesthetic contemplation?

Seeing production and consumption as not just intertwined but in some sense identical abolishes at a stroke the ontology of nature versus humanity, or the animal side of us versus the human side. It is something like what Agamben is after in his citation of Benjamin's celebration of sexual pleasure as a way out of the human/nature defile.[111] This thought affects ontology, ethics, and politics. The edifice of aesthetic environmentalism and ambience stands upon philosophically and socially solidified notions of sheer consumption, hence consumerism, defined as not-production. It seems objectively true: the Third World produces, the First consumes. Environmentalist ethics is predicated on this distinction—is it too outrageous to say that it helps sustain it? The Puritan-derived idea of wilderness is a way of performing abstinence—and likewise vegetarianism, and forms of environmentalist lifestyle: abstaining from gasoline, television, "technology" . . . The hale-and-hearty Marxoid version instigates guilt about consumerism, a guilt that is well within the parameters of the beautiful soul. For Marx, like Freud, sensuousness is only barely catered for in modern life, far from being a world of crazed pleasure. It is supremely important to think our way through pleasure and consumption, and in particular the relationship between sensuousness and the aesthetic dimension.

Dark Ecology

Lingering in the mirror world of the beautiful soul, we discern the key in the aesthetic itself. Having identified the notion of pleasure as a significant place in the argument about ecology, we soon discover pleasure's apparent opposite, the thing that we want to avoid, like all animals—pain. Ecomimesis offers the illusion of a false immediacy that is belied by the immersed yet laid-back aesthetic distance it demands. Nature, if it is anything at all, is what is immediately given, which at its simplest is pain. But in attending to environmental phenomena, aesthetic but not aestheticized, we are never sure whether they are real, originals, or copies. A melancholy emerges. It is well represented in John Carpenter's film *The Thing,* where the supposedly horrific alien is none other than the reproductive, simulative process of nature itself.[112] This reproductive process is prefigured by a computer chess program, with which the male protagonist plays, and loses, at the start of the film. Incensed by his loss, he throws a glass of whiskey onto the keyboard, destroying the computer whom he calls "bitch." When it appears, the monster (Latin *monstrare:* to display), who appears either in the guise of some other whom it has assimilated, or as bursting and pouring out of that guise in an attempt to escape, emits a sound like running water, or steam coming out of a hole, which when it gets louder resembles a melancholy roar. The Thing is destined never to be Itself. What is most horrific about it is its physical similarity to the Nietzschean crew of American explorers who attack it with flamethrowers, whose screams are indistinguishable from the Thing's slow yelping, which is never entirely distinct from the sound of a decelerated voice saying "I." In the sadness of its very capacity *not* to present immediacy, the aesthetic dimension gives body to the immediacy that hyper-aesthetic ecomimesis, pretending to be anti-aesthetic, wishes to force down our throats.

The fragile "I" addresses, or denies, this situation. *As I write . . . I am immersed in nature.* The second phrase is the metaphorical sum of the endless listing procedures of ecomimesis. "I am immersed in nature"; "I am at one with the cosmos"—these are forms of the Cretan liar paradox, a sentence such as "I am lying," whose truth claim contradicts its semantic form. Even if "I" could be immersed in nature, and still exist as an *I,* there would remain the *I* who is telling you this, as opposed to the *I* who is immersed. If we are even able to achieve ecology without nature, it will be difficult, if not impossible, and even undesirable, to achieve ecology without a subject. If reason, devoid of sadistic instrumentality, is openness to nonidentity, that is still a kind of subjectivity. We cannot come up with a "new and improved" version of identity that will do without the paradoxes and aporias associated with it.

I am immersed in nature is not a mantra whose repetition brings about its content. Thinking so is wishful thinking, otherwise known as beautiful soul syndrome. The ultimate fantasy of ambience is that we could actually achieve ecology without a subject. Ecological awareness would just happen to us, as immersively and convincingly as a shower of rain. Experimental art is not all that far from conservative ecocriticism in this regard. Both crave an automated form of ecological enjoyment. This automation is called "nature." Ecology without nature must come up with something quite different. Ecology without nature is not automated. It does not appeal to a continuum that subtends the passing show of life. Its ethics look more like perversion—or like acknowledging the perverse quality of *choice* in itself—the shutting down of possibilities, the acceptance of death. It is what *Walden* calls "liv[ing] deliberately"—without having to retreat to the woods to do so.[113]

This is *critical* choice. Consumerist ideological choice preserves the idea that we still have a choice. Critical choice shuts down the possibility of choosing again. It is a quantum choice, a "wave reduction" of choices, a one-shot deal. There is a virtue to ambient poetics. It shows us as many possibilities as possible, all superposed like Schrödinger's cat, which before we choose to observe it, remains dead and alive at the same time. As a fantasy form of consumerism, ambience exhibits a bewildering range of choices. Ambience shows us, as it were, the different kinds of shampoo in the supermarket, the supermarket shelves, the walls of the supermarket; the sound of the parking lot outside; the noise of birds and airplanes in the sky; the smell of toxic fumes. The bewildering quality of ambience intoxicates and renders inoperative the belief that there is a "thing" called nature that is "out there" beyond us. But if we dwell in ambience we make a mistake. If we "choose" it, we actually reproduce bohemian Romantic consumerism perfectly. Indeed, ideology may have become even stronger than before, since now it has been chosen reflexively. If ambience becomes the answer to all our problems, ideology really is "new and improved." It might be amusing to think that we have outwitted Heidegger or kitsch environmentalism with our inclusion of technological and artificial things in our utopian immersive space. But dwelling in ambience is not an example of critical choice.

Critical choice is a precarious leap. We will need to act on global warming, *even if* we are not strictly "responsible" for it, *even if* it will not come about. Critical choice is the way in which the beautiful soul grasps the world it has shunned. There is a note of existentialism here. Kierkegaard describes the beautiful soul in the shockingly intimate fiction, the "Seducer's Diary" in *Either/Or*.[114] The seducer sees love not as a conscious choice, hard and radically contingent, undermining self-assurance; but as the ambience in which the ego can bathe. He is obsessed with the atmosphere in which the seducee appears to him as a distanced aesthetic object, even and especially when she is sexually intimate with him. This is not simply a matter for the imagination, but of location in actually existing space: "If one sits in the middle of the room, in both directions one has a view beyond anything in the foreground, on both sides one has the endless horizon, one is alone in the wide ocean of the atmosphere."[115] Kierkegaard takes the beautiful soul through a further iteration in the aestheticization of ethics in the later section, a series of letters written to the seducer from someone praising the merits of marriage.[116] Further and further, higher and higher refinements of the aesthetic attitude do not hold out any hope that it is going to work well. Even the mystic, who wants to participate directly in the godhead, just as deep ecology wishes to immerse itself in nature, misses the object, by abstracting the choice: "his love for God has its highest expression in a feeling, a mood; in the evening twilight, in the season of mists, he melts with vague movements into one with his God."[117]

The aesthetic is not so easy to shed, however. This problem plagued Kierkegaard himself, who with all his talk of the corruption of "the aesthetic sphere" used aesthetic forms and who, at the very moment he was writing *Either/Or,* described himself as a *flâneur*.[118] We could do with a Keirkegaardian revelation of ecological writing's complicity with an infantilizing aestheticization that paradoxically works for the other side, turning the world into manipulable objects.[119] The aesthetics of nature writing is based on the ideology of raw materials and property. Nevertheless, in accomplishing his critique of the beautiful soul, Kierkegaard shuns the aesthetic dimension *too soon,* trapping himself at the Looking Glass House.[120] Instead, we should not give up on the aesthetic dimension, which is, ultimately, the reverberation of sentience (pain). If, as Derrida observes, there are only different forms of narcissism rather than narcissism and something else, the true escape from narcissism would be a dive further into it, and an extension of it (Derrida's word) to include as many other beings as possible.[121] By heightening the dilemma of a body and a material world haunted by mind(s), we care for the ecosystem, which in sum is interconnectedness. The ecological thought, the thinking of interconnectedness, has a dark side embodied not in a hippie aesthetic of life over death, or a sadistic-sentimental Bambification of sentient beings, but in a "goth" assertion of the contingent and necessarily queer idea that we want to stay with a dying world: *dark ecology.*

Now is a time for grief to persist, to ring throughout the world. Modern culture has not yet known what to do with grief. Environmentalisms have both stoked and assuaged the crushing feelings that come from a sense of total catastrophe, whether from nuclear bombs and radiation, or events such as climate change and mass extinction. Ecopsychology, pioneered by Theodore Roszak, is a form of Romantic ecology that encourages people to situate their individual suffering in a wider ecosystemic field: "Let the 'you' become the Earth and all our fellow creatures upon it. Only follow where ecological science leads in its honest effort to understand the uncanny intricacy that links us to our planetary habitat."[122] If we get rid of the grief too fast, we eject the very nature we are trying to save.

Joanna Macy and others in the nuclear guardianship movement have suggested that instead of trying to get over grief, to shut off the terrible trauma of the current ecological crisis, we simply stay with it.[123] We acknowledge it in all its meaninglessness. Žižek puts it this way in a profound passage on environmentalism.[124] Ecological apocalypticism, which closely resembles Kierkegaard's death wish for the planet, risks shutting down the admission of this meaninglessness: "Aye, let the storm break forth in still greater violence, making an end of life, and of the world . . . and in pent-up resentment sweep away the mountains and the nations and the achievements of culture."[125] Apocalypticism tries to see beyond death, to remain sighted after there is nothing left to see. In ecological apocalyptic fantasies of the last man, everyone dies— except for the viewer or the reader. They reproduce a fundamental Cartesian and semantic split between the "I" who is narrating, and the "I" who is the subject of the story.

The beautiful soul is dissolved when we recognize that we did it, we caused environmental destruction, not *you,* whoever you are.[126] Although ecological texts frequently strive to disconfirm the end of the world, their rhetoric of ecological apocalypticism revels in the idea that nature will be permanently "gone." We imagine our *own* death via nature. This has nothing to do with nature. To truly love nature would be to love what is nonidentical with us. What could be less "us" than the Cartesian idea of sheer extension? Instead of trying endlessly to get rid of the subject–object dualism, dark ecology dances with the subject–object duality: Cartesianism suffused with desire and passion— to love the thingness, not in a Heideggerian sense, but actually the mute, objectified quality of the object, its radical nonidentity. Nature is *not* a mirror of our mind. Ecological criticism should admit to the unnaturalness both of the object and of the subject: ecological desire is not chaste. The desire for a "natural" state (natural food, natural relationships, and so on) masks a compelling enjoyment.

In elegy, the person departs and the environment echoes our woe. In ecological lament, we fear that we will go on living, while the environment disappears around us. Ultimately, imagine the very air we breathe vanishing—we will literally be unable to have any more elegies, because we will all be dead. It is strictly impossible for us to mourn this absolute, radical loss. It is worse than losing our mother. It resembles the heterosexist melancholy that Judith Butler brilliantly outlines in her essay on how the foreclosure of homosexual attachment makes it impossible to mourn for it.[127] (In general, a partnership between queer theory and ecological criticism is long overdue.) We can't mourn for the environment because we are so deeply attached to it—we *are* it. Just as for Butler "the 'truest' gay male melancholic is the strictly straight man," so the truest ecological human is a melancholy dualist.[128] For Freud, melancholy is a refusal to digest the object, a sticking in the throat, an introjection. Melancholia is an irreducible component of subjectivity, rather than one emotion among many, despite recent attempts to categorize it differently. It is precisely the point at which the self is separated from, and forever connected to, the mother. Dark ecology is based on negative desire rather than positive fulfillment. It is saturated with unrequited longing. It maintains duality, if not dualism. Dark ecology is a politicized version of deconstructive hesitation or aporia. Can we be sure that that's an unfeeling machine "over there," a vermin, the evil thing? Dark ecology is a melancholic ethics. Unable fully to introject or digest the idea of the other, we are caught in its headlights, suspended in the possibility of acting without being able to act. Thus is born the awareness of the intensity and constraint of critical choice. Reframing the beautiful soul is a profound environmental act.

Luc Ferry proposes Kantian-Judaic duty as a way to be kind to animals.[129] We can because we must. But this decision is always born from an irresolvable gap. Bruno Latour defers to Kant on this point: "We can define morality as *uncertainty* about the proper relation between means and ends, extending Kant's famous definition of the obligation 'not to treat human beings simply as means but always also as ends'—provided that we *extend it to nonhumans as well,* something that Kantianism, in a typically modernist move, wanted to avoid."[130] There is something aporetic in our uncertainty as to whether animals are human or not. They remain *analogous* to the human, as our words for mimesis demonstrate, in their interchangeability with our words for primates and hominids. This melancholy attitude has an aesthetic form, in *noir* stories that establish that the narrator or protagonist is radically involved with his or her world, and thus responsible for it.

Against the affirmative talk of "dwelling" and the false immediacy of ecomimesis, the aesthetic dimension itself *does* embody, in the negative, an ecology without nature. While the classic Sherlock-Holmes type is the detective as the master, floating above the story and knowing the answer beforehand, the *noir* detective story implicates the detective in the plot. The *noir* detective finds that he is caught in a story that has crept up on him or her from behind his or her back, like history or like nature. Ecological politics has a *noir* form. We start by thinking that we can "save" something called "the world" "over there," but end up realizing that we ourselves are implicated. This is the solution to beautiful soul syndrome: reframing our field of activity as one for which we ourselves are formally responsible, even guilty.[131] It is a kind of "action," but a theoretical one. Dark ecology undermines the naturalness of the stories we tell about how we are involved in nature. It preserves the dark, depressive quality of life in the shadow of ecological catastrophe. Instead of whistling in the dark, insisting that we're part of Gaia, why not stay with the darkness?

Blade Runner is the best contemporary reading of *Frankenstein*.[132] In a version of Romantic irony, the detective Deckard becomes implicated in his analysis of the replicant femme fatale, realizing that he may be (may be) a replicant himself. The story has a pervasive atmosphere of undigested grief. Does this atmosphere have anything to benefit ecological critique? In 2019, what makes you human is your emotional response to animal suffering ("boiled dog," an upturned tortoise), while humanoid replicants are exploited and "retired" (killed) if they resist. This illusion of psychological depth, extracted in face-to-face interviews, is almost an ecomimetic ethics, like the eighteenth-century cult of sensibility. The replicants cannot identify with this sensibility, cannot put themselves into a tortoise's shoes. Yet they weep like little children because their emotional age is far younger than their implanted memories would suggest. But Deckard profoundly puts himself into the replicants' shoes. Deckard's uncanny dream, which makes us suspect that it is an implanted memory (and hence that he is not a human but a replicant) is of a *fantasy* animal, a unicorn. Society assumes the replicants

188 · Ecology without Nature

are "evil." Animals are respected, but when the stranger is too close for comfort, he or she becomes threatening. But in the story, the replicants turn out to be protagonists, fired with a revolutionary politics. *Frankenstein* and *Blade Runner* enjoin us to love people even when they are not people.

Far from being rational self-interest, ecological thought is shot through with desire. The task is to love the automatic *as* automatic. In order to mean anything at all, this love must be more excessive, exuberant, and risky than a bland extension of humanitarianism to the environment. Humanitarianism would leave the environment just as it is, as an Other "over there," a victim. In *Blade Runner* Deckard orders the femme fatale to say that she loves him and to ask him to kiss her. This could be a violation. Or perhaps it respects the fact that she *is* a doll, that to go on and on about how much he loves her would not convince her, but that to *stage* the love as a perverse script would speak the truth. It would acknowledge the objectal quality of the beloved, and thus to love her for herself rather than as a copy of a human.

Nature and *the body* have become Donna Haraway's cyborg, and *Frankenstein* and *Blade Runner* are allegories for how to carry on in a cyborg world. It is time to modify Donna Haraway's cyborg manifesto, which still brilliantly articulates the paradoxes of politicized identity. "I'd rather be a cyborg than a goddess," she writes.[133] I'd rather be a zombie than a tree hugger.[134] Leslie Marmon Silko's *Almanac of the Dead* is a vast chronicle of the undead Native Americans that refuses to become a work of mourning for them.[135] Deep Ecology buries the dead too fast (reducing everything to an expression of Gaia), while modernity tries to torch them in a familiar story of a war against matter. Meanwhile clouds of radioactive waste haunt the world. So while we campaign to make our world "cleaner" and less toxic, less harmful to sentient beings, our philosophical adventure should in some ways be quite the reverse. We should be finding ways to stick around with the sticky mess that we're in and that we are, making thinking dirtier, identifying with ugliness, practicing "hauntology" (Derrida's phrase) rather than ontology.[136] So out with the black clothes, eyeliner, and white makeup, on with the spangly music: dark ecology.

Here is the bizarre paradox. Since the machine (sheer automated extension) now stands at the basis of our models of mind, body, animal, and ecosystem, solidarity has, unexpectedly, become a *choice*. Marx sketches the possibility of arriving at a *collective* rather than a *community:* "[The indigenous farmer] has as little torn himself free from the umbilical cord of his tribe or community as a bee has from his hive . . . From the standpoint of the peasant and the artisan, capitalist co-operation does not appear as a particular historical form of co-operation; instead, co-operation itself appears as a historical form peculiar to, and specifically distinguishing, the capitalist process of production."[137] Because of the very same negative conditions, cooperation "takes place spontaneously and naturally" rather than being enforced.[138] How do collectives emerge? This is a question of which certain forms of modern biology, notably sociobiology, are fond. For E. O. Wilson the humanities and social sciences stack neatly on top of biology, chemistry, and physics.[139] In mathematics, chaos theory has also conceptualized how seemingly random events could coalesce "spontaneously and naturally." But these theories often repeat capitalist ideology. The behavior of the stock market comes to resemble that of clouds.[140] Magically, ant colonies cohere somewhere in between sheer anarchy and a minimal sense of order, rather like the citizens of Texas.[141] There is something of this in the idea of "natural capitalism" attuned to the rhythms and resources of the planet. It would somehow spontaneously emerge because it is more logical, and more profitable.[142]

This is a political version of the "new and improved" problem. Some special form of "emergence" (like Lyotard's "nuance") resides mysteriously "in between" conventional categories of order and chaos.[143] In an ultimate aestheticization of politics, we can sit back, relax, and let the automated process of self-organizing labor do it for us. Far from appearing in their uniqueness, difference, and strangeness, animals and the weather stand in for an all-too-human politics. There is a note of this in Hardt and Negri's *Empire,* a work of left uplift. The *feel* of being a communist, a description of which closes the book in an evocation of the ecologically inclusive St. Francis, resembles the feel of consumerism in its celebration of "irrepressible lightness and joy."[144] Cooperation here is not chosen.[145]

The problem of organization and control became a feature of modern art, giving rise to a new organicism. "Emergent" forms of organization are related to the old-fashioned Romantic organicism, which was also a way of resolving, aesthetically, the problems of mechanization. Environmental art, employing external, mechanical, or stochastic (random) processes of composition, is a form of new organicism. The old organicism promoted the idea that *genius* (the Classical notion of a demonic spirit that intervened between the world of gods and that of humans) was now *inside* the creative artist. One could *be* a genius. The genius created works of *art*, rather than *craft*, opening up a class distinction at the level of production. These creations behaved like autonomous beings with their own "life." Organic form was "the sign of a life which is able to shape and develop itself from within: the form corresponds to the life rather than to an external model."[146]

In the new organicism, genius is relocated outside the artist, who becomes the facilitator, the conductor. The artist establishes certain parameters, and then watches to see what will happen. In effect, he or she assumes the attitude of the consumerist. Consider a score by La Monte Young, one of the inventors of the sound-and-light Dream Syndicate in New York City: "Turn a butterfly (or any number of butterflies) loose in the performance area . . . the doors and windows may be opened, and the composition finishes when the butterfly flies away."[147] Content fits form, just as in the old organicism. There is no predetermined closure. But this fit takes place on the "outside," in the real rather than in the imaginary. Or at least, that is the idea.

Externalized *genius* has returned to the idea of the *genius loci,* the spirit of the place, which the artist tries to capture, albeit with more technically sophisticated means (subsonic microphones, stochastic techniques, improvisation). The air is a deformed, shapeless, exteriorized version of the poetic self. In diastic poetry by Jackson Mac Low or Jeffrey Robinson an algorithmic process determines what words are selected from a base text: say a combination of letters in a word is chosen—the poet finds words in the base text that begin with the letter in that word. Romanticism, especially as propounded by Coleridge, distinguished between *imagination,* which produced organic form by finding a form that seamlessly matched its content; and *fancy,* which imposed a mechanical form from the outside. The new organicism discovers that fancy is really an inverted form of imagination. One can trace a poetic lineage from the Romantic period toward postmodernism and L=A=N=G=U=A=G=E poetry. Far from escaping Romanticism, contemporary art falls back into its gravitational field. As Peter Otto puts it, "It is because we still belong to the era opened by Romanticism that our modernity continues to reinvent and reshape itself in Romanticism's forms."[148] Organicism values spontaneous generation. A poem could grow like a cucumber, given the right conditions. And it values an exact fit of content and form. The new organicism discovers a parallel between automated artistic production and ecosystems. For our purposes, there is a third term involved: *automated capitalism,* and the ravages of the "invisible hand" of the free market.

The new organicism is possibly even stranger than the old one. In the new organicism, "emergent" formal organization—compared with the growth of flowers or the spread of clouds—depends upon the operation of some essentially algorithmic process. The composition process is as mechanized as possible. It seldom, if ever, occurs to the exponents of the new organicism to reverse the terms of their analogy. If emergent algorithmic machine processes resemble the natural world, then there is a way in which the natural world is thoroughly automated, mechanical, and repetitive. Retroactively, we discern that organicism always contained a material, even mechanical, automated component, a component latent in the word *organism* itself (Greek *organon,* machine, tool).[149] This idea is attractive to posthuman thinking that is uneasy about traditional ideas of nature. It finds in thinkers such as Humberto Maturana and Francisco Varela a way of viewing what are traditionally called subjects and objects as an open system of feedback loops, and develops an idea of "autopoesis" close to the revised organicism I am describing here.[150] But for reasons given throughout this book, I do not believe this wishful thinking will hold. It is not as if there is anything beyond or behind (outside, as I have already said) the inside–outside distinction, upon which depend all other distinctions.

Coleridge was on to this when he backed away from his initial fascination with the Aeolian harp, an environmental instrument that predates the world of the art installation. Aeolian harps were considered demonic in the Middle Ages, precisely because they summoned the energy of (evil) nature.[151] But in the Romantic period, writers such as Coleridge and Percy Shelley became intrigued with the idea that art, and moreover, human consciousness itself, had the qualities of an Aeolian harp. Far from flying high in idealist abstraction, Romantic writers generated material theories of consciousness "emerging" from organized matter, like strong artificial intelligence theory today. Turing's original idea for computers was for a machine that could become any machine, and that could program itself. In the Romantic period, Charles Babbage drew up the first models for computers (the Difference Engine and Analytical Engine) using the mechanical Jacquard looms that had been doing artisans out of a job. They were "programmed" by Byron's daughter Ada.

The new, ambient organicism inverts the Romantic idea that inner truth generates its own body like DNA—without the spontaneous choice of an "author." In comparing artistic production to natural systems, the new organicism opens up possibilities for seeing nature as pure mechanism, as a sequence of algorithmic processes, for instance, in the recent phenomenon of art that produces "Electronic Life Forms," small solar-powered machines that emit sounds and move. Algorithms are on both sides of the analogy. Art becomes a monitoring instrument, a radio telescope, or a weather balloon. There are some further curiosities. First, is there an algorithm for nature as a whole? Some artists are excited to compare their work with cloud formations. But they do so not in order to compare *this* piece of music with *those* particular clouds out there, but with some general principle of cloud formation, and, even more generally, with something called nature that emerges out of chaotic flows. Politically, this is a form of libertarianism. John Cage's idea that music just happened directly contradicted the Marxist musicology of Adorno, for whom art was a place where the "violence" of choice assumed its full being, albeit one that was redeemed by the special status and qualities of art.

Comparing an algorithmic process with another algorithmic process, however, is not as seductive as saying that my poem resembles the tidal patterns in San Francisco Bay. If ecosystems operate according to some mechanical processes, there is no mystery to them. Ambient art seeks the invisible footprints of the real. But as soon as it makes them visible, they are not themselves any more. In adopting the scientific language of chaos theory and emergent systems, it cannot have it both ways and retain the invisibility of what it discovers. Ultimately, ambient art becomes science, pure and simple. Many modern artists pose themselves in a scientific manner. But this pose *is* a pose. They want to be the Romantic genius and the postmodern doorkeeper for the *genius loci* at the very same time. They want their consumption, nay consumerism, to be admired as a form of production. "Behold my buying habits and mixing skills," cries the DJ. The artist, the genius, is a *reader,* and maybe always was. Romantic poems appear to read themselves, suspended in some impossible place "in between" production and consumption. We are back to beautiful soul syndrome, which is another phrase for the agony of choice.

If art and nature are both algorithmic, then the unknown-ness of the unknown, the invisibility that ambient art tries to glimpse, is already visible. It is predetermined, a "known unknown" in the horrible language of Donald Rumsfeld, the U.S. Secretary of Defense at the time of this writing. The butterfly is released into the auditorium in the expectation that the audience will hear noise as music until the butterfly leaves. The radio telescope is tuned to deep space in the expectation that certain frequencies will announce the existence of alien beings. As was once said in computer programming circles, "bullshit in, bullshit out." Preserving the invisibility of the invisible would mean dropping the idea that an algorithmic process should characterize environmental artistic practice, or its content.

If art really *did* become more like science, then *irony* would be less an aesthetic pose, a slogan on a T-shirt, and more of a willingness to be wrong: to encounter nonidentity. Irony is the refreshing and consistent noncoincidence of what is in our heads with what is the case. Far from being a symptom of political or spiritual burn-out, it is the oil that keeps the engine running. Under its influence, the mysterious quality of nature would disappear, an advance for radical politics: Blake was forever associating "mystery" with the ideological power of nature. Environmental art seems to want to have it both ways: to be predictable and mysterious, to create mystery machines that can be downloaded off the Internet without a copyright fee, but retaining an aura of artistry.

The mechanical process that "is nature" is *monstrous*. To see this properly would retain the unknown-ness of the unknown, but not as an aesthetic mystery. It approaches the psychoanalytic idea of *drive,* the repetitive, cycling processes that operate sentient beings. The ultimate trajectory of the "new and improved" school of revisionary aesthetics would transfer art away from objects of desire and toward objects of the drive. These drives, these cycling processes have a certain right to remain unconscious, unknown. To tamper with them by bringing them into consciousness (chant this mantra and improve your sex drive!) bears the hallmark of fascist organization. A "rights of the unconscious" underpins the rights of nature. But the issue goes beyond that of the right to be left alone, for unconscious images to proliferate and link together in peace without ideological fixation. (We could always make *that* play into an ideological game park.)

We are stuck with the perverse necessity of choosing to help the other(s) fulfill their drive. This is the plot of *AI,* a film that Stanley Kubrick left to Steven Spielberg to make, in this very gesture acknowledging its basic theme of the rights of automated beings. Spielberg's inevitably kitschy, schmaltzy movie, heavy on special effects and low on acting, depicts far-future machines fulfilling the perceived needs (or programmed drives?) of a nearer-future machine, a little boy replicant. The story resembles Stravinsky's *Petroushka*. We are never able to tell, even at the end, whether the boy machine really has a soul, or whether this is also an inert "thing that thinks" (*res cogitans,* in Cartesian). The environment is always thematically present, as the far-future Ice Age, and as the "continual whirr of machines" at the disturbing fairgrounds at which robots ("mecha") are executed (or dismantled?) for human ("orga") enjoyment. But it is also theoretically present in the deadlock of an ethics of automation: we won't ever know whether we are doing machines a favor.

Ecocritique must carefully distinguish the necessity of helping the other(s) fulfill their drive from the reactionary "right to life" and also from Leopold's conservative "land ethic": "A thing is right when it tends to preserve the integrity, stability, and beauty of the biotic community. It is wrong when it tends otherwise."[152] Integrity, stability, and beauty are all aesthetic criteria. The presence of "beauty" in the trio only serves to divert attention from the organicism of integrity and stability. Leopold's "community" hesitates between an image of a group of conscious beings and an animated version of ambience. Essays such as "Thinking Like a Mountain" prepare for it.[153] Leopold was well aware that he was constrained to argue for environmentalism in aesthetic terms.[154] His argument is precisely Kantian: "The outstanding characteristic of perception is that it entails no consumption and no dilution of any resource."[155] This perception of wild nature is therefore consumerism without consumption, the pure form of consumerism.

In the Romantic period, art already interrogated the idea of organicism that came close to a politics of the drive, as an ultimate form of ecological politics. *Frankenstein* is an ecological novel precisely *not* because it compels us to care for a preexisting notion of nature, but because it questions the very idea of nature. Far from standing in for irreducible particularity—and hence ironically generalizing that very particularity—the creature represents alienated generality. In the sense that his existence subtends our personhood, he figures forth an essentialist view of nature. But insofar as this nature is abject and its stitches are showing, this "essence" includes arbitrariness and supplementarity. The creature is made out of any body, anybody. Frankenstein's creature is not even an other because he cannot return our gaze or act as blank screen. He is a horrific abject that speaks beautiful Enlightenment prose, a piece of butcher's meat with blinking eyes. This artificial object bleeds and speaks plangently of vegetarianism and compassion, while committing murders and blaming them on *his* environment—people. As Franco Moretti and Chris Baldick have argued, throughout the nineteenth century the creature was viewed as the working-class, creation of the bourgeoisie. He is also an object of homophobic fascination: Frankenstein's pursuit of him indicates a burning desire.[156] Criticism has, in addition, found in the creature the inconsistent object of racist fantasy.[157] The creature wants precisely not to be left alone, like a wilderness, but to have someone stay true to his own desire, to build him a mate so he can leave in peace, reproducing his drive. Does he point the way toward a posthuman ecology, or toward a humanity to come? I often think that the trouble with posthumanism is that we have not yet achieved humanity, and that humanity and posthumanity have no time for what Derrida calls the animal that therefore I am.

Caring for the creature would acknowledge the monstrosity at the heart of the idea of nature. It would involve a fetishist ethics—in the normative view, a kind of decadence—that would deform the eroticized objectification (what we call "nature") that is the mode of ecologically destructive enjoyment. This is what Adorno sees as the dissolution of the destructive idea of "progress" by paradoxically decadent ethical acts, giving the example of extreme forms of justice in animal rights. There *is* beauty in the beautiful soul: "The ideal of complete, life-renouncing distance from purpose, even if narrow-minded and willfully obstinate, [is] the reverse image of the false purposiveness of industry, in which everything is for something else."[158] *Frankenstein* is about how social conditions are not yet established for such "twisted" ethical forms to take place. Frankenstein's creature is the distorted, ambient category of the environment pulled around to the "front" of the reader's view, the "answer of the real" whose very form embodies a terrible split: the horrific ugliness of alienated social cruelty, and the painful eloquence of enlightened reflection. There would be no need for beautiful souls without such ugly objects. If a poisoned rainforest could speak, it would sound like Frankenstein's creature. Ecocritique must attend to such auguries of innocence.

The augury of *Frankenstein* is the reverse of deep ecology. The task becomes to love the disgusting, inert, and meaningless. Ecological politics must constantly and ruthlessly reframe our view of the ecological: what was "outside" yesterday will be "inside" today. We identify with the monstrous thing. We ourselves are "tackily" made of bits and pieces of stuff. The most ethical act is to love the other precisely in their artificiality, rather than seeking to prove their naturalness and authenticity. Deep ecology ironically does not respect the natural world as actual contingent beings, but as standing in for an idea of the natural. Deep ecology goes to extremes on this point, insisting that humans are a viral supplement to an organic whole.

Dark ecology, by contrast, is a perverse, melancholy ethics that refuses to digest the object into an ideal form. In a brilliantly contorted sentence, a miniature masterpiece of dialectics, Adorno describes genuine progress: "Progress means: humanity emerges from its spellbound state no longer under the spell of progress as well, itself nature, by becoming aware of its own indigenousness to nature and by halting the mastery over nature through which nature continues its mastery."[159] In its refusal to produce an idea of nature as a way of being, dark ecology is one of the aspects of this "halting," generating not the relaxing ambient sounds of ecomimesis, but the screeching of the emergency brake. Dark ecology, if it were ever to have been practiced, would have enjoined us to love the replicant *as* replicant and not as potential full subject: appreciating what in us is most objectified, the "thousand thousand slimy things." This is the truly ecological-ethical act. In this respect, dark ecology diverges from those Romanticisms that follow a Hegelian dialectic, the story of the reconciliation of the self to the other, who turns out to be the self in disguise.[160] It gets over the dilemma of the beautiful soul, not by turning the other into the self, but perversely, by leaving things the way they are. In order to be itself, forgiveness would not expect the frog to turn into a prince as soon as we kissed it. To forgive, then, would be a fundamentally ecological act, an act that redefined ecology in excess of all its established concepts, an act of radically being-with the other. And being-here, being literally on this earth *(Da-sein)*, would entail a need for forgiveness, an equally radical assumption that whatever is *there* is our responsibility, and ultimately, "our fault."[161]

Loving the thing *as* thing, not as a person in disguise, assumes two forms. First, we have the ethical choice as perverse leap: choosing to identify with the replicant, on condition that we preserve the artificiality of the other and do not try to naturalize or collapse otherness. Second, we have the spontaneous continuity of fascination in the claustrophobic environment: "I blessed [the monstrous other] unaware" (Coleridge, *The Ancient Mariner* 4.285). What could be more claustrophobic than a realm, however vast, from which there is no exit from your state of mind? This is the ocean in *The Ancient Mariner*, part 4. Surely this is where we are now—however huge the earth is, its toxicity makes it very claustrophobic. As long as there really is no exit and we can't achieve a sadistic/aesthetic distance, the phobic fascination turns into kindness, the continuous attention that awareness keeps placing on the object.

These two moments are the ethical inverse of environmental art. Putting a frame around nothing (minimalism) corresponds to the second form of ethical act, since we're just "letting whatever occur in the frame"—and the frame becomes claustrophobic precisely because what is *outside* it is now *included*. Exhibiting a frameless formless thing corresponds to the first ethical choice. We are compelled to identify with the object, and can't quite maintain the appropriate aestheticizing distance. Dark ecology holds open the space of what used to be called the aesthetic, until something better comes along. Ironically, what is most problematic about ecomimesis—the idiotic "extension" of writing going on and on—is in this respect its saving grace, an inconsistency that enables us to take it out of the frame called Nature. This inconsistency with its ideological content is why it can be orientalist, or artificial, as well as "natural."

Really Deep Ecology

The present ecological emergency demands that you need not be comfortable in order to do theory. This is where John Clare's profound poems of depression come to mind. Clare is usually framed as a proto-ecological poet of minute particulars, a genuine and genuinely disturbing working-class presence in the revised Romantic canon. Far from being tangential to the general nature poetry project, the depression poems are essential to it. They stage the idea of *being here* in its most profound, formal way. Beyond any specific ecological content, indeed, often in spite of it, the narrator remains. Of all the humors, melancholy was the closest to the earth. In his study of German tragic drama, Benjamin explores the heavy materialism of the Baroque, whose emotional analogue, he claims, is the relentless melancholy of the drama's protagonists.[162] Isn't this lingering with something painful, disgusting, grief-striking, exactly what we need right now, ecologically speaking?

Take the poem "I Am."

> I AM: yet what I am, none cares or knows,
>   My friends forsake me like a memory lost;
> I am the self-consumer of my woes,
>   They rise and vanish in oblivious host,
> Like shades in love and death's oblivion lost;
> And yet I am, and live with shadows tost
>
> Into the nothingness of scorn and noise,
>   Into the living sea of waking dreams,
> Where there is neither sense of life or joys,
>   But the vast shipwreck of my life's esteems;

> And een the dearest—that I love the best—
> Are strange—nay, stranger than the rest.
>
> I long for scenes where man has never trod;
> A place where woman never smiled or wept;
> There to abide with my Creator, GOD,
> And sleep as I in childhood sweetly slept:
> Untroubling and untroubled where I lie;
> The grass below—above the vaulted sky.[163]

The title's Cartesian reference should be obvious. Now you might think that this was Cartesian subjectivity at its darkest hour—the subject as pure empty self-reference, or S in Lacanian. And you would be right. At first glance, the closest we get to ecology is the last couplet, where the narrator wishes for an impossible relief. And even here there is an ambiguity in the sense of "above": is the narrator lying with the sky above him, or lying "above . . . the sky" in heaven? But the very form of this yearning and impossibility is precisely the *most* ecological thing about the poem. I am reminded of Adorno's remarks on the idea of peace, quoted in Chapter 1. The narrator's identity has shrunk to the pure open empty set of blank consciousness, filled with ambient noises and disturbing otherness. There is an extraordinary enactment of this between the first and second stanzas, where the reader's eyes have to "toss" themselves into the nothingness between an immense gap between lines in order to arrive at the end of the phrase (6–7). The narrator is so untogether, as they say in California, compared with Heidegger's peasant woman, whose shoes connect her to feudal rhythms. Here they are, *right here,* on the earth, feeling like shit. Why did we think that the deepest ecological experience would be full of love and light? I am, therefore I doubt, therefore I think, therefore I am, therefore I doubt—I wish life were simple.

The doubt is so very corrosive, that before we get to the grass and sky, we have a ghostly, ambient version of an environment formed from the narrator's scooped-out insides (7–12). The narrator is painfully aware that the otherness that surrounds him does not truly exist: it is a "nothingness of scorn and noise" (7). Does "I am" (1), like an Old English riddle in which the poem declares itself to be something ("I am . . . an onion"), not point out the status of the poem itself, a spectral quasi-object suspended in nothingness, an inconsistent bunch of squiggles that cannot ever know itself as such?[164] This depressive Romantic poem comes curiously close to Mallarmé's experiments with crossed-out words. In both cases, the sheer opacity of the poem becomes its subject, involving us in a paradox, since it is precisely the "lack of content" that gives the poem its opacity. Behind the vapor and mist we glimpse a dull inertia, symbolized by the dash, that quintessential gesture of sensibility, and hence the illusion of deep subjectivity. In the printed text, the dash becomes the sheer inert breath between signs, making us aware of the throat in which that breath is sticking. Wherever you go, here, even here, you are. The poem's inertia, its gravitational field, does not allow the doubting part to escape into some abstract realm beyond grass and sky, but in an extraordinary way, connects grass and sky to depression and doubt. We are a long way from traditional, organicist readings of Clare. We are also a long way from the therapeutic poetics of John Stuart Mill's reading of Wordsworth, celebrated in Jonathan Bate's *Romantic Ecology*.[165] Clare wants us to stay in the mud, rather than pull ourselves out of it. If we read the last line of "I Am" literally, this is exactly where we are.[166]

We may now read Clare's ecological-poetic career backward from the startling event of "I Am." At first, it might appear that "I Am" is a drastic, even tragic departure from an original ecological sensibility. Clare seems to embody the latest form of his poetic selfhood as an empty nothingness that can only yearn for an earth minimalistically conceived as grass and sky, like a character in a Beckett play looking out of a window. "I Am," however, has a retroactively corrosive effect on Clare's oeuvre. It helps us to see how, even from the point of view of the supposed self-contained, organic, feudal village, Clare was writing poetry *for another*. Bate's biography makes this very point, perhaps inadvertently and ironically, since it ostensibly puts a certain ecology firmly at the heart of Clare's poetics—an ecology marked by close, local observation of feudal vestiges of community and custom obliterated by capitalist procedures such as Enclosure. Writing itself, publication, editors in London, and circulation of writing, all come to stand in for this obliteration. But even when he was writing without a view to publication, Clare's work was displaced *from the inside* by an awareness of the other. He read his poems anonymously to his relatives out of an embarrassed fear that they would despise his work if they knew it was by him.[167] It had to sound as if it came from somewhere else in order to receive validation. Rusticity was itself a poetic trope of which Clare was well aware. And his poetic love of nature was itself a displacement from normative village life.[168]

It all comes down to the question of writing, which, confirming Derrida's view, carries the burden of all that seems wrong about language:

it is never really *yours,* it is always dispersed, differential, and so forth. Recent textual criticism has sought to discover an original, authentic Clare behind or before the corruption of London, capitalism, and so on, metonymies (or metaphors?) for the spacing and displacing actions of grammar. Ecological literary criticism has assumed this task as its own, discovering a natural Clare beneath the artificiality.[169] But Bate himself observes that the image of an authentic, ungrammatical Clare corrupted by revision is part of a fantasy of ownership in which Clare the primitive becomes an object of consumerism.[170] A painful awareness of grammar always bisected Clare's poetics, even (especially) in those moments when he was angry about grammar.

The space of the village, even if it was indeed feudal, was always already crisscrossed with otherness. There was no *there* there that was not already aware of *another there.* "I Am" is the stunning moment at which this otherness is perceived as intrinsic to the self, at a terrible cost. Clare does not know who he is, as a horribly vivid letter from the asylum indicates.[171] But this not-knowing is also a hard-won moment of actual subjectivity, in which, if we are to take Clare as an ecopoet seriously, we have lost nature, but gained ecology.

Clare gives us the feeling of environment as open mind. Consider the weird ending of "Mouse's Nest," which opens up the landscape: "The water oer the pebbles scarce could run / And broad old cesspools glittered in the sun" (13–14).[172] Clare helps us to feel the existential quality of doubt. This is by no means eco-skepticism—quite the opposite in fact. The poetic language is tied irrevocably to the earth's emotional gravity. Doubt—the effect of things ceasing to be what you expect—mingles with a heavy sadness, a lingering quality, even of dread, which situates the sonnet in an oppressive summer sunlight, an intense environment from which there is no escape. Faith is no longer a question of belief, of cleaving to ideas in your head, but of an existential remaining in place. The existential "thisness" of the glittering cesspools is surely an environmental analogue for the anti-aesthetic grotesqueness of the close-up of the mouse and her young, which surprises the narrator and defeats trite ecological sentimentality.[173]

This is incredibly good news for ecocriticism. Even here, even at the limits of subjectivity, we find closeness to the earth. It is quite the opposite of what we might expect. Environment as theory, as wonder, as doubt, does not achieve escape velocity form the earth, but, in fact, sinks down into it further than any wishful thinking, any naive concept of interconnectedness could push us. This is the place reached in

Shelley's extraordinary essay "On Love," where the very feelings of loneliness and separation, rather than fantasies of interconnectedness, put us in touch with a surrounding environment.[174] Dark ecology tells us that we can't escape our minds. Far from giving us a liturgy for how to get out of our guilty minds, how to stick our heads in nature and lose them, Clare helps us to stay right here, in the poisoned mud. Which is just where we need to be, right now.

"The woods are lovely dark and deep" (Robert Frost, "Stopping by the Woods on a Snowy Evening," 13).[175] But dark ecology is no solution to the problem of nature, which has more in common with the undead than with life. Nature is what keeps on coming back, an inert, horrifying presence and a mechanical repetition. Environmentalism cannot mourn the loss of the environment, for that would be to accept its loss, even to kill it, if only symbolically. The task is not to bury the dead but to join them, to be bitten by the undead and become them. Adorno: "The voice of deluded, unreflective progress drones in the insistence upon [sexual] taboos for the benefit of the unity of the nature-dominating ego."[176]

Paradoxically, the best way to have ecological awareness is to love the world as a person; while the best way to love a person is to love what is most intimate to them, the "thing" embedded in their makeup. We are caught on a Möbius strip. Blake sums it up in "The Fly," a Cartesian meditation:

> Little Fly
> Thy summers play,
> My thoughtless hand
> Hath brush'd away.
>
> Am not I
> A fly like thee?
> And art not thou
> A man like me?
>
> For I dance
> And drink & sing
> Till some blind hand
> Shall brush my wing.
>
> If thought is life
> And strength & breath.
> And the want
> Of thought is death.

> Then am I
> A happy fly,
> If I live,
> Or if I die.[177]

On the one hand, the Cartesian view ("thought is life"—I think there-fore I am) condemns us to be no better than flies, since our physical form does not determine our "thought." We are caught in the cycle of life and death. It does not matter whether we live or die. On the other hand (Blake's songs are always reversible), we have achieved an identity with the fly beyond the usual sentimental identification through dis-tance, the "pity" that that is contingent upon an imbalance of power, as in Blake's own "The Human Abstract": "Pity would be no more, / If we did not make somebody Poor" (1–2). The fly is not humanized; rather, the human becomes a fly. The last lines twist the logic of the beautiful soul. Instead of bemoaning the fate of living beings with *King Lear* ("As flies to wanton boys are we to the gods" (4.1.37)), the poem iden-tifies with the "evil" (the "thoughtless," "blind" mechanical operation) and with the insect.

Instead of imagining limitation *outside,* the conservative ecological view, we recognize *internal* limits, as in *Frankenstein,* which is about accepting limitations in a progressive manner—social mediation is re-quired to aid the creature.[178] The beautiful soul cannot go on dreaming endlessly.[179] The dreamy quality of immersion in nature is what keeps us separate from it. We are humans dreaming that we are flies, like Chuang Tzu, the philosopher who dreamt that he was a butterfly and could then never be sure whether he was a butterfly dreaming that he was a man. If we identify with the fly, we dispel the dream. We have lost nature, but gained a collective. The beautiful soul awakens to this conscious determination *(Begriff).*[180] We can have ecological sympathy, but it is *eccentric* rather than *concentric,* to borrow the language Lacan uses to describe the displaced Cartesian self.[181] Blake imagines lions having sympathy for lost little girls and weeping ruby tears (43–48).[182] In "Alastor," his poem about the differences between abstract Nature and concrete sentient beings, Percy Shelley visualizes an antelope looking at a poet in a forest clearing. Rather than taking pity on the animal world in a soft-focus version of the normal sadistic distance, we glimpse humans through nonhuman eyes (103–106).[183]

We can't quite call this *pantheism,* like the young Wordsworth and Coleridge. We don't know whether the physical world, or even animals, are subjects . . . yet. And that is precisely the slit, the gap, the space for which ambience does not account. Perhaps the view should be named ~~pantheism~~. It is rather like Spinoza's critique of the anthropomorphic idea of "man" itself. But unlike many ecological thinkers, who tread a Spinozan path, we have forged it via Kant and Descartes, who, most of all, helped thinking to maintain its distance toward the animal and the environment. If we can find ecology even here, there is hope.

Critical choice does not rise above consumerism or ideology only to collapse back into it. Rather than the pursuit of the illusion that one *still* has a choice—which is no choice at all—the true ecological choice is a form of radical commitment, a shutting-down of choice. At this level, *choice* and *acceptance* become the same thing. Paradoxically, consumerism gave us the idea, also repeated in philosophical texts, that there is such a thing as consciousness, with or without certain contents (such as ideas about ecology). Critical choice commits to consciousness, which remains at best a tenuous advertisement for a state of affairs in which we have given up generating ways of being, however ecological they might be.

We have given up obtaining satisfaction from the environment imagined as an unconscious process. Unfortunately, no such soothing relaxation tape remains, as waves of radiation from what we ignored for too long disjoint our bodies and our world. Lacan described the judo with which one could make us beautiful souls own up to our complicity: "It is hardly a question of adapting to [the reality the beautiful soul accuses], but to show it that it is only too well adapted, since it assists in the construction of that very reality."[184] This is not fair. It is ruthless. But "kindness"—tolerating the distance of the beautiful soul—could be worse. It runs the risk of calling upon "the obscene, ferocious figure of the superego . . . in which there is no other way out . . . than to make the patient sit down by the window and show him all the pleasant aspects of nature, adding 'Go out there. Now you're a good child.' "[185] If we keep tolerating the distance, we get stuck with ecomimesis.

So we have bottomed out, which is only the beginning of the rest of our ecological life. It is a strange ground, discernible in and as our experience of groundlessness. We have admitted that yes, we have a mind and that this mind fantasizes about nature in its struggle to think itself out of the history it has created. We should rewrite Freud's *Wo Es war, soll Ich werden* ("Where It (id) was, there shall I (ego) be"). However disappointing it is to do without the oceanic sway, *where nature was, there shall we be.* As I said in the Introduction, no one likes it when you mention the unconscious, not because you are saying taboo things, but because you are depriving the ego of its necessary fantasy support. Ecology, if it means anything at all, means being *without* nature. When we drag it front and center, against our ideological interests, it stops being a world in which we can immerse ourselves.

Hegel says that Descartes is the *terra firma* of philosophy, the stage at which "like the sailor after a long voyage, we can at last shout 'Land ho,'" and in that phrase we may find the groundless ground of ecology without nature.[186] We find ourselves back at the front door of the house of so-called Western philosophy, staring at the doorbell marked Descartes. The question *then* becomes: is it possible to separate Descartes' view of *res* from the idea that animals have no soul and can therefore be vivisected?[187] How far *down* into Descartes' thinking does this idea go? Does the approach to nature as *res* entail thinking of it as a vivisectable being to whom we can do infinite sadistic violence as "possessors and masters of nature"?[188] To introduce doubt about Descartes is a Cartesian maneuver. To be truly theoretical is to doubt. This is not the same thing as saying, with the opponents of solutions to global warming, that "we need more evidence." The only firm ethical option in the current catastrophe, as I observed before, is admitting to the ecologically catastrophic in all its meaningless contingency, accepting responsibility groundlessly, whether or not "we ourselves" can be proved to be responsible.[189] But this too is more a leap of doubt than a leap of faith. Can we be environmentalists, and environmentalist writers, without a hemorrhage of irony, sense of humor, and sensitivity to the illusory play of language? As long as there is environmental passion, there also lives more faith in honest doubt about the environment, and environmental art and aesthetics, than in the outworn creeds of nature.

You would be forgiven for thinking that this book has read like a critique of deep ecology. But I long to characterize what I am aiming for as "really deep ecology." I have not been writing against a deep green view, if to be deep green means to take seriously the idea of philosophical reflection. Ironically, to contemplate deep green ideas deeply is to let go of the idea of Nature, the one thing that maintains an aesthetic distance between us and them, us and it, us and "over there." How deep does deep ecology want to go? In a truly deep green world, the idea of Nature will have disappeared in a puff of smoke, as nonhuman beings swim into view. Then comes the next step. We must deal with the idea of distance itself. If we try to get rid of distance too fast, in our rush to join the nonhuman, we will end up caught in our prejudice, our concept of distance, our concept of "them." Hanging out in the distance may be the surest way of relating to the nonhuman.

Instead of positing a nondualistic pot of gold at the end of a rainbow, we could hang out in what feels like dualism. This hanging out would be a more nondual approach. Instead of trying to pull the world out of the mud, we could jump down into the mud. To emerge from the poisoned chrysalis of the beautiful soul, we admit that we have a choice. We choose and accept our own death, and the fact of mortality among species and ecosystems. This is the ultimate rationality: holding our mind open for the absolutely unknown that is to come. Evolution will not be televised. One cannot have a video of one's own extinction. A warning to deep ecology: if we aestheticize this acceptance, we arrive at fascism, the cult of death. Instead, ecological criticism must politicize the aesthetic. We choose this poisoned ground. We will be equal to this senseless actuality. Ecology may be without nature. But it is not without us.

Notes

Introduction

1. John M. Meyer, *Political Nature: Environmentalism and the Interpretation of Western Thought* (Cambridge, Mass.: MIT Press, 2001), 22.
2. Ibid.
3. Terre Slatterfield, Scott Slovic, and Terry Tempest Williams, "Where the Power Lies: Seeking the Intuitive Language of Story," in Terre Slatterfield and Scott Slovic, eds., *What's Nature Worth? Narrative Expressions of Environmental Value* (Salt Lake City: University of Utah Press, 2004), 61–81 (62).
4. Terre Slatterfield and Scott Slovic, "Introduction: What's Nature Worth?" in Slatterfield and Slovic, *What's Nature Worth?*, 1–17 (14).
5. John Elder, *Reading the Mountains of Home* (Cambridge, Mass.: Harvard University Press, 1998), 116.
6. Meyer, *Political Nature*, 18.
7. Simone de Beauvoir, *The Second Sex,* trans. and ed. H. M. Parshley, intro. Margaret Crosland (1952; repr., New York: Knopf, 1993), 147–209.
8. Talking Heads, *Stop Making Sense* (Sire Records, 1984), sleeve note.
9. Walter Benn Michaels, *The Shape of the Signifier* (Princeton, N.J.: Princeton University Press, 2004), 118–128.
10. Jonathan Bate, *Romantic Ecology: Wordsworth and the Environmental Tradition* (London: Routledge, 1991) and *The Song of the Earth* (Cambridge, Mass.: Harvard University Press, 2000); James McKusick, *Green Writing: Romanticism and Ecology* (New York: St. Martin's Press, 2000); Karl Kroeber, *Ecological Literary Criticism: Romantic Imagining and the Biology of Mind* (New York: Columbia University Press, 1994).
11. T. V. Reed, "Toward an Environmental Justice Ecocriticism," in Joni Adamson, Mei Mei Evans, and Rachel Stein, eds., *The Environmental Jus-*

tice Reader: Politics, Poetics, and Pedagogy (Tucson: University of Arizona Press, 2002), 125–162.

12. Terre Slatterfield, Scott Slovic, and John Daniel, "From Image to Event: Considering the Relations between Poetry and Prose as Conveyors of Environmental Values," in Slatterfield and Slovic, *What's Nature Worth?*, 160–185.

13. Meyer, *Political Nature*, 149–151.

14. See Luc Ferry, *The New Ecological Order,* trans. Carol Volk (Chicago: University of Chicago Press, 1995), 71.

15. See for example Elaine Scarry, *On Beauty and Being Just* (Princeton, N.J.: Princeton University Press, 1999).

16. Georg Wilhelm Friedrich Hegel, *Introductory Lectures on Aesthetics,* trans. Bernard Bosanquet, intro. and commentary Michael Inwood (Harmondsworth: Penguin, 1993), 85–88; Oscar Wilde, "The Critic as Artist," in *The Complete Works of Oscar Wilde,* intro. Vyvyan Holland (London: Collins, 1966), 1009–1059.

17. Timothy W. Luke, *Ecocritique: Contesting the Politics of Nature, Economy, and Culture* (Minneapolis: University of Minnesota Press, 1997), xi–xiii.

18. Theodor W. Adorno, *Negative Dialectics,* trans. E. B. Ashton (New York: Continuum, 1973), 5 ("Dialectics is the consistent sense of nonidentity"), 147–148, 149–150.

19. Georg Wilhelm Friedrich Hegel, *Hegel's Phenomenology of Spirit,* trans. A. V. Miller, analysis and foreword by J. N. Findlay (Oxford: Oxford University Press, 1977), 19, 24–26, 31.

20. Peter Fritzell, *Nature Writing and America: Essays upon a Cultural Type* (Ames: Iowa State University Press, 1990), 87.

21. Raymond Williams's exploration remains helpful. "Nature," in *Keywords: A Vocabulary of Culture and Society* (London: Fontana Press, 1988), 219–224. See also "Ecology" (110–111).

22. For an account of the tribulations of Spinozism, for instance, see Jonathan Israel, *Radical Enlightenment: Philosophy and the Making of Modernity 1650–1750* (Oxford: Oxford University Press, 2001), 157–327.

23. Edward Casey, *The Fate of Place: A Philosophical History* (Berkeley: University of California Press, 1997), 162–179.

24. Ibid., 77, 98, 142–150.

25. John Locke, *An Essay Concerning Human Understanding,* trans. Peter H. Nidditch (Oxford: Clarendon Press, 1979), II.23.23–24 (308–309).

26. This is a perennial theme in Canghuilhem and Foucault. See Georges Canghuilhem, *The Normal and the Pathological* (New York: Zone Books, 1991), 233–288.

27. Edmund Burke, *A Philosophical Enquiry into the Origin of Our Ideas of the Sublime and the Beautiful,* ed. J. T. Boulton (Oxford: Basil Blackwell, 1987). See Immanuel Kant, *Critique of Judgment,* trans. Werner S. Pluhar (Indianapolis, Ind.: Hackett, 1987), 138–139.

28. Kant, *Critique of Judgment,* 135.

29. Fredric Jameson, "Globalization and Political Strategy," *New Left Review,* second series 4 (July–August 2000): 49–68 (68).

30. Bruno Latour, *Politics of Nature: How to Bring the Sciences into Democracy* (Cambridge, Mass.: Harvard University Press, 2004), 7–8, 25–26.

31. See for example John Milton, *Paradise Lost* 8.140–158, a description of other worlds; *Paradise Lost,* ed. Alastair Fowler (London: Longman, 1971).

32. William Wordsworth, "Tintern Abbey," in *Lyrical Ballads, and Other Poems, 1797–1800,* ed. James Butler and Karen Green (Ithaca, N.Y.: Cornell University Press, 1996), 98–100.

33. John Gatta, *Making Nature Sacred: Literature, Religion, and Environment in America from the Puritans to the Present* (Oxford: Oxford University Press, 2004).

34. Jacques Derrida, "Violence and Metaphysics," in *Writing and Difference,* trans. Alan Bass (London: Routledge and Kegan Paul, 1978), 79–153 (151–152).

35. David Simpson, *Romanticism, Nationalism and the Revolt against Theory* (Chicago: University of Chicago Press, 1993), 4, 10, and *passim.*

36. For a useful discussion of ecocriticism's view of "theory," see Thomas Hothem, "The Picturesque and the Production of Space: Landscape Description in an Age of Fiction" (Ph.D. dissertation, University of Rochester, 2003), 36; Dana Phillips, "Ecocriticism, Literary Theory, and the Truth of Ecology," *New Literary History* 30.3 (1999): 577–602 (578).

37. Jacques Derrida, "How to Avoid Speaking: Denials," in Sanford Budick and Wolfgang Iser, eds., *Languages of the Unsayable: The Play of Negativity in Literature and Literary Theory* (Stanford, Calif.: Stanford University Press, 1996), 3–70.

38. Donna Haraway, *The Companion Species Manifesto: Dogs, People, and Significant Otherness* (Chicago: Prickly Paradigm Press, 2003).

39. Theodor Adorno, *Aesthetic Theory,* trans. and ed. Robert Hullot-Kentor (Minneapolis: University of Minnesota Press, 1997), 65.

40. Angus Fletcher, *A New Theory for American Poetry: Democracy, the Environment, and the Future of Imagination* (Cambridge, Mass.: Harvard University Press, 2004), 122–123.

41. Raymond Williams, *Culture and Society: Coleridge to Orwell* (London: Chatto and Windus, 1958; repr., London: The Hogarth Press, 1987).

42. See for example Ted Hughes, "Writing about Landscape," in *Poetry in the Making: An Anthology of Poems and Programmes from "Listening and Writing"* (London: Faber and Faber, 1967), 74–86 (76).

43. Adorno, *Aesthetic Theory,* 233.

44. Walter Benjamin, "The Work of Art in the Age of Mechanical Reproduction," in *Illuminations,* ed. Hannah Arendt, trans. Harry Zohn (London: Harcourt, Brace and World, 1973), 222–223.

45. Herbert Marcuse, *An Essay on Liberation* (Boston: Beacon Press, 1969), 31. See Timothy W. Luke, "Marcuse and the Politics of Radical Ecology," in Luke, *Ecocritique,* 137–152.

46. Herbert Marcuse, *The Aesthetic Dimension: Toward a Critique of Marxist Aesthetics,* trans. Herbert Marcuse and Erica Sherover (Basingstoke: Macmillan, 1986), 72.
47. Adorno, *Aesthetic Theory,* 310.
48. Benjamin, "The Work of Art," 217–251.
49. Robert Kaufman, "Red Kant, or the Persistence of the Third *Critique* in Adorno and Jameson," *Critical Inquiry* 26 (Summer 2000): 682–724.
50. Ibid., 711.
51. Slavoj Žižek, *The Indivisible Remainder: An Essay on Schelling and Related Matters* (London: Verso, 1996), 194.
52. Public Image Limited, *The Greatest Hits, So Far* (Virgin, 1990).
53. Kant, *Critique of Judgment,* 108.

1. The Art of Environmental Language

Epigraph to Chapter 1, "To the Reader," by Denise Levertov, from *Poems 1960–1967,* copyright © 1961 by Denise Levertov. Reprinted by permission of New Directions Publishing Corp., Pollinger Limited, and the proprietor.
1. Jacques Derrida, "Signature Event Context," in *Margins of Philosophy,* trans. Alan Bass (Chicago: University of Chicago Press, 1982), 307–330 (328).
2. Charles Dickens, *Bleak House,* ed. Norman Page, intro. J. Hillis Miller (Harmondsworth: Penguin, 1985), 49–50.
3. For further discussion, see David Simpson, *Situatedness, or, Why We Keep Saying Where We're Coming From* (Durham, N.C.: Duke University Press, 2002), 1–16, 22, 101.
4. Denise Levertov, *Poems 1960–1967* (New York: New Directions, 1983).
5. Henry David Thoreau, *Walden and Civil Disobedience,* intro. Michael Meyer (1854; repr., Harmondsworth: Penguin, 1986), 45.
6. Maurice Blanchot, *The Space of Literature,* trans. Ann Smock (1955; repr., Lincoln: University of Nebraska Press, 1982), 28–30.
7. Aldo Leopold, *A Sand County Almanac, and Sketches Here and There,* intro. Robert Finch (1949; repr., Oxford: Oxford University Press, 1989).
8. Roland Barthes, "From Work to Text," in *Image, Music, Text,* trans. Stephen Heath (London: Fontana, 1977), 155–164 (159).
9. Ibid., 159.
10. Richard A. Lanham, *A Handlist of Rhetorical Terms: A Guide for Students of English Literature* (Berkeley: University of California Press, 1969), 52.
11. Angus Fletcher, *A New Theory for American Poetry: Democracy, the Environment, and the Future of Imagination* (Cambridge, Mass.: Harvard University Press, 2004), 117–118.
12. Simpson, *Situatedness,* 14.
13. Lawrence Buell, *The Environmental Imagination: Thoreau, Nature Writing, and the Formation of American Culture* (Cambridge, Mass.: Harvard University Press, 1995), 10.

14. James McKusick, *Green Writing: Romanticism and Ecology* (New York: St. Martin's Press, 2000), 1.
15. Lanham, *Handlist of Rhetorical Terms*, 36, 49.
16. Dana Phillips, *The Truth of Ecology: Nature, Culture, and Literature in America* (Oxford: Oxford University Press, 2003), 71.
17. Brian Eno, *Ambient 1: Music for Airports* (EG Records, 1978), sleeve note.
18. Leo Spitzer, "Milieu and Ambiance," in *Essays in Historical Semantics* (1948; repr., New York: Russell and Russell, 1968), 179–316.
19. See Michael Bull and Les Back, "Introduction: Into Sound," in Michael Bull and Les Back, eds., *The Auditory Culture Reader* (Oxford: Berg, 2003), 1–18; David Toop, *Ocean of Sound: Aether Talk, Ambient Sound and Imaginary Worlds* (London: Serpent's Tail, 1995) and *Haunted Weather: Music, Silence and Memory* (London: Serpent's Tail, 2004).
20. Michel Chion, *Audio-Vision: Sound on Screen*, ed. and trans. Claudia Gorbman (New York: Columbia University Press, 1994), 109–111.
21. Jean Baudrillard, "Mass Media Culture," in *Revenge of the Crystal*, trans. Paul Foss and Julian Pefanis (London: Pluto Press, 1990), 63–97 (65), offers some thoughts on contemporary nature as simulacrum.
22. Terre Slatterfield and Scott Slovic, "Introduction: What's Nature Worth?" in Terre Slatterfield and Scott Slovic, eds., *What's Nature Worth? Narrative Expressions of Environmental Value* (Salt Lake City: University of Utah Press, 2004), 1–17 (15).
23. Buell, *Environmental Imagination*, 98.
24. *TV Garden*, 1982 version. Single-channel video installation with live plants and monitors; color, sound; variable dimensions. Collection of the artist.
25. William Wordsworth, *Lyrical Ballads with Other Poems*, 2 vols. (London: T. N. Longman and O. Rees, 1800), 1.xxxiii–xxxiv.
26. Roman Jakobson, "Closing Statement: Linguistics and Poetics," in Thomas A. Sebeok, ed., *Style in Language* (Cambridge, Mass.: MIT Press, 1960), 350–377.
27. Ibid., 356.
28. "Hello, you're on the air," from "Back Side of the Moon," The Orb, *The Orb's Adventures beyond the Ultraworld* (Island Records, 1991).
29. Viktor Shklovsky, "Art as Technique," in Raman Selden, ed., *The Theory of Criticism from Plato to the Present: A Reader* (London: Longman, 1995), 274–276 (274).
30. In Toop, *Haunted Weather*, 239–240.
31. Philippe Lacoue-Labarthe and Jean-Luc Nancy, *The Literary Absolute: The Theory of Literature in German Romanticism* (Albany: State University of New York Press, 1988), 57–58. For further discussion, see Scott Cutler Shershow, *The Work and the Gift* (Chicago: University of Chicago Press, 2005), 165–182.
32. Thoreau, *Walden*, 168–169.
33. *Oxford English Dictionary*, "timbre," *n.* 3.
34. Jacques Derrida, "Tympan," in *Margins of Philosophy*, ix–xxix (xvi).

35. Roland Barthes, "The Grain of the Voice," in *Image, Music, Text,* 179–189.
36. Slavoj Žižek, *The Indivisible Remainder: An Essay on Schelling and Related Matters* (London: Verso, 1996), 99–103, 108–109.
37. "Le fond de cette gorge, à la forme complexe, insituable, qui en fait aussi bien l'objet primitif par excellence, l'abîme de l'organe féminin"; Jacques Lacan, "Le rêve de l'injection d'Irma," in *Le séminaire de Jacques Lacan,* ed. Jacques-Alain Miller (Paris: Editions du Seuil, 1978), 2.193–204 (196); Sigmund Freud, *The Interpretation of Dreams,* in *The Standard Edition of the Complete Psychological Works of Sigmund Freud,* ed. and trans. James Strachey, 24 vols. (London: Hogarth, 1953), 4.106–120.
38. Martin Heidegger, "The Origin of the Work of Art," in *Poetry, Language, Thought,* trans. Albert Hofstadter (New York: Harper and Row, 1971), 15–87 (26).
39. Ibid., 25.
40. Peter Wollen, "Blue," *New Left Review,* second series 6 (November–December 2000): 120–133 (121, 123).
41. See, for instance, Julia Kristeva, "About Chinese Women," trans. Séan Hand, in Toril Moi, ed., *The Kristeva Reader* (Oxford: Blackwell, 1986), 138–159 (157).
42. Douglas Khan, "Death in Light of the Phonograph: Raymond Roussel's *Locus Solus,*" in Douglas Khan and Gregory Whitehead, eds., *Wireless Imagination: Sound, Radio, and the Avant-Garde* (Cambridge, Mass.: MIT Press, 1994), 69–103 (93).
43. Celeste Langan, "Understanding Media in 1805: Audiovisual Hallucination in *The Lay of the Last Minstrel,*" *Studies in Romanticism* 40.1 (Spring 2001): 49–70.
44. Tzvetan Todorov, *The Fantastic: A Structural Approach to a Literary Genre,* trans. Richard Howard (Cleveland: Case Western Reserve University Press, 1973), 41–57.
45. Immanuel Kant, *Critique of Judgment,* trans. Werner S. Pluhar (Indianapolis, Ind.: Hackett, 1987), 97–140 (99, 112–113, 123).
46. See Markman Ellis, *The Politics of Sensibility: Race, Gender and Commerce in the Sentimental Novel* (Cambridge: Cambridge University Press, 1996); Jerome McGann, *The Poetics of Sensibility: A Revolution in Literary Style* (New York: Clarendon Press, 1996); G. J. Barker-Benfield, *The Culture of Sensibility: Sex and Society in Eighteenth-Century Britain* (Chicago: University of Chicago Press, 1992). For the ways in which poetics took account of emerging brain science, see Alan Richardson, *British Romanticism and the Science of the Mind* (Cambridge: Cambridge University Press, 2001).
47. Maurice Merleau-Ponty, *Phenomenology of Perception,* trans. Colin Smith (London: Routledge and Kegan Paul, 1996), 61.
48. John Locke, *An Essay Concerning Human Understanding,* trans. Peter H. Nidditch (Oxford: Clarendon Press, 1979), 301–304 (II.22.10–13).
49. Deidre Lynch, *The Economy of Character: Novels, Market Culture, and the Business of Inner Meaning* (Chicago: University of Chicago Press, 1998).

50. Murray Krieger, *Ekphrasis: The Illusion of the Natural Sign* (Baltimore, Md.: Johns Hopkins University Press, 1992); James Heffernan, *Museum of Words: The Poetics of Ekphrasis from Homer to Ashbery* (Chicago: University of Chicago Press, 1993).

51. Toop, *Ocean of Sound,* 15.

52. Jacques Derrida, "Différance," in *Margins of Philosophy,* 6, 26. For a contrary view, see Kate Rigby, "Ecstatic Dwelling: Cosmopolitan Reinhabitation in Wordsworth's London," paper given at the annual conference of the North American Society for Studies in Romanticism, Boulder, Colo., September 9–12, 2004.

53. For an example, see Kate Rigby, "Earth, World, Text: On the (Im)possibility of Ecopoiesis," *New Literary History* 35.3 (2004): 427–442.

54. Kant, *Critique of Judgment,* 106.

55. Ibid., 113.

56. Jonty Semper, *Kenotaphion* (Locus +/Charrm, 2002). The Two Minutes' Silence was adopted from the three minutes of silence held during the Boer War. Sir Percy Fitzpatrick, who promoted the idea, wrote: "Silence, complete and arresting, closed upon the city, the moving awe-inspiring silence of a great Cathedral where the smallest sound must seem a sacrilege." See Adrian Gregory, "The Silence and History," sleeve note, also available at *http://www.kenotaphion.org/.*

57. John Cage, *A Year from Monday* (Middletown, Conn.: Wesleyan University Press, 1967), 134.

58. Thomas De Quincey, "On the Knocking at the Gate in MacBeth," in *The Works of Thomas de Quincey,* ed. Edmund Baxter, Frederick Burwick, Alina Clej, David Groves, Grevel Lindop, Robert Morrison, Barry Symonds, and John Whale, 21 vols. (London: Pickering and Chatto, 2000), 3.152–153 (vol. 3, ed. Burwick).

59. *Oxford English Dictionary,* "syncope," *n.* 1, 4.

60. Jacques Attali, *Noise: The Political Economy of Music,* trans. Brian Massumi, foreword by Fredric Jameson, afterword by Susan McClary (Minneapolis: University of Minnesota Press, 2003), 34–36, 111–112, 122–123.

61. Robert Freedman et al., "Linkage of a Neurological Deficit in Schizophrenia to a Chromosome 15 Locus," *http://www.pnas.org/cgi/content/abstract/94/2/587.* See also *http://narsad.org/news/newsletter/profiles/profile2003-06-25c.html.*

62. Alvin Lucier, *I Am Sitting in a Room* (Lovely Music, 1990).

63. See for example Andy Goldsworthy, *Time* (London: Thames and Hudson, 2000).

64. Jacques Derrida, "Violence and Metaphysics," in *Writing and Difference,* trans. Alan Bass (London: Routledge and Kegan Paul, 1978), 79–153 (151–152).

65. Jacques Derrida, *Dissemination,* trans. Barbara Johnson (Chicago: University of Chicago Press, 1981), 54, 104, 205, 208, 222, 253.

66. There is only enough space to mention briefly Derrida's *Glas* ("clang"),

which is in part a meditation on the idea of bells and tongues; Jacques Derrida, *Glas*, trans. John P. Leavey Jr. and Richard Rand (Lincoln: University of Nebraska Press, 1986).

67. David Harvey, *Justice, Nature and the Geography of Difference* (Oxford: Blackwell, 1996), 243, 246.
68. Roger Penrose, *The Emperor's New Mind: Concerning Computers, Minds, and the Laws of Physics* (Oxford: Oxford University Press, 1990), 231–236, 243, 248–250, 250–251, 255–256.
69. Ibid., 126.
70. Geoffrey Hartman, *The Fateful Question of Culture* (New York: Columbia University Press, 1997), 158.
71. Georges Teyssot, "The American Lawn: The Surface of Everyday Life," in Georges Teyssot, ed., *The American Lawn* (New York: Princeton Architectural Press, 1999), 1–39 (5–8). The Archigram Monte Carlo Project (1970) featured a collage of images of people on lawns entitled *Ambience* (176).
72. Bruno Latour, *Politics of Nature: How to Bring the Sciences into Democracy* (Cambridge, Mass.: Harvard University Press, 2004), 58.
73. Yve-Alain Bois and Rosalind Kraus, *Formless: A User's Guide* (New York: Zone Books, 1997), 79.
74. Ibid., 26–29.
75. Ibid., 90.
76. Slavoj Žižek, *The Fragile Absolute: Or, Why Is the Christian Legacy Worth Fighting For?* (London: Verso, 2000), 21–40.
77. Jean-François Lyotard, "After the Sublime, the State of Aesthetics," in *The Inhuman: Reflections on Time*, trans. Geoffrey Bennington and Rachel Bowlby (Cambridge: Polity Press, 1991), 140. See David Cunningham, "Notes on Nuance: Rethinking a Philosophy of Modern Music," *Radical Philosophy* 125 (May–June 2004): 17–28.
78. Gilles Deleuze and Félix Guattari, *A Thousand Plateaus: Capitalism and Schizophrenia*, trans. Brian Massumi (Minneapolis: University of Minnesota Press, 1987), 3–25; Sadie Plant, *Zeroes + Ones* (London: Fourth Estate, 1998).
79. Paul Miller, *Rhythm Science* (Cambridge, Mass.: MIT Press, 2004).
80. Gilles Deleuze and Félix Guattari, "make rhizome everywhere," in *A Thousand Plateaus*, 191.
81. Bruce Smith, "Tuning into London c. 1600," in Bull and Back, *The Auditory Culture Reader*, 127–135 (131–132).
82. Aristotle, *On the Art of Poetry*, in *Classical Literary Criticism: Aristotle, Horace, Longinus*, trans. T. S. Dorsch (Harmondsworth: Penguin, 1984), 31, 35.
83. Henry George Liddell and Robert Scott, *A Greek-English Lexicon*, rev. and augmented by Henry Stuart Jones et al. (Oxford: Clarendon Press, 1968), *rhapsodes*.
84. *Oxford English Dictionary*, "rhapsody," *n.* 1, 2.

85. Plato, *Plato; Two Comic Dialogues: Ion, Hippias Major,* trans. Paul Woodruff (Indianapolis, Ind.: Hackett, 1983), 26 (534a).
86. Ibid.
87. Ibid.
88. Marcel Detienne, *Dionysos at Large,* trans. Arthur Goldhammer (Cambridge, Mass.: Harvard University Press, 1989), 55.
89. Plato, *Plato,* 535.
90. Ibid.
91. Detienne, *Dionysos at Large,* 53.
92. An aptly ambient example is André Breton, "Intra-Uterine Life," from *The Immaculate Conception,* in *What Is Surrealism? Selected Writings,* ed. Franklin Rosemont (London: Pluto Press, 1978), 49–61 (49–50).
93. André Breton, "The Automatic Message," in *What Is Surrealism?,* 97–109 (98).
94. Richardson, *Mind,* 39–65, 66–92.
95. William Wordsworth, *The Prelude* 1.1, in *The Thirteen Book Prelude,* ed. Mark Reed (Ithaca, N.Y.: Cornell University Press, 1991).
96. Friedrich Nietzsche, *The Birth of Tragedy,* in Albert Hofstadter and Richard Kuhns, eds., *Philosophies of Art and Beauty: Selected Readings in Aesthetics from Plato to Heidegger* (Chicago: University of Chicago Press, 1976), 513–514.
97. Ibid., 500–501.
98. Heidegger, "Origin," 33–34.
99. Ibid., 35.
100. Ibid., 19, 32, 45, 42–43.
101. Martin Heidegger, "Letter on Humanism," in *Basic Writings,* ed. David Farrell Krell (New York: Harper and Row, 1977), 210.
102. Aristotle, *Poetry,* 35.
103. *Weltarm,* "poor in world": "Plant and animal . . . have no world." Heidegger, "Origin," 43.
104. David Abram, "Speaking with Animal Tongues," essay for the Acoustic Ecology Institute, *http://www.acousticecology.org/writings/animaltongues.html.*
105. Edward Thomas, *The Collected Poems of Edward Thomas,* ed. R. George Thomas (Oxford: Oxford University Press, 1981). By permission of Oxford University Press.
106. Martin Heidegger, "Time and Being," in *On Time and Being,* trans. Joan Stambaugh (New York: Harper and Row, 1972), 18.
107. Emmanuel Levinas, "There Is: Existence without Existents," in Seán Hand, ed., *The Levinas Reader* (Oxford: Blackwell, 1989), 29–36 (30).
108. Ibid., 30, 30–31, 32.
109. Allen Grossman with Mark Halliday, *The Sighted Singer; Two Works on Poetry for Readers and Writers* (Baltimore, Md.: Johns Hopkins University Press, 1992), 211.
110. Denise Gigante, "After Taste: The Aesthetics of Romantic Eating" (Ph.D.

dissertation, Princeton University, 2000). Samuel Taylor Coleridge, *The Rime of the Ancient Mariner,* in *Coleridge's Poetry and Prose,* ed. Nicholas Halmi, Paul Magnuson, and Raimonda Modiano (New York: Norton, 2004).

111. *Coleridge's Poetry and Prose,* ed. Nicholas Halmi, Paul Magnuson, and Raimonda Modiano (New York: Norton, 2004).

112. Henry David Thoreau, *The Maine Woods* (Harmondsworth: Penguin, 1988), 93.

113. Ibid., 94.

114. *Oxford English Dictionary,* "handsel," *n.* 1–3.

115. Thoreau, *The Maine Woods,* 95.

116. Stanley Allan Tag, "Growing Outward into the World: Henry David Thoreau and the Maine Woods Narrative Tradition 1804–1886" (Ph.D. dissertation, University of Iowa, 1994).

117. John M. Meyer, *Political Nature: Environmentalism and the Interpretation of Western Thought* (Cambridge, Mass.: MIT Press, 2001), 41.

118. Ibid., 34, 137–138.

119. Val Plumwood, *Environmental Culture: The Ecological Crisis of Reason* (London: Routledge, 2002), 230.

120. Ibid., 230–231.

121. Toop, *Ocean of Sound,* 1–2.

122. Slavoj Žižek, *Looking Awry: An Introduction to Jacques Lacan through Popular Culture* (Cambridge, Mass.: MIT Press, 1992), 132, 135–137; Slavoj Žižek, *The Sublime Object of Ideology* (London: Verso, 1989), 74–75, 76–79. In general, the seventh chapter of *Looking Awry* is a sustained analysis of the rhetoric and politics of the sinthome. The term is a pun on St. Thomas, who had to insert his fingers into the gaping wound in the side of the risen Christ, who had returned to convince Thomas of His reality. For Lacan, the sinthome is neither symptom nor fantasy but "the point marking the dimension of 'what is in the subject more than himself' and what he therefore 'loves more than himself' " (Žižek, *Looking Awry,* 132).

123. See Žižek's discussion of Ridley Scott's film *Alien* (*Sublime Object,* 79). It also squares with Lacan's view of subjecthood as a hole in the real caused by the removal of a "little bit" of it, that nevertheless results in the *framing* of reality (see Jacques-Alain Miller's explanation in Žižek, *Looking Awry,* 94–95).

124. See Jacques Derrida, "There Is No *One* Narcissism (Autobiophotographies)," in *Points: Interviews, 1974–1994,* ed. Elisabeth Weber, trans. Peggy Kamuf et al. (Stanford, Calif.: Stanford University Press, 1995), 196–215 (199).

125. Pink Floyd, "Echoes," *Meddle* (EMI, 1971); The Beatles, "I Am the Walrus," *Yellow Submarine* (EMI, 1967).

126. Maurice Merleau-Ponty, "The Intertwining—The Chiasm," in *The Visible and the Invisible,* ed. Claude Lefort, trans. Alfonso Lingis (Evanston, IL: Northwestern University Press, 1968), 130–155.

127. Slavoj Žižek, *For They Know Not What They Do: Enjoyment as a Political Factor* (1991; repr., London: Verso, 1994), 76.

128. Gary Snyder, *Mountains and Rivers without End* (Washington, D.C.: Counterpoint, 1996).

129. J. B. Lamarck, "Preliminary Discourse," in *Zoological Philosophy* (Chicago: University of Chicago Press, 1984), 15.

130. Paul Ricoeur, *The Rule of Metaphor: Multi-Disciplinary Studies of the Creation of Meaning in Language,* trans. Robert Czerny, with Kathleen McLaughlin and John Costello (Toronto: University of Toronto Press, 1977), 43.

131. Lord George Gordon Byron, Letter to Annabella Milbanke, November 29, 1813, in *Byron's Letters and Journals,* ed. Leslie Marchand, 12 vols. (London: John Murray Publishers, 1973–1982), 3.179 (vol. 3, 1974).

132. Ricoeur, *Rule of Metaphor,* 43.

133. Theodor Adorno, *Aesthetic Theory,* trans. and ed. Robert Hullot-Kentor (Minneapolis: University of Minnesota Press, 1997), 63–64.

134. See Douglas Khan, *Noise Water Meat: A History of Sound in the Arts* (Cambridge, Mass.: MIT Press, 2001), 161–199.

135. Sigmund Freud, *Beyond the Pleasure Principle,* in *Standard Edition,* 18.62. In Hartman's haunting phrase, "we call peace what is really desolation" (*Culture,* 191). See Freud 30–31, 47, 67, 76 (on the "Nirvana" principle).

136. Theodor W. Adorno, "Sur l'Eau," in *Minima Moralia: Reflections from Damaged Life,* trans. E. F. N. Jephcott (London: Verso, 1978), 155–157 (157).

137. Mary Shelley, *The Last Man: By the Author of "Frankenstein,"* 3 vols. (London: Henry Colburn, 1826), 3.1–3.

138. William Wordsworth, "Note on The Thorn," in *William Wordsworth: The Major Works,* ed. Stephen Gill (Oxford: Oxford University Press, 1984), 594.

139. Goethe was the first to theorize the notion of the afterimage. Johann Wolfgang von Goethe, *Theory of Colours,* trans. Charles Lock Eastlake (London: Frank Cass, 1967), 16–28.

140. James A. Snead, "Repetition as a Figure of Black Culture," in Henry Louis Gates Jr., ed., *Black Literature and Literary Theory* (London: Routledge, 1984), 59–80.

141. William Wordsworth, "There Was a Boy," in *Lyrical Ballads.*

142. Thomas De Quincey, *Recollections of the Lakes and the Lake Poets,* ed. David Wright (Harmondsworth: Penguin, 1970), 119–206 (160).

143. Ibid.

144. Wordsworth, preface to the *Lyrical Ballads,* 746.

145. Kant, *Critique of Judgment,* 130.

146. Ibid., 131.

147. Julia Kristeva, *Revolution in Poetic Language,* trans. Margaret Waller, in Moi, *The Kristeva Reader,* 89–136 (120).

148. Ibid., 121.

2. Romanticism and the Environmental Subject

1. This is one of Basho's most famous haikus. See Matsuo Basho, *The Essential Basho*, trans. Sam Hamill (Boston: Shambhala, 1999).
2. Leo Spitzer, "Milieu and Ambiance," in *Essays in Historical Semantics* (1948; repr., New York: Russell and Russell, 1968), 179, 183, 186–187, 201–207.
3. Ibid., 206–207.
4. Ursula K. Heise, "Sense of Place and Sense of Planet: A Polemic," paper given at the MLA Convention, Philadelphia, December 27–30, 2004.
5. William Shakespeare, *The Tempest*, in *The Complete Works*, ed. Peter Alexander (London: Collins, 1951).
6. Timothy Morton, *The Poetics of Spice: Romantic Consumerism and the Exotic* (Cambridge: Cambridge University Press, 2000), 9–10, 90–104, 167–168, 234–235.
7. Raymond Williams, *Culture and Society: Coleridge to Orwell* (London: Chatto and Windus, 1958; repr., London: The Hogarth Press, 1987), 234–238; *Culture* (London: Fontana Press, 1989), 10–14. See David Simpson, "Raymond Williams: Feeling for Structures, Voicing 'History'," in Christopher Prendergast, ed., *Cultural Materialism on Raymond Williams* (Minneapolis: University of Minnesota Press, 1995), 29–49.
8. See Tilottama Rajan, *Deconstruction and the Remainders of Phenomenology: Sartre, Derrida, Foucault, Baudrillard* (Stanford, Calif.: Stanford University Press, 2002).
9. Jacques Derrida, *Of Grammatology*, trans. Gayatri Chakravorty Spivak (Baltimore, Md.: Johns Hopkins University Press, 1987), 101–140; Maureen McLane, *Romanticism and the Human Sciences: Poetry, Population, and the Discourse of Species* (Cambridge: Cambridge University Press, 2000), 33–35, 48–62.
10. Karl Marx, *Selected Writings*, ed. David McLellan (Oxford: Oxford University Press, 1977), 224–225.
11. Alan Bewell, *Romanticism and Colonial Disease* (Baltimore, Md.: Johns Hopkins University Press, 2000), 30–31, 244–245.
12. Ulrich Beck, *Risk Society: Towards a New Modernity*, trans. Mark Ritter (London: Sage, 1992), 13–28.
13. Ibid., 19.
14. Ernst Bloch, quoted in Mike Davis, "The Flames of New York," *New Left Review* 12 (November–December 2001): 34–50 (41).
15. David Harvey, *Justice, Nature and the Geography of Difference* (Oxford: Blackwell, 1996), 241.
16. Henri Lefebvre, *The Production of Space*, trans. Donald Nicholson-Smith (1974; repr., Oxford: Blackwell, 1991), 191, 346–347, 348–351, 359–360.
17. Rem Koolhaas, "Junkspace," *October* 100 (Spring 2002): 175–190.
18. Ibid., 177.
19. Marc Augé, *Non-Places: Introduction to an Anthropology of Supermoder-*

nity, trans. John Howe (London: Verso, 1995), 111; see also 2–3, 31–32, 34, 44–45, 94, 97–98.

20. Karl Marx, *Capital*, trans. Ben Fowkes, 3 vols. (Harmondsworth: Penguin, 1990), 311.
21. See Beck, *Risk Society*, 39.
22. Peter Wollen, "Blue," *New Left Review*, second series 6 (November–December 2000): 133. Kevin McLaughlin has explored the role of paper as a modern metaphor for this potential energy, in *Paperwork: Fiction and Mass Mediacy in the Paper Age* (Philadelphia: University of Pennsylvania Press, 2005), 6–11.
23. Marx, *Capital*, 556.
24. Ibid., 889.
25. Koolhaas, "Junkspace," 186.
26. Gilles Deleuze and Félix Guattari, *Anti-Oedipus: Capitalism and Schizophrenia*, trans. R. Hurley, M. Seem, and H. Lane (Minneapolis: University of Minnesota Press, 1983), 17–18, 42.
27. Ibid., 2.
28. I take the name from the famous Sound Factory club in New York City in the 1990s.
29. Lindsay Waters, "Come Softly, Darling, Hear What I Say: Listening in a State of Distraction—A Tribute to the Work of Walter Benjamin, Elvis Presley, and Robert Christgau," *boundary 2* 30.1 (Spring 2003): 199–212.
30. Slavoj Žižek, "How Did Marx Invent the Social Symptom?" in *The Sublime Object of Ideology* (London: Verso, 1991), 11–53; Terry Eagelton, *Ideology: An Introduction* (London: Verso, 1991), 40.
31. Amiri Baraka, "Something in the Way of Things (in Town)," The Roots, *Phrenology* (MCA, 2002).
32. Marx, *Capital*, 366–367.
33. Friedrich Engels, *The Condition of the Working Class in England*, ed. Victor Kiernan (1845; repr., Harmondsworth: Penguin, 1987), 86.
34. Jonathan Bate, *Romantic Ecology: Wordsworth and the Environmental Tradition* (London: Routledge, 1991), 36–61.
35. Georges Teyssot's *The American Lawn* (New York: Princeton Architectural Press, 1999) indicates the frisson of kitsch and high modernism that the lawn produces. Moreover, the association between lawn and canvas was part of lawn aesthetics: Alessandra Ponte, "Professional Pastoral: The Writing on the Lawn, 1850–1950," in *The American Lawn*, 89–115 (101–102).
36. T. J. Clark, "In Defense of Abstract Expressionism," *October* 69 (Summer 1994): 23–48.
37. For a comprehensive discussion see Thomas Hothem, "The Picturesque and the Production of Space: Suburban Ideology in Austen," *European Romantic Review* 13.1 (March 2002): 49–62.
38. Virginia Scott Jenkins, *The Lawn: A History of An American Obsession* (Washington, D.C.: Smithsonian Institution Press, 1994), 4.

39. Tom Fort, *The Grass Is Greener: Our Love Affair with the Lawn* (London: HarperCollins, 2001), 149.

40. Official Monticello website, *http://www.monticello.org/jefferson/planta tion/home.html*.

41. Thorstein Veblen, *The Theory of the Leisure Class: An Economic Study of Institutions* (New York: Dover, 1994), 82.

42. Ibid., 83.

43. John Keats, *The Complete Poems,* ed. John Barnard (Harmondsworth: Penguin, 1987).

44. Marx, *Capital,* 462.

45. Ibid., 532–533.

46. Marx, *The Communist Manifesto,* in *Selected Writings,* ed. David McLellan (Oxford: Oxford University Press, 1977), 227.

47. Marx, *Capital,* 365.

48. Charles Dickens, *Hard Times* (Oxford: Oxford University Press, 1998), 1.

49. Marx, *Capital,* 638.

50. Alfred W. Crosby, *Ecological Imperialism: The Biological Expansion of Europe, 900–1900* (Cambridge: Cambridge University Press, 1993), 77, 298–299.

51. Peter Kitson, in Tim Fulford, Peter Kitson, and Debbie Lee, *Literature, Science and Exploration in the Romantic Era: Bodies of Knowledge* (Cambridge: Cambridge University Press, 2005), 171–175.

52. David Simpson, "How Marxism Reads 'The Rime of the Ancient Mariner,'" in Paul H. Fry, ed., *Samuel Taylor Coleridge: The Rime of the Ancient Mariner; Complete, Authoritative Texts of the 1798 and 1817 Versions with Biographical and Historical Contexts, Critical History, and Essays from Contemporary Critical Perspectives* (Boston: Bedford Books of St. Martin's Press, 1999), 148–167 (155–157).

53. Vandana Shiva, *Biopiracy: The Plunder of Nature and Knowledge* (Boston: South End Press, 1997).

54. *USA Today,* June 26, 2000, *http://www.usatoday.com/life/health/genetics/ lhgec068.html*.

55. Martin Heidegger, *Being and Time,* trans. Joan Stambaugh (Albany: State University of New York Press, 1996), 98. Heidegger sees this ignorance as a creation of "modern technology" rather than capitalism, a relentless desire to see and know everything, to be in all places at once. Martin Heidegger, *On Time and Being,* trans. Joan Stambaugh (New York: Harper and Row, 1972), 7. In opposition to this, Heidegger asserts a philosophy of opacity and obscurity. Nearness is not the same as knowledge.

56. Franco Moretti, "Graphs, Maps, Trees: Abstract Models for Literary History 2," *New Left Review,* second series 26 (March–April 2004): 79–103.

57. Bruce R. Smith, *The Acoustic World of Early Modern England: Attending to the O-Factor* (Chicago: University of Chicago Press, 1999). Auditory cultural studies is proliferating. See Michael Bull and Les Back, eds., *The Auditory Culture Reader* (Oxford: Berg, 2003). See also Smith's remarks in

"Poetry and Theory: A Roundtable," *PMLA* 120.1 (January 2005): 97–107 (102–104).

58. Reissued on CD as *Songs of the Humpback Whale* (Living Music, 1998; vinyl, 1970); *Deep Voices: Recordings of Humpback, Blue and Right Whales* (Living Music, 1995).

59. David Toop, *Haunted Weather: Music, Silence and Memory* (London: Serpent's Tail, 2004), 191–192.

60. Marc Redfield, "Radio-Nation: Fichte and the Body of Germany," paper presented at the annual conference of the North American Society for Studies in Romanticism, Tempe, Arizona, September 14–17, 2000.

61. Heidegger, *Being and Time*, 53–54, 61–62, 94–105.

62. Ibid., 65–67.

63. Ibid., 96.

64. J. R. R. Tolkien, *The Hobbit* (1937; repr., London: Unwin, 1977), 249; *The Lord of the Rings* (1954; repr., London: Unwin, 1977), 1.43.

65. Georg Wilhelm Freidrich Hegel, *Introductory Lectures on Aesthetics*, trans. Bernard Bosanquet, intro. and commentary Michael Inwood (1886; repr., Harmondsworth: Penguin, 1993), 70–75.

66. Dana Phillips, *The Truth of Ecology: Nature, Culture, and Literature in America* (Oxford: Oxford University Press, 2003), 71.

67. The phrase "The Question of the Animal" is the subtitle of Cary Wolfe, ed., *Zoontologies* (Minneapolis: University of Minnesota Press, 2003). Wolfe's introduction powerfully outlines the stakes (ix–xxiii).

68. Giorgio Agamben, *The Open*, trans. Kevin Attell (Stanford, Calif.: Stanford University Press, 2004), 39–43.

69. Edmund Husserl, *The Essential Husserl: Basic Writings in Transcendental Phenomenology*, ed. Donn Welton (Bloomington: Indiana University Press, 1999), 155.

70. Martin Heidegger, "The Origin of the Work of Art," in *Poetry, Language, Thought*, trans. Albert Hofstadter (New York: Harper and Row, 1971), 43. See Jacques Derrida, *Of Spirit: Heidegger and the Question*, trans. Geoffrey Bennington and Rachel Bowlby (Chicago: University of Chicago Press, 1991), 47–57.

71. Jacques Derrida, " 'Eating Well,' or, the Calculation of the Subject," in *Points: Interviews, 1974–1994*, ed. Elisabeth Weber, trans. Peggy Kamuf et al. (Stanford, Calif.: Standford University Press, 1995), 255–287 (277).

72. Denise Levertov, "Some Affinities of Content," in *New and Selected Essays* (New York: New Directions, 1992), 1–21; "The Poet in the World," *New and Selected Essays*, 129–138.

73. David Clark, "On Being 'the Last Kantian in Nazi Germany': Dwelling with Animals after Levinas," in Jennifer Ham and Matthew Senior, eds., *Animal Acts: Configuring the Human in Western History* (New York: Routledge, 1997), 165–198; a revision appears in Barbara Gabriel and Susan Ilcan, eds., *Postmodernism and the Ethical Subject* (Kingston: McGill–Queen's University Press, 2004), 41–75.

74. Tolkien, *Lord of the Rings*, 2.254.

75. Jacques Derrida, Givanna Borradori (interviewer), *Philosophy in a Time of Terror: Dialogues with Jürgen Habermas and Jacques Derrida* (Chicago: University of Chicago Press, 2003), 85–172 (129). Derrida's seminal statement on hospitality is "Hostipitality," in *Acts of Religion,* ed., trans., and intro. Gil Anidjar (London: Routledge, 2002), 356–420.

76. Timothy Morton, *Shelley and the Revolution in Taste: The Body and the Natural World* (Cambridge: Cambridge University Press, 1994), 155.

77. Paul Hamilton, *Metaromanticism: Aesthetics, Litertature, Theory* (Chicago: University of Chicago Press, 2003), 261–262.

78. Hegel, *Aesthetics,* 73.

79. *The Observer,* February 22, 2004.

80. Paul Virilio, *Popular Defense and Ecological Struggles,* trans. Mark Polizzotti (1978; repr., New York: Semiotext(e), 1990), 50, 72.

81. See for example Emily Thompson, *The Soundscape of Modernity* (Cambridge, Mass.: MIT Press, 2002).

82. David Simpson, *Romanticism, Nationalism and the Revolt against Theory* (Chicago: University of Chicago Press, 1993), 72.

83. Herbert Marcuse, *One-Dimensional Man: Studies in the Ideology of Advanced Industrial Society,* 2nd ed., intro. Douglas Kellner (1964; repr., Boston: Beacon Press, 1991), *passim* but especially 14, 26–27, 36–37, 59, 61, 80–83. See Timothy Luke, "Marcuse and the Politics of Radical Ecology," in *Ecocritique: Contesting the Politics of Nature, Economy, and Culture* (Minneapolis: University of Minnesota Press, 1997), 137–152.

84. Phillips, *Truth of Ecology,* 67.

85. Arne Naess, *Ecology, Community, and Lifestyle: A Philosophical Approach* (Oslo: University of Oslo Press, 1977), 56.

86. Blaise Pascal, *Pensées,* trans. A. J. Krailsheime (Harmondsworth: Penguin, 1995), 201.

87. Maurice Blanchot, *The Space of Literature,* trans. Ann Smock (1955; repr., Lincoln: University of Nebraska Press, 1982), 217.

88. *Oxford English Dictionary,* "field," *n.* III.17.a.

89. Roger Penrose, *The Emperor's New Mind: Concerning Computers, Minds, and the Laws of Physics* (Oxford: Oxford University Press, 1990), 185.

90. Husserl, *The Essential Husserl,* 159.

91. Edward Casey, *The Fate of Place: A Philosophical History* (Berkeley: University of California Press, 1997), 151–161.

92. Luc Ferry, *The New Ecological Order,* trans. Carol Volk (Chicago: University of Chicago Press, 1995), 21–24, 47–49, 53–54, 69, 70, 122, 140–141.

93. Michel Serres, *The Natural Contract,* trans. Elizabeth MacArthur and William Paulson (Ann Arbor: University of Michigan Press, 1998), 34.

94. Edmund Husserl, *Cartesian Meditations: An Introduction to Phenomenology,* trans. Dorion Cairns (The Hague: Martinus Nijhoff, 1973), 1. Cited in David Simpson, "Putting One's House in Order: The Career of the Self in Descartes' Method," *New Literary History* 9 (1977–1978): 101n10.

95. Dalia Judowitz, *Subjectivity and Representation in Descartes: The Origins of Modernity* (Cambridge: Cambridge University Press, 1988). The possibility that Descartes' use of fiction reflects a deep tendency toward dissimulation can be found in Louis E. Loeb, "Is There Radical Dissimulation in Descartes' *Meditations?*" in Amélie Oksenberg Rorty, ed., *Essays on Descartes' Meditations* (Berkeley: University of California Press, 1986), 243–270.

96. Simpson, *Theory*, 88.

97. *Oxford English Dictionary*, "field," *n.* III.17a–d.

98. Husserl, *Essential Husserl*, 166–170.

99. David Abram, *The Spell of the Sensuous: Perception and Language in a More-Than-Human World* (New York: Pantheon, 1996), 202–203.

100. Ibid., 203–210.

101. Mary Klages has argued that the sentimentalization of disability in the nineteenth century has resulted in a view that communication is a transcendence of disability. Mary Klages, *Woeful Afflictions: Disability and Sentimentality in Victorian America* (Philadelphia: University of Pennsylvania Press, 1999).

102. Rod Giblett, *Postmodern Wetlands: Culture, History, Ecology* (Edinburgh: Edinburgh University Press, 1996), 237.

103. Donna Haraway, "A Cyborg Manifesto: Science, Technology, and Socialist-Feminism in the Late Twentieth Century," in *Simians, Cyborgs, and Women: The Reinvention of Nature* (London: Routledge, 1991), 149–181 (152).

104. Lynn Margulis, *Symbiosis in Cell Evolution* (New York: W.H. Freeman, 1981); Lynn Margulis and Dorion Sagan, *Microcosmos: Four Billion Years of Evolution from Our Microbial Ancestors* (Berkeley: University of California Press, 1997).

105. Bruno Latour, *We Have Never Been Modern*, trans. Catherine Porter (Cambridge, Mass.: Harvard University Press, 2002), 49–55. See also Latour, *Politics of Nature: How to Bring the Sciences into Democracy* (Cambridge, Mass.: Harvard University Press, 2004), 22–25.

106. Latour, *Politics of Nature*, 24. See also Latour, *Pandora's Hope: Essays on the Reality of Science Studies* (Cambridge, Mass.: Harvard University Press, 1999), 174–215.

107. Abram, *Spell of the Sensuous*, 66.

108. Georges Bataille, *The Accursed Share: An Essay on General Economy*, vol. 1, trans. Robert Hurley (New York: Zone Books, 1988), 19–26.

109. Ibid., 20.

110. Paul Hawken, Amory Lovins, and L. Hunter Lovins, *Natural Capitalism: Creating the Next Industrial Revolution* (Boston: Little, Brown, 1999).

111. Peter Stallybrass and Allon White, *The Politics and Poetics of Transgression* (London: Methuen, 1986), 23–25.

112. Allen Ginsberg, *Collected Poems 1947–1980* (New York: Harper, 1988).

113. Neil McKendrick, John Brewer, and J.H. Plumb, *The Birth of a Consumer*

Society: The Commercialization of Eighteenth-Century England (Bloomington: Indiana University Press, 1982).

114. Morton, *Shelley,* 13–21, 30–38.

115. Morton, *Poetics of Spice,* 5, 9–11.

116. Pierre Bourdieu, *Distinction: A Social Critique of the Judgement of Taste,* trans. Richard Nice (London: Routledge, 1989), 34–44.

117. I develop this term following Colin Campbell, *The Romantic Ethic and the Spirit of Modern Consumerism* (Oxford: Basil Blackwell, 1987); "Understanding Traditional and Modern Patterns of Consumption in Eighteenth-Century England: A Character-Action Approach," in John Brewer and Roy Porter, eds., *Consumption and the World of Goods* (London: Routledge, 1993), 40–57.

118. Emily Jenkins, *Tongue First: Adventures in Physical Culture* (New York: Henry Holt, 1998).

119. Timothy Murphy, "William Burroughs Between Indifference and Revalorization: Notes towards a Political Reading," *Angelaki* 1.1 (1993): 113–124.

120. Morton, *Poetics of Spice,* 23.

121. Sigmund Freud, *Civilization and Its Discontents,* in *The Standard Edition of the Complete Psychological Works of Sigmund Freud,* ed. and trans. James Strachey, 24 vols. (London: Hogarth, 1953), 11.64–65.

122. Percy Bysshe Shelley, "On Life," in *Shelley's Prose: Or The Trumpet of a Prophecy,* ed. David Lee Clark (London: Fourth Estate, 1988), 171–175 (174).

123. John Keats, letter to Richard Woodhouse, October 27, 1818, in *Poetical Works and Other Writings of Keats,* 8 vols., ed. H. Buxton Forman (New York: Phaeton, 1970), 7.129.

124. John Keats, letter 159, in *The Letters of John Keats, 1814–1821,* 2 vols., ed. Hyder F. Rollins (Cambridge, Mass.: Harvard University Press, 1958); *Arabian Nights' Entertainments,* ed. Robert L. Mack (Oxford: Oxford University Press, 1995), 658–659.

125. Ludwig Feuerbach, *Gesammelte Werke II, Kleinere Schriften,* ed. Werner Schuffenhauer (Berlin: Akadamie-Verlag, 1972), 4.27; Jean-Anthelme Brillat-Savarin, *The Physiology of Taste,* trans. Anne Drayton (Harmondsworth: Penguin, 1970), 13.

126. Jack Turner, *The Abstract Wild* (Tucson: University of Arizona Press, 1997), 32.

127. Immanuel Kant, *Critique of Judgment,* trans. Werner S. Pluhar (Indianapolis, Ind.: Hackett, 1987), 108.

128. Jean-Paul Sartre, *Being and Nothingness: An Essay on Phenomenological Ontology,* trans. and ed. Hazel Barnes (New York: The Philosophical Library, 1969), 341–345 (342).

129. John Gatta, *Making Nature Sacred: Literature, Religion, and Environment in America from the Puritans to the Present* (Oxford: Oxford University Press, 2004), 15–33, 88–99.

130. Bate, *Romantic Ecology,* 14–16.

131. John Carey, *What Good Are the Arts?* (London: Faber and Faber, 2005), 3–64.

132. Terry Eagleton, *Literary Theory: An Introduction* (Oxford: Basil Blackwell, 1993), 24–25, 28–29.

133. Charles Baudelaire, "Correspondences," in *The Poems and Prose Poems of Charles Baudelaire,* ed. James Huneker (New York: Brentano's, 1919).

134. Thoreau, *Walden,* 156–168 (my emphasis).

135. Toop, *Haunted Weather,* 45.

136. Timothy Morton, "Consumption as Performance: The Emergence of the Consumer in the Romantic Period," in Timothy Morton, ed., *Cultures of Taste/Theories of Appetite: Eating Romanticism* (London: Palgrave, 2004), 1–17.

137. Theodor Adorno, *Aesthetic Theory,* trans. and ed. Robert Hullot-Kentor (Minneapolis: University of Minnesota Press, 1997), 140, 154, 159.

138. Karl Marx, "Toward a Critique of Hegel's *Philosophy of Right:* Introduction," in *Selected Writings,* ed. David McLellan (Oxford: Oxford University Press, 1977), 71.

139. Georg Wilhelm Friedrich Hegel, *Hegel's Phenomenology of Spirit,* trans. A. V. Miller, analysis and foreword by J. N. Findlay (Oxford: Oxford University Press, 1977), 383–409.

140. Moltke S. Gram, "Moral and Literary Ideals in Hegel's Critique of 'The Moral World-View,' " *Clio* 7.3 (1978): 375–402 (390).

141. David Icke, *It Doesn't Have to Be Like This: Green Politics Explained* (London: Green Print, 1990).

142. Timothy Morton, "Environmentalism," in Nicholas Roe, ed., *Romanticism: An Oxford Guide* (Oxford: Oxford University Press, forthcoming), 696–707.

143. Arthur Schopenhauer, *The World as Will and Representation,* 2 vols., trans. E. F. J. Payne (New York: Dover, 1969), 411.

144. Ibid., 412.

145. Ibid., 390.

146. Roland Emmerich (director), *The Day After Tomorrow* (20th Century Fox, 2004).

147. Malcolm Bull, "Where Is the Anti-Nietzsche?" *New Left Review,* second series 3 (May/June 2000): 121–145.

148. Ibid., 144–145.

149. In Marx, *Selected Writings,* 7–8.

150. James Treadwell, *Interpreting Wagner* (New Haven, Conn.: Yale University Press, 2003), 78–79.

151. Alan Gurganus, "Why We Fed the Bomber," *New York Times,* June 8, 2003; Jeffrey Gettleman, "Eric Rudolph: America's Terrorist, North Carolina's Folk Hero," *New York Times,* June 2, 2003.

152. See Phillips, *Truth of Ecology,* 159–172.

153. Penrose, *Emperor's New Mind,* 250–251; see 231–236, 243, 248–250, 255–256.

154. Hegel, *Phenomenology,* 389–390.

155. Ibid., 399.

156. Adorno, *Aesthetic Theory,* 64.

157. Derrida, *Of Grammatology,* 162.

158. James Boswell, *Boswell's Life of Johnson* (London: Oxford University Press, 1965), 333.

159. John McDowell, *Mind and World* (Cambridge, Mass.: Harvard University Press, 2003).

160. Ibid., 12–13.

161. Adorno, *Aesthetic Theory,* 179.

162. Ibid., 219.

163. Don DeLillo, *White Noise* (Harmondsworth: Penguin, 1986), 258.

164. Stanley Donen (director), *Bedazzled* (20th Century Fox, 1967).

165. Hegel, *Aesthetics,* 54–55.

166. Louis Althusser, "Ideology and the State," in *Lenin and Philosophy and Other Essays,* trans. Ben Brewster (New York: Monthly Review Press, 1971), 176.

167. Ibid., 173.

168. Marjorie Levinson, "The New Historicism: Back to the Future," in Marjorie Levinson et al., eds., *Rethinking Historicism—Critical Readings in Romantic History* (New York: Basil Blackwell, 1989), 18–63.

169. Theodor W. Adorno, *Kierkegaard: Construction of the Aesthetic,* trans. and ed. Robert Hullot-Kentor (Minneapolis: University of Minnesota Press, 1999, 40–46.

170. Pink Floyd, "Grantchester Meadows," *Ummagumma* (EMI, 1969). Words and Music by Roger Waters. © Copyright 1970 (Renewed) and 1980 Lupus Music Co. Ltd., London, England. TRO-Hampshire House Publishing Corp., New York, controls all publication rights for the U.S.A. and Canada. Used by Permission.

171. Samuel Taylor Coleridge, *Coleridge's Poetry and Prose,* ed. Nicholas Halmi, Paul Magnuson, and Raimonda Modiano (New York: Norton, 2004), 180.

172. Abram, *Spell of the Sensuous,* 266.

173. John Cage, "Composition as Process," in *Silence: Lectures and Writings* (Middletown, Conn.: Wesleyan University Press, 1961), 51.

174. Celeste Langan, "Understanding Media in 1805: Audiovisual Hallucination in *The Lay of the Last Minstrel,*" *Studies in Romanticism* 40.1 (Spring 2001): 49–70.

175. Abram, *Spell of the Sensuous,* 282n2. The anxiety about writing is common in autobiographical texts. See Paul De Man's interpretation of Proust's inversions of inside and outside: "Reading," in *Allegories of Reading* (New Haven, Conn.: Yale University Press, 1979), 57–78.

176. Edmund Burke, *A Philosophical Inquiry into the Origin of Our Ideas of the Sublime and the Beautiful,* ed. Adam Phillips (Oxford: Oxford University Press, 1998), 31.

177. Hegel, *Aesthetics*, 78.
178. The phrases belong to Wordsworth ("She dwelt among untrodden ways"), Charlotte Turner Smith (*Beachy Head*, 349, in *The Poems of Charlotte Smith*, ed. Stuart Curran [Oxford: Oxford University Press, 1993]), and Robert Frost, respectively.
179. Georg Wilhelm Friedrich Hegel, *Lectures on the Philosophy of Religion*, ed. Peter C. Hodgson, trans. R.F. Brown, P.C. Hodgson, and J.M. Stewart, with the assistance of H.S. Harris (Berkeley: University of California Press, 1988), 253–254, 265nn183,185, 266n188, 504–505; Georg Wilhelm Friedrich Hegel, *The Philosophy of History*, trans. J. Sibree, prefaces by Charles Hegel and J. Sibree, new introduction by C.J. Friedrich (1900; repr., New York: Dover Publications, 1956), 171; *Hegel's Logic*, 3rd ed., trans. William Wallace, foreword by J.N. Findlay (1873; repr., Oxford: Oxford University Press, 1975), 125, 127–128.
180. Hegel, *Phenomenology*, 395, 398–399.
181. See David Simpson, "Romanticism, Criticism and Theory," in Stuart Curran, ed., *The Cambridge Companion to British Romanticism* (Cambridge: Cambridge University Press, 1993), 10.
182. Georg Wilhelm Friedrich Hegel, *Aesthetics: Lectures on Fine Art*, 2 vols., trans. T.M. Knox (Oxford: Clarendon Press, 1975), 1.527.
183. Hegel, *Phenomenology*, 400.
184. Adorno, *Aesthetic Theory*, 103.
185. Bate, *Romantic Ecology*, 7–8.
186. Abram, *Spell of the Sensuous*, 39.
187. See David Simpson, *Situatedness, or, Why We Keep Saying Where We're Coming From* (Durham, N.C.: Duke University Press, 2002), 234.
188. Heidegger, "Origin," 33.
189. Sigmund Freud, "A Child Is Being Beaten," in *Standard Edition*, 17.179–204.
190. Abram, *Spell of the Sensuous*, 31–32, 42–43, 78.
191. Heidegger, *Being and Time*, 62, 83–94.
192. See Jacques Derrida, "The Rhetoric of Drugs," in *Points*, 228–254 (234–235).
193. Carl G. Jung, "The Difference between Eastern and Western Thinking," in *The Portable Jung*, ed. and intro. Joseph Campbell, trans. R. F. C. Hull (Harmondsworth: Viking Penguin, 1971; repr., New York: Penguin, 1976), 487.
194. See for example Geoffrey Hartman, *The Fateful Question of Culture* (New York: Columbia University Press, 1997), 70–71, 158.
195. "'Mont Blanc': Shelley's Sublime Allegory of the Real," in Steven Rosendale, ed., *The Greening of Literary Scholarship* (Iowa City: University of Iowa Press, 2002), 207–223 (214, 221).
196. Herbert Marcuse, *The Aesthetic Dimension: Toward a Critique of Marxist Aesthetics*, trans. Herbert Marcuse and Erica Sherover (Basingstoke: Macmillan, 1986), 37–38.

197. Hegel, *History,* 171.
198. Hegel, *Religion,* 252–254.
199. Hegel, *History,* 171.
200. Chögyam Trungpa, *Training the Mind and Cultivating Loving-Kindness* (Boston: Shambhala, 1993), 35–36.
201. Laura Brown, *Alexander Pope* (Oxford: Basil Blackwell, 1985), 28–45.
202. Theodor Adorno and Max Horkheimer, *Dialectic of Enlightenment,* trans. John Cumming (London: Verso, 1979), 61.

3. Imagining Ecology without Nature

1. Kristin Ross, *The Emergence of Social Space: Rimbaud and the Paris Commune* (Minneapolis: University of Minnesota Press, 1988), 47–74, 102.
2. Alain Badiou, *Ethics: An Essay on the Understanding of Evil,* trans. and intro. Peter Hallward (London: Verso, 2001), 40–57.
3. Scott Shershow has powerfully demonstrated this linkage. *The Work and the Gift* (Chicago: University of Chicago Press, 2005), 193–205. See Jean-Luc Nancy, *The Inoperative Community,* trans. Peter Connor et al. (Minneapolis: University of Minnesota Press, 1991).
4. Martin Heidegger, "Building Dwelling Thinking," in *Poetry, Language, Thought,* trans. Albert Hofstadter (New York: Harper and Row, 1971), 143–161 (153). See also "The Thing," in *Poetry, Language, Thought,* 163–186 (174). This is not just a matter of Old English but also of Latin. The *res* in *res publica* (republic) is the public "thing," that is, the transactions of an assembly. The resonance of *res* is both "object" and "circumstance," as well as "dealings" (Ethan Allen Andrews, *A Latin Dictionary: Founded on Andrews' Edition of Freund's Latin Dictionary,* rev. and enl. Charlton T. Lewis [Oxford: Clarendon Press, 1984]). See Bruno Latour, *Politics of Nature: How to Bring the Sciences into Democracy* (Cambridge, Mass.: Harvard University Press, 2004), 54.
5. See for example Emmanuel Levinas, "Ethics and Politics," in *The Levinas Reader* (Oxford: Blackwell, 1989), 289–297 (294); *Totality and Infinity: An Essay on Exteriority,* trans. Alphonso Lingis (Pittsburgh, Penn.: Duquesne University Press, 1969).
6. Jacques Derrida, "Hostipitality," in *Acts of Religion,* ed., trans., and intro. Gil Anidjar (London: Routledge, 2002), 356–420.
7. Robert Bernasconi, "Hegel and Levinas: The Possibility of Forgiveness and Reconciliation," *Archivio di Filosofia* 54 (1986): 325–346; "Levinas Face to Face with Hegel," *Journal of the British Society for Phenomenology* 13 (1982): 267–276.
8. Christof Koch, *The Quest for Consciousness: A Neurobiological Approach* (Englewood, Colo.: Roberts & Co., 2004), 33, 35, 83–84, 140–144, 250–255, 264–268.
9. See for example John M. Meyer, *Political Nature: Environmentalism and the Interpretation of Western Thought* (Cambridge, Mass.: MIT Press, 2001), 47.

10. See for example Gary Polis, ed., *Food Webs at the Landscape Level* (Chicago: University of Chicago Press, 2004).

11. That is, with reading. See David Abram, *The Spell of the Sensuous: Perception and Language in a More-Than-Human World* (New York: Pantheon, 1996), 131, 282n2.

12. James Henry Leigh Hunt, "A Now, Descriptive of a Hot Day," *The Indicator* 1 (1820): 300–302.

13. See for example David Robertson, *Ecohuman's Four Square Deck/Deal* (Davis, Calif.: Printed for the author, 2002), a deck of fifty-two cards like a deck of playing cards, which can be shuffled to give various instructions and observations concerning a tour beginning in Europe and ending in New York City; and *Freakin Magic Playing Cards* (Davis, Calif.: Printed for the author, 2003), based on a circumambulation of Yucca Mountain. Or see *http://www.davidrobertson.org/*.

14. William Wordsworth, *"The Ruined Cottage" and "The Pedlar,"* ed. James Butler (Ithaca, N.Y.: Cornell University Press, 1979).

15. Edward Thomas, *The Collected Poems of Edward Thomas,* ed. R. George Thomas (Oxford: Oxford University Press, 1981). By permission of Oxford University Press.

16. Wilfred Owen, *The Complete Poems and Fragments,* ed. Jon Stallworthy, 2 vols. (London: Chatto & Windus, 1983).

17. W. G. Sebald, *On the Natural History of Destruction,* trans. Anthea Bell (1999; repr., New York: Random House, 2003).

18. William Blake, *The Complete Poetry and Prose of William Blake,* rev. ed., ed. D. V. Erdman (New York: Doubleday, 1988).

19. Walter Benjamin, "Notes to the Theses on History," in *Gesammelte Schriften,* ed. Theodor Adorno and Gersshom Scholem, 7 vols. (Frankfurt am Main: Surkhamp, 1972–1989), 1.1232.

20. Mary Favret, "War, the Everyday, and the Romantic Novel," paper given at "New Approaches to the Romantic Novel, 1790–1848: A Symposium," the University of Colorado, Boulder, October 5–6, 2001.

21. William Blake, "Auguries of Innocence," in *The Complete Poetry and Prose of William Blake.*

22. James E. Wilson, *Terroir* (Berkeley: University of California Press; San Francisco: Wine Appreciation Guild, 1998); Patrick Bartholomew Reuter, "Terroir: The Articulation of Viticultural Place" (Master's Thesis, University of California, Davis, 1999).

23. Theodor W. Adorno, *Negative Dialectics,* trans. E. B. Ashton (New York: Continuum, 1973), 200.

24. For a decisive account, see Marjorie Levinson, "Pre- and Post-Dialectical Materialisms: Modeling Praxis without Subjects and Objects," *Cultural Critique* (Fall 1995): 111–120.

25. Clement Greenberg, "The Avant-Garde and Kitsch," in Gillo Dorfles, ed., *Kitsch: The World of Bad Taste* (New York: Bell, 1969), 116–126.

26. *Oxford English Dictionary,* "kitsch." German philology speculates that

kitsch derives from the English "sketch," though there is little or no evidence to prove it (Winfried Schleiner, private communication). The modern edition bundles *A Sand County Almanac* with *Sketches Here and There*, which turn out to be anything but sketchy in their outlining of the land ethic. *Kitsch* stems from the verb meaning "to put together sloppily." For a decisive analysis see Susan Stewart, *On Longing: Narratives of the Miniature, the Gigantic, the Souvenir, the Collection* (Chapel Hill, N.C.: Duke University Press, 1993), 166–169.

27. Arjun Appadurai, ed., *The Social Life of Things: Commodities in Cultural Perspective* (Cambridge: Cambridge University Press, 1986), 13, 15–17; Susan Sontag, "Notes on 'Camp,' " in *Against Interpretation* (1966; repr., New York: Doubleday, 1990), 275–292; Andrew Ross, "Uses of Camp," in *No Respect: Intellectuals and Popular Culture* (London: Routledge, 1989), 135–170.

28. Theodor Adorno, *Aesthetic Theory*, trans. and ed. Robert Hullot-Kentor (Minneapolis: University of Minnesota Press, 1997), 67.

29. Ibid., 66.

30. Yve-Alain Bois and Rosalind Kraus, *Formless: A User's Guide* (New York: Zone Books, 1997), 117–124.

31. Brian Eno, *Ambient 1: Music for Airports* (EG Records, 1978), sleeve note.

32. Adorno, *Aesthetic Theory*, 103.

33. Nicholas Collins, sleeve note in Alvin Lucier, *I Am Sitting in a Room* (Lovely Music, 1990).

34. Paul Hamilton, *Metaromanticism: Aesthetics, Litertature, Theory* (Chicago: University of Chicago Press), 102–104.

35. Adorno, *Aesthetic Theory*, 67.

36. Bois and Kraus, *Formless*, 118.

37. Terry Eagleton, *Literary Theory: An Introduction* (1983; repr., Oxford: Basil Blackwell, 1993), 82.

38. Georg Wilhelm Friedrich Hegel, *Hegel's Phenomenology of Spirit*, trans. A. V. Miller, analysis and foreword by J. N. Findlay (Oxford: Oxford University Press, 1977), 399.

39. David V. Erdman, *Blake: Prophet Against Empire*, 2nd ed. (New York: Dover, 1991), 133; see also 123–124.

40. Gerda Norvig has read Thel as a figure for theory: "Female Subjectivity and the Desire of Reading in(to) Blake's *Book of Thel*," *Studies in Romanticism* 34.2 (1995): 255–271.

41. William Galperin, *The Return of the Visible in British Romanticism* (Baltimore, Md.: Johns Hopkins University Press, 1993), 13, 53–55, 71; Jennifer Jones, "Virtual Sublime: Sensing Romantic Transcendence in the Twenty-First Century" (Ph.D. dissertation, University of California, Santa Barbara, 2002).

42. See Timothy Morton, "Wordsworth Digs the Lawn," *European Romantic Review* 15.2 (March 2004): 317–327.

43. Adorno, *Aesthetic Theory*, 67.

44. Samuel Taylor Coleridge, *Coleridge's Poetry and Prose*, ed. Nicholas Halmi, Paul Magnuson, and Raimonda Modiano (New York: Norton, 2004).

45. Jean-Paul Sartre, *Being and Nothingness: An Essay on Phenomenological Ontology*, trans. and ed. Hazel Barnes (New York: The Philosophical Library, 1969), 601–615. Sartre's view of woman/sex as a "hole" (613–614) is relevant to the earlier discussion of space as invaginated sinthome. For parallels between Romantic and existential disgust, see Denise Gigante, "The Endgame of Taste: Keats, Sartre, Beckett," *Romanticism on the Net* 24 (November 2001), *http://users.ox.ac.uk/~scat0385/24gigante.html*.

46. Stanley Cavell, *In Quest of the Ordinary: Lines of Skepticism and Romanticism* (Chicago: University of Chicago Press, 1988), 61.

47. Sartre, *Being and Nothingness*, 609.

48. Timothy Morton, "Blood Sugar," in Timothy Fulford and Peter Kitson, eds., *Romanticism and Colonialism: Writing and Empire, 1780–1830* (Cambridge: Cambridge University Press, 1998), 87–106.

49. Samuel Taylor Coleridge, *The Collected Works of Samuel Taylor Coleridge*, vol. 1 *(Lectures 1795 on Politics and Religion)*, ed. L. Patton and P. Mann (London: Routledge and Kegan Paul; Princeton, N.J.: Princeton University Press, 1971), xxxviii, 235–237, 240, 246–248, 250–251.

50. Sartre, *Being and Nothingness*, 609.

51. Julia Kristeva, *Powers of Horror: An Essay on Abjection* (New York: Columbia University Press, 1982), 1–31.

52. See *http://www.joannamacy.net/html/nuclear.html*.

53. Milan Kundera, *The Unbearable Lightness of Being* (New York: Harper, 1999), 248.

54. Slavoj Žižek, *The Indivisible Remainder: An Essay on Schelling and Related Matters* (London: Verso, 1996), 218–220.

55. See for example Kate Rigby, "Earth, World, Text: On the (Im)possibility of Ecopoiesis," *New Literary History* 35.3 (2004): 439.

56. Jacques Derrida, "How to Avoid Speaking: Denials," in *Derrida and Negative Philosophy*, ed. Harold Coward and Toby Foshay (Albany: State University of New York Press, 1992), 74.

57. Martin Jay, *Force Fields: Between Intellectual History and Cultural Critique* (New York: Routledge, 1993), 1–3, 8–9.

58. Walter Benjamin, "Theses on the Philosophy of History," in *Illuminations*, ed. Hannah Arendt, trans. Harry Zohn (London: Harcourt, Brace and World, 1973), 253–264 (261).

59. Karl Kroeber, *Ecological Literary Criticism: Romantic Imagining and the Biology of Mind* (New York: Columbia University Press, 1994), 42.

60. Joseph Carroll, *Evolution and Literary Theory* (Columbia: University of Missouri Press, 1995), 2.

61. Walter Benjamin, "The Work of Art in the Age of Mechanical Reproduction," in *Illuminations*, 222–223.

62. Ibid., 223.

63. Slavoj Žižek, "The One Measure of True Love Is: You Can Insult the Other," interview with Sabine Reul and Thomas Deichmann, *Spiked Magazine*, November 15, 2001, *http://www.spiked-online.com/Articles /00000002D2C4.htm*.

64. Martin Heidegger, "The Origin of the Work of Art," in *Poetry, Language, Thought*, 34.

65. See David Simpson, *Situatedness, or, Why We Keep Saying Where We're Coming From* (Durham, N.C.: Duke University Press, 2002), 234. Simpson compares Heidegger's peasant with Malinowki's primitivist image of Pacific islanders.

66. Adorno, *Negative Dialectics*, 365.

67. See Howard Eiland, "Reception in Distraction," *boundary 2* 30.1 (Spring 2003): 51–66.

68. Benjamin, "Work of Art," 239.

69. Eiland, "Reception in Distraction," 60–63.

70. Benjamin, "Work of Art," 240.

71. Gernot Böhme, *Atmosphäre: Essays zur neuen Ästhetik* (Frankfurt am Main: Suhrkamp, 1995), 66–84.

72. Robert E. Norton, *The Beautiful Soul: Aesthetic Morality in the Eighteenth Century* (Ithaca, N.Y.: Cornell University Press, 1995), 1–8, 277–282.

73. Latour, *Politics of Nature*, 56.

74. Robert Kaufman, "Aura, Still," *October* 99 (Winter 2002): 45–80 (49). Kaufman quotes Adorno, *Aesthetic Theory*, 269, 245.

75. Adorno, *Aesthetic Theory*, 269, 245.

76. Maurice Blanchot, *The Space of Literature*, trans. Ann Smock (1955; repr., Lincoln: University of Nebraska Press, 1982), 224.

77. David Harvey, *Justice, Nature and the Geography of Difference* (Oxford: Blackwell, 1996), 391–397, 403–438.

78. Raymond Williams, *The Country and the City* (Oxford: Oxford University Press, 1975), 233 and 233–247 *passim*.

79. Luc Ferry, *The New Ecological Order*, trans. Carol Volk (Chicago: University of Chicago Press, 1995), 91–107.

80. Giorgio Agamben, *The Open: Man and Animal*, trans. Kevin Attell (Stanford, Calif.: Stanford University Press, 2004), 85–87.

81. I borrow the phrase from Edward Casey, *Getting Back into Place: Toward a Renewed Understanding of the Place-World* (Bloomington: Indiana University Press, 1993).

82. Heidegger, "Origin," 41–42.

83. Martin Heidegger, "Building Dwelling Thinking," in *Poetry, Language, Thought*, 143–161 (152–153).

84. Ibid., 150.

85. Meyer Shapiro, "The Still Life as a Personal Object: A Note on Heidegger and Van Gogh," in Marianne L. Simmel, ed., *The Reach of Mind: Essays in Memory of Kurt Goldstein* (New York: Springer, 1968), 203–209.

86. Timothy Morton, " 'Twinkle, Twinkle, Little Star' as an Ambient Poem; a Study of a Dialectical Image; with Some Remarks on Coleridge and

Wordsworth," in James McKusick, ed., "Romanticism and Ecology," *Romantic Praxis* (November 2001), *http://www.rc.umd.edu/praxis/ecology/*.

87. Heidegger, "Building Dwelling Thinking," 154.
88. Heidegger, "Origin," 54–55.
89. Ibid., 49, 46–47.
90. Avital Ronell, *The Telephone Book: Technology, Schizophrenia, Electric Speech* (Lincoln: University of Nebraska Press, 1989), 26–83 (28).
91. I take the term *textmark* from Jonathan Bate, *The Song of the Earth* (Cambridge, Mass.: Harvard University Press, 2000), 175.
92. Martin Heidegger, "Supplement," in *The Metaphysical Foundations of Logic*, trans. M. Heim (Bloomington: Indiana University Press, 1984), 221.
93. Edward Casey, *The Fate of Place: A Philosophical History* (Berkeley: University of California Press, 1997), 259.
94. Jacques Lacan, "The Agency of the Letter in the Unconscious or Reason Since Freud," in *Ecrits: A Selection*, trans. Alan Sheridan (London: Tavistock Publications, 1977), 146–178 (166).
95. René Descartes, *Meditations and Other Metaphysical Writings*, trans. and intro. Desmond M. Clarke (Harmondsworth: Penguin, 2000), 19.
96. See Harvey, *Justice*, 167–168.
97. Sigmund Freud, "The Uncanny," in *The Standard Edition of the Complete Psychological Works of Sigmund Freud*, ed. and trans. James Strachey, 24 vols. (London: Hogarth, 1953), 17.218–252 (246, 252).
98. Thoreau's word. Henry David Thoreau, *Walden and Civil Disobedience*, intro. Michael Meyer (1854; repr., Harmondsworth: Penguin, 1986), 372.
99. See Kenneth R. Johnston, "Wordsworth and *The Recluse*," in Stephen Gill, ed., *The Cambridge Companion to William Wordsworth* (Cambridge: Cambridge Univeristy Press, 2003), 70–89 (86).
100. I am grateful to Andrew Hageman for pointing this out to me.
101. The Cure, "A Forest," *Seventeen Seconds* (Elektra/Asylum, 1980).
102. Freud, "The Uncanny," 17.237. For a comprehensive study see Robert Pogue Harrison, *Forests: The Shadow of Civilization* (Chicago: University of Chicago Press, 1993), especially 2, 5, 84, 186.
103. Blanchot, *Space of Literature*, 256–260.
104. Johnston, "Wordsworth and *The Recluse*," 81.
105. Blake, *Complete Poetry and Prose*, 667.
106. I follow the argument in Theodor Adorno and Max Horkheimer, *Dialectic of Enlightenment*, trans. John Cumming (London: Verso, 1979).
107. Keith Basso, *Wisdom Sits in Places: Landscape and Language among the Western Apache* (Albuquerque: University of New Mexico Press, 2000), 27.
108. Jacques Derrida, "Hostipitality."
109. Karl Marx, "Comments on Adolph Wagner," in *Selected Writings*, ed. David McLellan (Oxford: Oxford University Press, 1977), 581.
110. John McDowell, *Mind and World* (Cambridge, Mass.: Harvard University Press, 1994), 115–119.
111. Agamben, *The Open*, 83–84.

112. John Carpenter (director), *The Thing* (Universal Studios, 1982).

113. Thoreau, *Walden*, 135.

114. Søren Kierkegaard, *Either/Or: A Fragment of Life*, trans. and intro. Alastair Hannay (London: Penguin, 1992), 243–376.

115. Ibid., 373.

116. Ibid., 381–474.

117. Ibid., 540.

118. Theodor W. Adorno, *Kierkegaard: Construction of the Aesthetic*, trans. and ed. Robert Hullot-Kentor (Minneapolis: University of Minnesota Press, 1999), 10.

119. Kierkegaard, *Either/Or*, 243–376.

120. Adorno, *Kierkegaard*, 40–46.

121. Jacques Derrida, "There Is No *One* Narcissism (Autobiophotographies)," in *Points: Interviews, 1974–1994*, ed. Elisabeth Weber, trans. Peggy Kamuf et al. (Stanford, Calif.: Stanford University Press, 1995), 199.

122. Theodore Roszak, "Where Psyche Meets Gaia," in Theodore Roszak, Mary E. Gomes, and Allen D. Kanner, eds., *Ecopsychology: Restoring the Earth, Healing the Mind* (San Francisco: Sierra Club Books, 1995), 1–17 (17).

123. Joanna Macy, "Working through Environmental Despair," in Roszak, Gomes, and Kanner, *Ecopsychology*, 240–259; *Despairwork: Relating to the Peril and Promise of Our Time* (Philadelphia: Library Company of Philadelphia, 1982).

124. Slavoj Žižek, *Looking Awry: An Introduction to Jacques Lacan through Popular Culture* (Cambridge, Mass.: MIT Press, 1992), 35–39.

125. Kierkegaard, in Adorno, *Kierkegaard*, 123–124.

126. See Jay Bernstein, "Confession and Forgiveness: Hegel's Poetics of Action," in Richard Eldridge, ed., *Beyond Representation: Philosophy and Poetic Imagination* (Cambridge: Cambridge University Press, 1996), 34–65.

127. Judith Butler, "Melancholy Gender/Refused Identification," in *The Psychic Life of Power: Theories in Subjection* (Stanford, Calif.: Stanford University Press, 1997), 132–150 (138–140).

128. Ibid., 147.

129. Ferry, *The New Ecological Order*, 53–54.

130. Latour, *Politics of Nature*, 155.

131. Slavoj Žižek, *The Sublime Object of Ideology* (London: Verso, 1989), 217.

132. Ridley Scott (director), *Blade Runner* (Blade Runner Partnership, The Ladd Company, Run Run Shaw, The Shaw Brothers, 1982).

133. Donna Haraway, "A Cyborg Manifesto: Science, Technology, and Socialist-Feminism in the Late Twentieth Century," in *Simians, Cyborgs, and Women: The Reinvention of Nature* (London: Routledge, 1991), 181.

134. This view is supported by Ursula K. Heise in "From Extinction to Electronics: Dead Frogs, Live Dinosaurs, and Electric Sheep," in Cary Wolfe, ed., *Zoontologies: The Question of the Animal* (Minneapolis: University of Minnesota Press, 2003), 59–81 (74–78); and by Louis H. Palmer III in "Articulating the

Cyborg: An Impure Model for Environmental Revolution," in Steven Rosendale, ed., *The Greening of Literary Scholarship* (Iowa City: University of Iowa Press, 2002), 165–177.

135. Leslie Marmon Silko, *Almanac of the Dead: A Novel* (New York: Simon and Schuster, 1991).

136. I borrow "hauntology" from Jacques Derrida, *Specters of Marx: The State of the Debt, the Work of Mourning, and the New International,* trans. Peggy Kamuf (London: Routledge, 1994), 161.

137. Karl Marx, *Capital,* 3 vols., trans. Ben Fowkes (Harmondsworth: Penguin, 1990), 452–453.

138. Ibid., 453.

139. E. O. Wilson, *Consilience: The Unity of Knowledge* (New York: Knopf, 1998).

140. James Gleick, *Chaos: Making a New Science* (New York: Viking, 1987), 152.

141. See for instance Steven Johnson, *Emergence: The Connected Lives of Ants, Brains, Cities, and Software* (New York: Scribner, 2001), 73–82.

142. Paul Hawken, Amory Lovins, and L. Hunter Lovins, *Natural Capitalism: Creating the Next Industrial Revolution* (Boston: Little, Brown, 1999).

143. Johnson, *Emergence,* 11–23.

144. Michael Hardt and Antonio Negri, *Empire* (Cambridge, Mass.: Harvard University Press, 2000), 413.

145. See Shershow, *Work and the Gift,* 56, 64, 220.

146. Peter Otto, "Literary Theory," in Iain McCalman, ed., *An Oxford Companion to the Romantic Age: British Culture 1776–1832* (Oxford: Oxford University Press, 1999), 378–385 (384).

147. La Monte Young, *Composition 1960 #5,* in *An Anthology* (New York: Heiner Friedrich, 1963). For further discussion of music that works with emergent form, see David Toop, *Haunted Weather: Music, Silence and Memory* (London: Serpent's Tail, 2004), 190–192.

148. Otto, "Literary Theory," 385.

149. See Williams, *Culture and Society,* 256–257.

150. See for example Cary Wolfe, *Critical Environments: Postmodern Theory and the Pragmatics of the "Outside"* (Minneapolis: University of Minnesota Press, 1998), 58, 67–68; and *Animal Rites: American Culture, the Discourse of the Species, and Posthumanist Theory* (Chicago: University of Chicago Press, 2003), 89.

151. Toop, *Haunted Weather,* 182–183.

152. Aldo Leopold, *A Sand County Almanac, and Sketches Here and There,* intro. Robert Finch (1949; repr., Oxford: Oxford University Press, 1989), 224–225.

153. Ibid., 129–137.

154. Leopold, "Conservation Esthetic," in *Sand County Almanac,* 165–177.

155. Ibid., 173.

156. Eve Kosofsky Sedgwick, *Between Men: English Literature and Homosocial Desire* (New York: Columbia University Press, 1985), 91–92, 116–117.

157. Elizabeth A. Bohls, "Standards of Taste, Discourses of 'Race', and the

Aesthetic Education of a Monster: Critique of Empire in *Frankenstein*," *Eighteenth-Century Life* 18.3 (1994): 23–36.

158. Theodor Adorno, "Progress," *The Philosophical Forum* 15.1–2 (Fall–Winter 1983–1984): 55–70 (61–63, 62).

159. Ibid., 61.

160. For example, see M. H. Abrams, *Natural Supernaturalism: Tradition and Revolution in Romantic Literature* (New York: W. W. Norton, 1973), 225–252, especially 241: "a union between the disalienated mind and a rehumanized nature."

161. Derrida, "Hostipitality."

162. Walter Benjamin, *The Origin of German Tragic Drama* (London: NLB, 1977), 200–233.

163. Edmund Blunden and Alan Porter, eds., *John Clare: Poems Chiefly from Manuscript* (London: Richard Cobden-Sanderson, 1920).

164. *Anglo-Saxon Poetry*, trans. and ed. S. A. J. Bradley (London: Dent, 1982), 372.

165. Jonathan Bate, *Romantic Ecology: Wordsworth and the Environmental Tradition* (London: Routledge, 1991), 14–16.

166. I am grateful to Tim Fulford for pointing this out.

167. Jonathan Bate, *John Clare: A Biography* (London: Picador; New York: Farrar, Straus and Giroux, 2003), 91.

168. Ibid., 206.

169. James C. McKusick, *Green Writing: Romanticism and Ecology* (New York: St. Martin's Press, 2000), 77–94 (especially 89, 91).

170. Bate, *Clare*, 563–575.

171. Ibid., 506.

172. John Clare, *John Clare*, ed. Eric Robinson and David Powell (Oxford: Oxford University Press, 1984).

173. John Goodridge has indicated to me that "cesspools" is a textual crux. Some scholars, including Goodridge and Robert Heyes, prefer "sexpools" (small pools formed in the hole left by turf cutting). I do not believe this affects my reading.

174. Percy Bysshe Shelley, "On Love," in *Shelley's Prose: The Trumpet of a Prophecy*, ed. David Lee Clark (London: Fourth Estate, 1988), 169–171 (170).

175. Robert Frost, *New Hampshire: A Poem with Notes and Grace Notes* (New York: Henry Holt, 1923). My thanks to John Felstiner for suggesting this quotation (and for pointing out the lack of commas in the manuscript).

176. Adorno, "Progress," 62.

177. Blake, *Complete Poetry and Prose*.

178. Hamilton, *Metaromanticism*, 146–147.

179. Benjamin C. Sax, "Active Individuality and the Language of Confession: The Figure of the Beautiful Soul in the *Lehrjahre* and the *Phänomenologie*," *Journal of the History of Philosophy* 11.4 (1983): 437–466.

180. I diverge here from the translation of *Begriff* as "notion," since that word does no justice to the element of inward, conscious conceptual essence Hegel is after here. *Begriff* was used by Kant to imply "concept." Notions are inherently suspect—we view them from the outside.

181. Lacan, "Agency," 165.

182. Blake, "The Little Girl Lost," in *The Complete Poetry and Prose.*

183. Percy Bysshe Shelley, *The Poems of Shelley,* ed. Kelvin Everest, K. Matthews, and Geoffrey Matthews (London: Longman, 1989).

184. Jaques Lacan, "The Direction of the Treatment and the Principles of Its Power," in *Ecrits,* 226–280 (236).

185. Ibid., 256.

186. Georg Wilhelm Friedrich Hegel, *Lectures on the History of Philosophy: The Lectures of 1825–1826,* 3 vols., ed. Robert F. Brown, trans. R.F. Brown and J.M. Stewart, with H.S. Harris (Berkeley: University of California Press, 1990), 3.131.

187. René Descartes, *Discourse on Method and Meditations on First Philosophy,* 4th ed., trans. Donald Cress (Indianapolis, Ind.: Hackett, 1999), 33.

188. Ibid., 35.

189. Žižek, *Looking Awry,* 35–39.

Index

Harvard University Press is a member of Green Press Initiative (greenpressinitiative.org), a nonprofit organization working to help publishers and printers increase their use of recycled paper and decrease their use of fiber derived from endangered forests. This book was printed on recycled paper containing 30% post-consumer waste and processed chlorine free.